AWAY FROM
BELOVED LOVER

AWAY FROM BELOVED LOVER

A Musical Journey through Cambodia

DEE PEYOK

GRANTA

Granta Publications, 12 Addison Avenue, London W11 4QR
First published in Great Britain by Granta Books, 2023

Map on page ix © Peter Hermes Furian/Shutterstock

The credits on pp. 329–31 constitute an extension of this copyright page.

A CIP catalogue record for this book is available from the British Library.

1 3 5 7 9 10 8 6 4 2

ISBN 978 1 78378 711 1
eISBN 978 1 78378 712 8

Typeset by Avon Dataset Ltd
Printed and bound by CPI Group (UK) Ltd, Croydon, CR0 4YY

www.granta.com

This book is dedicated to all of the musicians
who lost their lives in the Cambodian genocide.

And to my son, Errol, that you may one
day understand why I missed reading
so many stories, to write this one.

Contents

Map   ix

List of illustrations   xi

A Note on Language   xiii

Preface   xv

1 The Golden Age: An Overview   1

2 Palace Music   35

3 Royal Rock 'n' Roll   66

4 Jivin' Jitterbugs 'n' the King of Cambodian
    Swing   91

5 Buried Treasure   112

6 The Blind Master   138

7 Old Pot Still Cooks Good Rice   155

8 Golden Voice Emperor   195

9 The Drakkar Band   234

10 Cambodia's First Guitar Band   264

Epilogue   301

Acknowledgements   320

Sources   321

Credits   329

Index   332

Illustrations

CVMA stands for the Cambodian Vintage Music Archive

1	Bokor Palace Hotel	xv
2	Sieng Vanthy, Yol Aularong and Pen Ram performing	1
3	Cambodian classical and folk instruments	6
4	Norodom Sihanouk	13
5	Cambodian 1960s/1970s record sleeves	21
6	The Khmer Rouge brotherhood	28
7	Cambodians working on an irrigation project, 1976	31
8	Svay Sor surveys his classroom	35
9	TVK network television, 1970	49
10	Apsara dancers, Royal Palace, 1960s	66
11	Apsara in 1964s	75
12	Lay Mealea and Joe Wrigley perform with their band, Miss Sarawan	91
13	Sieng Dy performing at the Magetat in 1969 film *Joie de Vivre*	103
14	Exterior of the Magetat	103
15	Chariya in the 1980s	109
16	Thach Soly	112
17	Sinan digitising his collection at the CVMA	119
18	Thach Soly with his band, Sophoan	127

19 Master Kong Nay   138
20 Kong Nay   153
21 Ros Sereysothea   155
22 Sinn Sisamouth and Ros Sereysothea   168
23 Ros Sereysothea record sleeve   169
24 Saboeun and the CVMA archive   172
25 Saboeun's wall of photos   174
26 Sinn Sisamouth and his beloved VW Bug   195
27 Vintage Sisamouth songbook   199
28 Sophorn, Oro, Dee Peyok, Gnut   205
29 Cover and page from 1950s RNK Radio
        programmes   209
30 Sinn Sisamouth record sleeve   215
31 Dee Peyok, Gnut, Oro, Martin Jay and Sophorn   226
32 Sinn Sisamouth's childhood home   232
33 Drakkar 1974 album cover   234
34 Touch Chhattha in the late 1960s   239
35 Baksey Cham Krong   264
36 Tana, Kagnol and Sothivann at the City
        Winery show   274
37 Lon Nol soldier running with gun and guitar   301
38 Nate Hun, CVMA co-founder, with his
        collection   310
39 Author in Bokor Palace ballroom   318

A Note on Language

All Cambodian names are written in the order they are traditionally addressed in Cambodian culture: last name, first name.
My translators and I have done our best to capture the correct
meaning of what was said in interviews, as well as accurate
transliterations of Cambodian names and places. As much of
the information in this book was gathered from Khmer-spoken
interviews – and I am not a fluent Khmer speaker and relied on
translators and translations – the nuances of a person's language
and delivery are sometimes missing from the dialogue.

Please note that members of the Cambodian Royal Family
are often known by their full names (e. g. Prince Norodom
Sihanouk) as well as their forename only (e. g. Prince Sihanouk).
This book's index uses the full version of their names with a
cross reference from the simpler form so please refer to it if
you are unsure about the identity of the various kings, queens,
princes and princesses.

As there are many Khmer consonants and vowels that don't
exist in English – and vice versa – the spellings of names that are
based on the most common known transliterations may vary from
their phonetic sound. Here is a quick guide on how to pronounce
a selection of names:

NAME	PRONUNCIATION
Lay Mealea	Lay Melee-a
Lim Sophorn	Lim Soporn
Mao Sareth	Mao Sarett
Mol Kagnol	Mol Ka-nole
Mol Kamach	Mol Kamack
Pen Ran	Pan Ron
Peou Sipho	Po Sipo
Ros Saboeun	Ros Saboorn
Sinn Sisamouth	Sinn Sisamoot
Touch Chhattha	Tuch Chattar
Touch Tana	Tuch Tanar
Yol Aularong	Yo Larong

Preface

Bokor Palace Hotel.

Cambodia: the land of water and rice, of myths and god-kings, folklore and wonder. It's a country that rewards the industrious, fattens the corrupt and regurgitates the poor. A place that both filled and broke my heart.

I first visited the country in 2012, joining a journalist friend who lived there to realize a lifelong dream to see the temples at Siem Reap. I crossed off the usual tourist tick-list: watched the sun rise over Angkor Wat, got lost among the overgrowth enveloping Ta Prohm temple, posed for headshots next to the four-sided Buddha heads of the Bayon temple. But it was an unexpected experience within the Dâmrei mountain range in southern Cambodia that would, unknown to me at the time, change the course of my life.

I'd heard it said that, 'Once you've seen the Dâmrei Mountains, you've seen Cambodia.' Steeped in sacred mythology of subaqueous kingdoms, serpent-headed queens and adventurous kings, 'the hump of an ox'– as its largest mountain, Bokor, is known to Cambodians – hosts natural wonders, Buddhist statues and colonial ruins. Bokor's rich history piqued our interest, so my husband Kevin and I packed a lunch of pilfered hotel breakfast rolls and jam, hired a moped from a nearby river town, and slowly climbed the 38 kilometres to the mountain's summit. Winding upwards, the new Chinese road that carried us cut through a lush chattering jungle that, I'd been told, still hid tigers and elephants deep within its midst. The higher we climbed the cooler and cleaner the mountain air became, the views – when they appeared – were breathtaking, and the road, refreshingly unfrequented. A flat tyre, a roadside puncture repair and a hat tip later – to the mammoth statue of Lok Yeay Mao (protector of travellers) – we parked our moped by the ruins of the French colonial hill town.

Looming large between a Catholic church and a crumbling hamlet, the art deco Bokor Palace Hotel had long been abandoned and stripped of all decadence. Its skin covered in bright red and green lichen and pockmarked by bullets, the building had survived the First Indochina War and the Vietnamese invasion in 1978, remaining unoccupied – save for the odd refugee and squatter – until the country opened up again in the 1990s.

It called to us in a voice that seemed to drown out all the other sights we'd planned to see that day. Without saying a word, Kevin made off towards the hotel on a de-mined path and, like an obedient starling, I followed. In the distance we could hear a familiar song, just within earshot. Smiling at each other in confusion, we tried to recall it from the recesses of our minds. The song grew louder with the approach of a young Cambodian man balancing a ghetto-blaster on his shoulder. We automatically stepped in time with the beat and his stride, three musketeers synchronously climbing the steps of the grand hotel. Entering the ballroom together, the sound of a Farfisa bounced off the empty walls. As our eyes adjusted to the gloom, nebulous art-deco remnants sharpened into focus under white render and thick dust. I drank it all in, until the inevitable light-bulb moment. I turned to Kevin as he turned to me, and we uttered in excited unison, 'A Whiter Shade of Pale!'

It was immediately obvious that we weren't listening to the original, but while the sound quality was third rate, the musicianship easily rivalled Procol Harum's 1967 release. The experience of hearing it there, sung in the Cambodian language, Khmer, was as bizarre as it was profound. When the singer launched in for the first line, his mellifluous voice took flight, filling every inch of cavernous space surrounding us. Captivated, I felt euphoric. It was a gospel-choir-in-church-crescendo sort of moment: feasting my eyes on grand curved staircases to either side of the room, a gargantuan fireplace ahead, the recording's echo reverberated off every beautiful surface the light hit. The moment seemed to last forever, and I've often wondered since, where my life would be had I not heard that song, there and then. If the timing was off, if our moped's front tyre hadn't blown on the ascent, if a frail old boy, who miraculously emerged from the mountainside vegetation, hadn't come to our rescue, would I be writing this book now?

It didn't take me long to track down some old Cambodian rock music. Boom Boom Records – a clothing shop that sold bootleg CDs – in Cambodia's capital, Phnom Penh, took me hurtling towards my future with a downloaded three-pack of rewritable discs. The albums were *Cambodian Rocks* (Parallel World), and *Cambodian Rocks, Volume Two* and *Three* (Khmer Rocks) and, though riddled with overdubs, I played them over and over. Nestled among psych stormers, ska and hard-rock rhapsodies was the 'A Whiter Shade of Pale' cover I'd heard on Bokor. It was performed by a singer called Sinn Sisamouth, who'd renamed it

'Away from Beloved Lover' (sometimes credited as 'Apart from Beloved Lover').

When I returned home to London I began to scour the internet and the vaults of the British Library for any answers to my endless questions about who the artists on those tracks were, and how their music had come about. But it seemed they'd left us grains of lost records in unearthed treasures, and a vast blue of mystery. I soon realized that the book I wanted to read didn't exist, that the information out there was thin, to say the least. In the absence of a forerunner and with 1960s musicians fast approaching their twilight years, this quest for knowledge called to me like a potent siren song. If I was going to find those answers, I knew that as mad as it sounded I was going to have to go back East and find them myself.

Sixteen months after our first encounter with the music, on 8 April 2014 Kevin and I set off once again, this time armed with enough savings to see us through a few months, and some leads on experts of Cambodian 1960s and 1970s popular music. We landed in Phnom Penh, feather-light with the freedom and optimism that comes with adventure, and as green as could be.

It wasn't long before Kevin found work teaching and we rented an apartment a stone's throw from Phnom Penh's red-light district. In a quiet alley just off Street 63, on the corner of Street 184, our one-bedroom first-floor apartment was bright, magnolia and spartan throughout, and wedged safely between our landlord's living quarters on the ground floor and his sons' bedrooms on the second floor. We had a gas camping stove to cook on, a military-green 1950s desk for writing, and a slim balcony that spanned the L-shaped apartment. Orchids were suspended from the balcony railings and I have countless memories of reclining on our hammock, watching the street come to life and fall asleep.

Cart-wielding street sellers would shout their wares down

below: cockles, coconuts, rambutans . . . *'Ah well! Dong, dong! Sao mao!'* I'd race down the steps, flip flops clacking, at the sound of the *'dong'* man for my daily coconut; an essential dehydration fix in the sweltering spring heat.

The neighbourhood was eclectic: a third of residents were from all corners of the globe and the rest were Phnom Penh locals. The Westerners on the street came in all shapes and sizes, and all manners of crazy. For a time, there was an Armenian gang living opposite who scared the living daylights out of us. They were replaced by a gun-wielding English pimp and his harem, who were less threatening but double the drama. Aside from our landlord, a policeman called Mr Nil Thera, and the tuk tuk drivers, we made friends with a gentle man with a birthmark on his face, though he never told us his name.

He lived opposite with his wife, daughter, mother and the patriarch of the family, who we called 'Granddad'. Granddad was an engineer by nature and a mechanic by trade. He could fix anything, from machines to broken chairs, and when he wasn't working he would upcycle metal and plastic rubbish into new toys for his granddaughter. Every day, he'd set up his air compressor, attach a head-torch to his Britpop bucket hat, crouch onto his skinny haunches – shirtless, in plaid boxers, never-ending cigarette hanging out of his mouth – and wait for business to pull up. On the rare occasions that he left his post, he would dust down a beautiful red 1960s Vespa and, slowly mounting it, would light a cigarette and start revving the engine loudly. Just when you thought he was going to turn into James Dean and shoot off like a lightning bolt into the city streets, he would slowly put-put away at an elderly pace, cigarette hanging from his mouth, looking every inch the rebel without a cause, but at a quarter of the speed.

And then there was Robert, an American writer in his seventies who would blast out Hendrix while walking around in his boxers. He always had a joint pressed to the side of his lips, his military dog tags resting under strands of long white hair, beating against his spindly frame as he restlessly moved from his computer to the sofa to the balcony all hours of the day and night. He hardly spoke, but on the rare occasions he did, he would shout strange musings at me across the balcony – 'You know, in Phnom Penh we don't have a pollution problem, we have a dust-in-the-air problem!' – then laugh maniacally.

I could go on, but it really was floors and floors of eccentric adventurers and wayward explorers on the balconies and inside the apartments all around us. They provided my imagination with wonderful fuel. In those early days, I'd observe from my hammock, making up stories for each of them, whole histories in fact, without us ever really saying a word to each other in our transient Cambodian world. It was from that little alley in the big city that I took my first giant step into the unknown.

AWAY FROM
BELOVED LOVER

I

The Golden Age: An Overview

Front, l–r: Sieng Vanthy, Yol Aularong, Pen Ram.

Southeast Asia, 1962. In Laos, Operation Pincushion was turning hill tribesmen into guerrillas. Totalitarian rule was enforced in Burma. The Stonehill scandal had erupted in the Philippines. South Vietnam's President Diệm was spending a quiet moment reading George Washington's biography when a faulty 500 lb bomb dropped through the ceiling of the palace library. In neighbouring Cambodia Prince Sihanouk's Sangkum Reastr Niyum party (the Community Favoured by the People) won every seat in their third consecutive election. The event marked seven years since the party's formation and the start of Cambodia's transition to independence – a transition that would end France's ninety-year colonial rule and see Cambodia's popular king, Norodom Sihanouk, abdicate the throne to take a political lead and be closer to the common folk.

Against a backdrop of corruption, war, crumbling colonies

and dissolving monarchies, the 1960s ushered in a period of fierce modernisation for every aspect of Southeast Asian life. From bricks and mortar to culture, Cambodia was rapidly changing. And in the spaces in between, rock 'n' roll burst onto the Cambodian music scene, igniting neighbouring household radios like wildfire, the establishment littering the pages of the national rag *La Dépêche du Cambodge* with readers' letters of disdain while the youth polished the packed mud of nightclub floors with the twist – hair flinging and hips gyrating to the sound of liberation.

Just as Sam Cooke and Chubby Checker were twisting their way into the US Billboard charts and Cliff Richard and the Shadows were topping the UK charts with one hit 45 after another, music broke new ground across Southeast Asia, from the emergence of Cambodian surf guitars to the go-go girls of Singapore. As Bob Dylan went electric to shouts of 'Judas!' from die-hard folkies, 'Luk Thung' country music went electric in its native Thailand, later paving the way for still popular Thai funk. The lyrics of Bob Dylan and Thailand's famous singer Sroeng Santi may have differed politically and culturally, but the universal themes of love and desire prevailed over all. Needless to say, the music of East and West merged across Southeast Asia to create the most fascinating *mélange* of instruments, attitude and expressionism.

In time, garage girl group Dara Puspita broke onto the scene in Indonesia, Burma's Bo Hein was pushing the boundaries of free jazz with the first hint of noise music long before it – or the drugs to tolerate it – were synthesized. The CBC Band were kicking out the jams on Vietnam's frontline and Roziah Latiff & the Jayhawkers straddled surf, exotica and rockabilly; Roziah's silk-spun voice captivating the rubber tappers of Singapore, their transistor radios strapped to their heads as they worked. While Phil Spector was creating his wall of sound in the West, Southeast

Asia was fuelling its own juggernaut of sound and, for a time, was unstoppable. The music that rippled through the subcontinent in the 1960s and 1970s was an expression of independence, resistance and the celebration of youth, often created under great social and political strain. Many of the artists eventually suffered, were constrained by, or silenced under, autocratic or extremist regimes, the Vietnamese War and, in Cambodia, civil war and genocide.

But 1962 marked a new dawn for Cambodian music. A buzz was humming as electrical volts sparked their way down the cables of new frontiers. Rock 'n' roll had arrived. For the kingdom whose capital, Phnom Penh, was dubbed the 'pearl of the Orient' and the 'Paris of the East' it was a time of prosperity, exploration and mobility; a period of development and opportunity. A country unshackling itself from almost ninety years of colonisation was breathing freely once more. Cambodia was embracing both its independence and its second 'golden age'. Its first had begun centuries before, when its magnificent temples were built by the first Cambodians: the 'Khmer'.

From Sanskrit scripts and temple carvings to passed-down folktales, the influence of Hinduism trickled into the earliest art forms created by the first Cambodians. Some of the rockers featured in this book cite influences as far back as 500 AD and as far reaching as the Dângrêk Mountains. I've marvelled at this, and I can't think of a scalable spiritual or artistic comparison between Anglo-Saxon culture and modern British music, except perhaps the odd medieval renaissance band, which in all seriousness does not garner quite the same sense of reverence. More musicians still harked back to the influence of the Angkorian period between 9th and 15th centuries, Cambodia's first golden age, when King Jayavarman II proclaimed the Khmer Empire independent from Java. The Khmers' power ceded from an abundance of natural resources, in particular the land and coastal trade routes from

China to India, and their empire stretched over modern-day Cambodia and, indeed, most of Southeast Asia. However, it was their skill at carving beauty out of stone that set the Khmer race apart. To my mind, no other civilization has rivalled such chisel artistry. It's what makes their exquisite temples a world heritage site. The importance of the temples – their architects, artefacts and the artisans who made them and serviced their courts – cannot be understated. They are as integral to Khmer culture now as they ever were, and remain a cultural touchstone for many musicians today.

Cambodians and tourists alike flock to the country's most famous temple complex, Angkor Wat – considered to be the largest religious site in the world. It is said to have taken at least thirty years to build and more stone than all of the Egyptian pyramids. More than 1,500 celestial beings are sculpted into the walls of Angkor Wat's gallery, and the temple is the emblem of Cambodia's national flag. Many of its courtly instruments can still be heard in cities and villages throughout Cambodia, and temple Sanskrit epics like *Reamker* (more widely known by its Hindi name *Ramayana*) are still taught in schools. Art and mythology seem to permeate the minds of all Cambodians, young and old.

Beyond the schools and temple frescoes is a land where oral history prevails over written history. Khmer proverbs, passed down through the generations in words and song, form the moral vertebrae of a country that lists its official religion – its spine – as Theravāda Buddhism. This ancient, most conservative branch of Buddhism rooted itself firmly in Khmer culture by the 13th century, just as the Angkor Empire was beginning its decline. As I journeyed through Cambodia, I took part in several Buddhist ceremonies – both individual and collective – and went on various road trips, including a tour with Cambodian musicians, where I also encountered remnants of animism. The first loggers, frightened of incurring the wrath of the forest spirits, would carve out small spirit houses and make offerings of food and shelter to the spirits. The pre-Buddhist bamboo houses of the original loggers are long gone but, on Buddhist holidays, there was no passing a roadside shrine without a superstitious traveller stopping the van to make a quick offering.

Nestled between Thailand, Vietnam and Laos, Cambodia's religious practices and cultural identity have ebbed and flowed, strengthened and weakened, transformed and transcended with centuries of invasions and land grabs from warring neighbours, and colonisation in the late eighteen hundreds. The age-old monarchy – a dynasty of god-kings in peasant eyes – was reduced to puppetry by the French imperialists. But while the colonists had a devastating impact on Cambodians' pride, the indigenous art and music, for the most part, remained unsullied.

The umbrella of classical folk – which evolved from ancient forms of Cambodian music – survived all this, and worse to come. Every style of classical folk has a place and purpose in Khmer society, and many of these musical forms keep ancient stories, myths and doctrines alive to this day. From meditative music to please the spirit, to melancholic ceremonial music that supposedly entranced elephants and their riders to walk in unison. The clashing symbols and operatic arias of Bassac theatre entertain villagers. The haunting chants of monks and *smot* singers cry dharmas to help spirits journey into the after-life. The wind section and percussion of twelve-drum arek orchestras sing and pound for rain, and the gongs of the *kongvong* keep the wailing skirl of the Royal Palace's orchestral oboe in check, as shadow puppets and ornately dressed dancers move to their rhythms. Short of travelling to Cambodia to pick up a CD directly from a war-maimed artist outside Angkor Wat, the US classical music label Celestial Harmonies' *Music of Cambodia* archives – recorded by producer David Parsons in the villages and temples of Cambodia in 1994 – are a good place to start.

The most popular style of all classical Khmer music is *mahori*, which means 'beauty', and in ancient times referred to 'the musicians at the temple'. Unlike *arek*, which evolved from tribal gong circles in the earliest villages, or *smot*, which established itself a few centuries ago on religious sites, *mahori* came from the royal court. This pre-Angkorian, more refined music still permeates much of Cambodian life to this day, from the gentle tinkling heard at Buddhist temples and tourist sites, to the CD so often blasting and distorting from a village-wedding marquee speaker at dawn.

Before France made Cambodia a protectorate, France's ally, Spain, sent Filipino soldiers from their colony to fight alongside the French–Spanish Expeditionary Force. The year was 1859, and the fight was for 'Cochinchina' – what is now called Vietnam. Cambodia welcomed these excursions across their land to keep their 'land-grabbing' neighbours at bay, and Cambodia's King Norodom I was said to have treated the Filipino soldiers with such

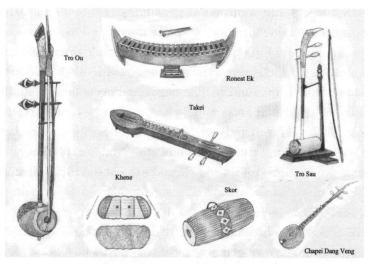

Cambodian classical and folk instruments.

esteem that a number of the soldiers chose to remain in service to him as palace guards at the Cambodian court after their tour of duty ended. Thirteen years later, King Norodom I went on a state visit to the Philippines, where he was serenaded with gun salutes, fireworks, balls and bands, playing both Spanish and Filipino military airs as well as indigenous music. Norodom fell in love not only with the country but with a young Filipino-Spanish woman called Josefa 'Pepita' Roxas y Manio. A devout Catholic, Josefa was said to have broken Norodom's heart, refusing his marriage proposal on the grounds of her allegiance to God. When it came time for the king to board his vessel back to Cambodia he was joined by a group of Filipino musicians. According to writer Luciano P. R. Santiago's detailed account, it was hoped that the musicians 'could console him with Tagalog *kundimans* [love songs] evoking Pepita's image, cherished by his healing heart'. The musicians were installed within the reed and brass bands of his Phnom Penh palace, and their music stimulated a long-lasting cultural exchange between the two countries. After the Philippine Constabulary Band formed at the palace in the early 1900s, there were numerous stories of Filipino big band musicians training Cambodian palace musicians.

The advent of gramophone recordings, 78 rpm records and the passing of the Philippines from the Spanish to the USA, who ruled between 1898 and 1946, brought American dances like the foxtrot and music genres such as blues, jazz and Latin to Manila's military big brass bands and its bars. The Filipino teachers brought clarinets, trumpets, trombones and saxophones with them across the South China Sea, and so great was their influence during Cambodia's colonial era – particularly in the training sphere – that Cambodians to this day still talk frequently of their place in Cambodia's musical history. They even categorize the music within its own genre: *pleng Manil* or 'Manila music'.

These musicians joined a long lineage of palace musicians,

dating back to the 6th century and the first indigenous Mon-Khmer ensembles. But the Filipinos weren't the first foreign influence. That came primarily from Cambodia's land neighbours – Thailand, Vietnam and Laos – and further frontiers, China and India, who held great sway over Khmer language, culture and religion. As a result of trade, war and land grabs, many classical and folk instruments were – and still are – shared between Cambodia, Thailand, Vietnam and Laos, the nations that had once made up the Khmer Empire: from the low tonal parps of the *khene* reed mouth organ of Laos's Hmong tribes and the warbling horns of Vietnam's coastal Cham people, to the *pinpeat/piphat* and *mahori* ensembles Cambodia and Thailand still share. But where Cambodian folk music remains absolutely indigenous and untouched is in the highlands of Ratanakiri and the lowlands of Mondulkiri, where tribes still beat to their own drum, pounding their fists against several hammered, bronze gongs and strumming a guitar-like instrument called a *gungteng*, unique to the region. In 2003 Sublime Frequencies label associate Laurent Jeanneau started gathering three years' worth of field recordings, later releasing them under the title *Ethnic Minority Music of Northeast Cambodia*. Raw and untamed, the moments Laurent captured opened up the region to the outside world, putting ethnic Cambodian music on the global map for the first time since it was first recorded and shared by colonists in the late 19th and early 20th centuries. Music made here is lower in pitch than that of the ethnic Vietnamese, softer and slower in rhythm than ethnic Thais' and Laotians'. Their song is easy, trancelike and hypnotic. Rooted in animism, the singers call to the forest spirits for rain, for a successful hunt, for peace and tranquillity.

But in the main, what we recognize as traditional Khmer music today – courtly orchestras like *pinpeat* and *mahori*, dominated by chattering wooden xylophones and chinking gongs – emerged much later during the Angkorian golden age when the palace orchestras reached their apex. At fifty ensembles strong, the lute and flute sections alone made up a hundred players.

After the fall of the Khmer Empire in the 15th century the palace orchestras fell into decline, but their proud heritage – etched on bas-reliefs and chronicled in ancestral Cambodian books – remained. By the 1800s the orchestras were building themselves back up and, a century on, the palace training ground was a noble rite of passage for many of Cambodia's 1960s stars. Here they mastered every well-respected form of music, from classical Khmer to jazz to Latin. They tapped the wooden xylophone keys of a *roneat* in the Royal Ballet's *pinpeat* orchestra, welcomed foreign dignitaries within the *mahori* ensemble's gong circle, and saluted the annual water festival in a thirty-three-player-strong post-colonial marching band. The array of musical styles and instruments students were exposed to – from playing Cambodia's oldest instrument (a gourd and bow called a *kse diev*) at a royal wedding, to squeezing an accordion at a royal dinner dance – would not only have great influence on their future careers, but on Cambodia as a whole. In Phnom Penh, horn sections called revellers to dancehall floors; in the countryside fanfare bands paraded through village squares; and in Cambodia's recording studios, a traditional Cambodian fiddle made from a coconut shell (called a *tro*) accompanied the clarinet.

Life under the French protectorate between 1863 and 1953 was described by French historian Alain Forest as 'painless', though many Cambodians regarded it as anything but. The country was foremost a buffer zone between French territory in South Vietnam and British territory in Siam – what is now called Thailand. But France wasted no time exploiting Cambodia's natural resources – predominantly rubber and rice. The French installed themselves as the ruling class, integrated the Cambodian and French economies, set about taxing Cambodians heavily and did relatively little to improve Cambodian lives.

There is a Tibetan proverb that says: 'A child without education is like a bird without wings.' In the case of the French in Cambodia, they built roads but they did not invest in education. In doing so, they maintained control of the oppressed; keeping production going and the widespread population of farmers ignorant. On the contrary, the French stroked the egos of the ruling Cambodian class in Phnom Penh, whispered of their cultural and historical supremacy over their Vietnamese, Thai and Chinese neighbours and minorities, igniting Khmer nationalism and a sense of allegiance to their new friends, the French. As a result, much of Cambodia's culture, society, customs and way of life remained intact despite occupation by the French. There were a few French schools in the capital for the Cambodian bourgeoisie, and much of their 'Frenchness' was shaped from childhood: from their primary education in the *lycée* school system Cambodia adopted, to higher education at French universities. It's in their gestures, their attitude and manners; in the case of Sihanouk it threaded through much of his foreign and domestic policy. The French left their trace in Khmer dictionaries with words derived from French: *pan* for bread (from the French *pain*), and *onglee* for English (derived from *Anglaise*). They left their mark on Cambodian cuisine: red curry was served with bread (not rice) and the popular dish *lok lak* was a Cambodian twist on the French dish *boeuf bourguignon*. Under the protectorate street signs directed people in French, women began to wear makeup and men buttoned down their shirts. New Roman Catholic church services were accompanied by pianists from the Royal Palace and the 1930s welcomed the Cambodian prose novel, the *pralomlok*. Even the translation of the word *pralomlok* – 'a story that is written to seduce the hearts of human beings' – reeks of French charm.

By the 1940s, growing resentment among the younger Cambodian bourgeoisie towards their French rulers was building momentum with the help of underground publications like the anti-colonial *Nagara Vatta* (*Notre Cité*) newspaper. After reclaiming Cambodia's borders from Japan, who occupied Cambodia during the Second World War, the French set up a vast youth corps programme to encourage patriotism towards not only a Cambodian's own heritage but, more importantly, towards the French imperial state. Unfortunately for the French, the plan backfired as communist propaganda booklets, Buddhist priests and nationalist insurgents infiltrated the groups and garnered a renewed Cambodian sense of nationalism towards their own country, the Buddhist monastic order and Cambodia's popular monarchy. This sentiment was bolstered by the anti-colonialist movement, the Khmer Issarak ('the Free Khmer'), which was established by exiled and rebel Khmers in Bangkok just as the war was ending. Over the next few years, with some support from Thailand, the guerrilla fighter faction of the movement grew, fuelled by the goal of Khmer independence from the French who were weakening as the war drew on.

On 3 May 1941 Cambodia's Prince Norodom Sihanouk was crowned king. An enigmatic and shrewd politician, the young king quickly learned to walk the fine line between the nationalists and the French, which he navigated masterfully towards independence. In 1946 Cambodia was granted self-rule, in 1949 the protectorate was abolished, and on 9 November 1953 Cambodia marked its full independence.

While the monarchy's power and privileges were relinquished from the French and reinstated, it wasn't enough for the ambitious thirty-one-year-old who, fresh from his political victory, had designs on government. By 1955 King Norodom Sihanouk had abdicated the throne, ceding power to his father, Suramarit, and a month later, formed his own centrist-right political party, the Sangkum Reastr Niyum (the Community Favoured by the People). The party's leader, Prince Sihanouk, was a populist authoritarian and the party – despite its name

– was a democratic sham. But Cambodian lives, by and large, were significantly improved under the Sangkum. Cambodia was free from foreign occupation and war and it was a time of peace and prosperity for most of its inhabitants. The number of modern school buildings, universities and teacher training centres grew, as did factories and jobs. The state invested in enterprise, which subsequently regulated goods and disrupted the Chinese merchants' monopoly. State co-operatives ran their own credit programmes, replacing the loan sharks – the average villager was better off.

The first order of business for the Sangkum was to develop Cambodia's industrial infrastructure, and they successfully nationalized many services, including banking, insurance and foreign trade. Training in France became a rite of passage for anyone looking for a good job within Sihanouk's new Cambodia. Children of the establishment were sent off to obtain degrees from French universities; government workers took training courses in France – and they all came back laden with heavy shellac 78s and gramophones. Traditional Khmer music recorded by the Asian arms of Western music label powerhouses, military fanfare, swing jazz and foreign performers sprung to life under the gramophone needle, bringing a *mélange* of East and West, old and new ideas and influences into the homes of Cambodia's middle and upper classes. French singers like Charles Aznavour, Édith Piaf, Georges Brassens and Yves Montand were popular with the bourgeoisie and the royals, including Sihanouk's mother, Queen Kossamak, who was the patron saint of Khmer dance and an admirer of them all.

In addition to his royal and political duties, Sihanouk was also a musician, songwriter, actor and film director, and he passionately supported the creative arts and festivals that celebrated both Cambodia's ancient Buddhist heritage and its emergent film industry. There was a huge expansion in building from the 1950s.

And it was this, the rapid urbanisation of Phnom Penh and other Cambodian cities over the next fifteen years, along with the development of arts and culture, that led to the Sangkum era being coined 'the golden age' – a second coming of the nation's Angkorian glory days.

With its capital shaping up to become a very modern metropolis, Sihanouk, ever the tightrope walker, encouraged nationalist pride, reverence and respect for Cambodia's deep cultural roots, as well as positioning the country for change. He wanted a statement that Cambodia was prepared to modernize its culture along with Western nations, and the arts provided the perfect vessel for this.

Norodom Sihanouk.

In late 1958 – eleven years after the first state-run radio station launched – Sihanouk laid the cornerstone of the building that was to house a 20-kilowatt medium-wave and a 15-kilowatt short-wave radio transmitter, given to him as gifts by China's premier, Zhou Enlai. Five months later, the new national broadcasting station,

Radiodiffusion Nationale Khmère (widely referred to as RNK for short) went live with its first test transmission. More radio stations were established in the coming years, the radio waves grew in strength as the portable radio took off. Local residents, bicycle carriage drivers and passers-by no longer needed to huddle together to listen to broadcasts through loud speakers on street corners.

Just as the bourgeoisie were silencing their gramophones to catch announcements and performances on the radio, average Cambodians could also now enjoy these programmes in the comfort of their own homes, with Cambodia soon having potentially the highest number of radios per capita in Southeast Asia. With the escalation of the Vietnam War in the 1960s, Cambodians were able to tune into American military radio shows from the likes of Voice of America (VOA) or the Armed Forces Vietnam Network (AFVN). Foreign music was no longer the commodity of the wealthy Cambodian record collector, and the UK and US hits of the decade – Bobby Bare's 'Detroit City', The Animals' 'We Gotta Get Out of This Place' and Jimi Hendrix's 'Purple Haze', among many others – flooded the airwaves on VOA and AFVN. At the same time pre-recorded Cambodian songs – the likes of Cambodian crooner Sinn Sisamouth's early Hong Kong recordings, or retro songstress Mao Sareth's melancholic doo-wop ballads – could finally go out to the masses.

The highly politicized broadcasts on RNK radio weren't Sihanouk's only mouthpiece. The working classes in the provinces adored him and their 'god-king' spent a great deal of time nurturing and maintaining this adoration, touring the countryside with his military bands, playing songs that celebrated their towns and his own political party, Sangkum Reastr Niyum. Whether breaking ground on a new building development or cutting the ceremonial ribbon of some remote water well project, the head of state, Sihanouk, would take the Yothea Phirum (Youth Band) to parp their brassy bugles. Industry mascot bands like Sonic Sing (Imports and Exports) and SKD (the alcohol and distillery band: Société Khmer des Distilleries) employed some of the finest musicians in Phnom Penh, cherry picked by master musicians to represent their sector and exhibit their industry power and popularity. The ensembles entertained workers and foreign dignitaries, and bands like the Dontrey Phirum (the police band) and the RNK radio band (sometimes called Kosnaka), played ceremonially to several thousand civilians in Veal Preah Man Park on what was once a manicured, grassy terrain in front of the National Museum of Cambodia, now laid to waste. Cambodia's big bands, traditional palace orchestras and radio stars were joined by students of schools like l'Université des Beaux-Arts in a cultural Petri dish where musicians spawned and proliferated throughout the 1950s and early 1960s.

It was under the watchful eye of the Royal Palace and the aforementioned Kosnaka band, in this melting pot of global musical influence, that a young singer from the north-east rose to stardom. He would eventually become Cambodia's most famous male singer of all time. With a back catalogue that spanned just about every musical genre, the prolific songwriter was estimated to have written anything from 1,000 to 4,000 songs in a career lasting less than two decades. He was a chameleon who could turn his hand to any style, from folk to rumba to music for popular dances like the cha-cha-cha and the jerk, as well as a popular Khmer circle dance called *romvong* and psychedelic rock 'n' roll. His name was Sinn Sisamouth.

To this day, every small child – from the rice-bowl countryside of Battambang to the international fee-paying schools of Phnom Penh – knows Sisamouth's music. He was a beloved, revered gentleman of the industry; women adored him and men wanted to be him. Popular artists came and went, but none were so adept at not only adopting trends, but setting them too. Throughout the 1960s and early 1970s he remained ahead of the curve and dominated the radio waves. Joining him on his ascent, in the dawn of the Sangkum era, was Cambodia's first guitar band, Baksey Cham Krong.

In December 1961 Sidney Furie's British musical *The Young Ones* was released. Featuring Cliff Richard, the movie helped propel Richard and his backing band, the Shadows, into a new stratosphere of global fame. That same autumn Hank Marvin and co. had toured Australia, Singapore and Malaysia, sparking the emergence of rock 'n' roll bands in just about every country in Southeast Asia. Thailand went so far as to name an entire movement after the band.

Baksey Cham Krong were huge fans of the Shadows and this influence inspired the band's move from their accordion-led folk and French cabaret roots to their reinvention as a surf rock band in the early 1960s. They were the band that triggered the rock scene and the careers of the *yé-yé* groups as they were then called: a term Cambodians took from the French, who'd originally coined the phrase to describe their own early rock bands. The word was a mimicry of 1960s British beat bands like the Beatles (hence the popular Beatles lyric 'yeah yeah' transliterated).

The Shadows may have been the catalyst for a movement, but they weren't the only European band to give Cambodian boys their teenage kicks. A vestige from the French protectorate, it was still fashionable among bourgeois parents of the 1960s to educate their children in France. The teenagers would return home for the holidays from boarding school or university laden down with the latest hits by France's Johnny Hallyday, Sylvie Vartan, Tino Rossi and Richard Anthony, the USA's Pat Boone, the Ventures and Trini Lopez, Canada's Paul Anka, and the UK's Beatles. One such traveller brought back a Chubby Checker record, a traineeship in ceramics and a dance move that rivalled Elvis's snake hips in the eyes of the Cambodian intelligentsia. That move was the twist, and his rocket ascent to stardom in front of the beaded curtains of the Kbal Thnal nightclub shook the establishment, broke the traditional dancefloor's circle formation and put rock 'n' roll on the map. Chum Kem, the godfather of Cambodian rock, shot to fame with his hit song 'Kampuchea Twist' in 1962.* It flooded the 'letters to the editor' of one national newspaper with comments of disgust from the old guard over Kem's vulgarity, which was countered by optimistic sympathizers and teenagers rejoicing in the liberation brought by Kem and his music.

The music industry of Kem's time may have been small in terms of numbers in the workforce, but it was industriously Cambodian in its approach to enterprise. Downtown Phnom Penh in the 1960s was littered with record labels like Wat-Phnom, Chan Chaya, Tep Niminth, Kampuchea Thas, Sakura, Samleng Thas Hors and Lac Sea, which produced Khmer, English and Chinese songs and had its own thriving vinyl pressing plant downtown. Musicians like Sinn Sisamouth started out his career recording live on Phnom Penh radio and later recording, mastering and pressing his singles in Hong Kong before the arrival of Cambodia's own pressing plant moved most production to within the capital. The growth of Phnom Penh's record labels, studios and the addition of the plant was more lucrative for Cambodia's square mile music industry, but the price tag of vinyl was still beyond the reach of many young music fans, and it warped easily in the tropical heat. By 1971 Cambodian vinyl came to be eclipsed by a cheaper format: the compact cassette. Every label had a cassette maker, and the new technology took off far quicker in the East than it did in the West; the music shops of the time and the homes of Cambodian teenagers were soon stocked full of cassettes thanks to their low cost.

---

* Sometimes published as 'Twist Twist Khnom'.

These music shops were scattered alongside cinemas on the boulevards around the downtown old market and the middle market, their reservations lined with the classic silhouettes of Simcas, Fiats, Citroëns and Triumphs that enveloped shadows of passing cyclo riders as they elegantly marched by in mid-air. These paid-carriage peddlers would sparsely dot the flowering boulevards to collect a fare before launching off across the city, languorously passing fountains, colonial mansions and modernist buildings as they traversed a spacious and clean capital poised to build its own, independent future. At night the music shops and cinemas pumped out the decibels, supplying a soundtrack to a paradise playground for teenagers lining up to see the latest films and perusing the racks for the newest arrivals in rock 'n' roll, cha cha cha and mambo. That buzz remains to this day along the central reservations of Phnom Penh's boulevards, with hip young things gathering under neon lights; music blasting and motorcycles whizzing by in the warm night air.

The Tonlé Sap River is where Phnom Penh's live music scene kicked off in the 1950s amid Cambodia's reclaimed independence from the French. Floating supper clubs like A-Rex – later known as the Lotus D'Or – played host to the Khmer bourgeoisie, foreign correspondents, dignitaries and a film producer or two, their twinkling lights reflected in the eyes of impoverished quayside dreamers. Onboard, black-tie house bands played jazz and classical repertoires accompanied by immaculate girls in a-line dresses, their canary song just cutting through the smoke and chatter as their vessels chugged their way downstream. Pristine waiters served dinner to dignitaries of old and neoterics and dilettantes of the new while singers like Sinn Sisamouth crooned jazz standards, before his female counterpart, Mao Sareth, lulled diners to the floor with bolero and rumba rhythms. On land, nightclubs like Kbal Thnal and Raja Palace were followed by a string of new openings from the Mekong, the

Olympia, Chaktomuk Dancing, la Lune, the Dancing Water and the Dancing Flower and, largest of all, the state-run Magasin D'état.

Allegedly worried that foreign dignitaries would be bored in Cambodia, Sihanouk instructed the building of the Magasin D'état – or 'Magetat', as it was commonly called – shortly after becoming head of state in 1955. On warm cicada nights, the Magetat's red leather booths enveloped friends and lovers; musicians performed in front of a rouged silk-curtain and patrons traversed the red and white themed dining room to tap their feet on the parquet dancefloor. Military men danced alongside embassy workers, and the girls gazed with Beatles-inspired adoration at the rock 'n' rollers who alternated every forty-five minutes with a full brass-band orchestra.

The Magetat helped launch and maintain the careers of many famous musicians, including members of the rock bands Apsara and Bayon and female singers like Huoy Meas, Cambodia's very own Édith Piaf. A host and announcer on RNK radio, singer and national treasure Huoy Meas made her way early on in an industry dominated by men. But within a short time the civil rights movement and the 1960s sexual revolution arrived in the West, and around the globe many nations were rewriting the conventions of the 1950s. In Cambodia some educated women were gaining positions within government and the economy, and women from the ruling classes were encouraged to take an interest in culture and the arts. In front of the camera, and on the grooves of records, the tide of sexism was turning. The arts paved the way of change for Cambodian women. Women with their own ideas and personas, women who sang of love and sex both passively and defiantly, even if their songs were most often written by men.

Petite balladeers like Sihanouk favourites Sieng Dy and So Savoeun both subscribed to Cambodia's *chbab srey* ('the Code of

Conduct for Women'). It was a code in poem form – undoubtedly written by a man in the 1800s – promoting 'quietness and harmonious and proper behaviours' in Cambodian women. Outwardly, Dy and Savoeun's attitude towards the men in their songs was submissive, complaisant, their stage presence stationary, their lyrics spiked with innocence, yearning and heartache. Dy and Savoeun's forerunners, songstresses of the late 1950s and early 1960s like Chhuon Malay and Mao Sareth abided by the same code too. When the twist arrived on Cambodian dancefloors, these singers struggled to loosen up their hip joints. They'd been raised on traditional Cambodian social dances like the *saravan* (a popular couples dance using the arms to mimic a bird in flight), the *chok krapeus* (the 'shrimp picking' dance; a line dance with fluid, gesticulating hand movements) and the popular circle dances *romvong, rom kbach* and *rom lam leav* which, to this day, look just as fitting on urban dancefloors as in the tribal forest clearings from which they originated. From here the singers transitioned easily to the precise, tidy, line-dancing movements of the Madison, but the twist engaged a part of the female anatomy that had been harnessed by tightly wrapped traditional skirts – called *sampots* – since the 1st century's Funan Empire.

However, as the 1960s progressed, and the miniskirt arrived, singers like Sieng Dy's sister, Sieng Vanthy, put her best go-go boot forward, rolling her hips across many a Phnom Penh dancefloor. Though no woman in Cambodian music embodied the liberation of the 1960s quite like Pen Ran. With her trademark backcombed bob, flirty poses, figure-hugging outfits and voguish moves, Ran flouted convention and injected post-war fun and the sexual revolution into her stage and vocal performances. The northern girl from humble beginnings shook things up and administered a good dose of sass and wit into the lyrics of her rock and go-go songs. Often ironic and witty, she challenged a male-led industry with feminist undertones, waving the flagpole of youth, freedom and independence with song titles like 'It's too Late, Old Man' and 'I'm a Maiden, not a Widow'. She wasn't afraid to experiment with different styles, and her repertoire crossed over psych, bolero, ska, Cuban music and even soul, her lion-hearted vocal and attitude earning her the moniker of 'our Cambodian soul singer'.

Ran's male counterpart was Liev Tuk. Influenced heavily by Wilson Pickett and James Brown, the rock star left his conventional start behind and carved out a niche for himself with his energetic live performances, coiffed hair and screeching vocals. Western influence extended to some of his covers, including a gritty, lyricized version of Booker T. & the MG's 'Hip Hug-Her' and a

Cambodian 1960s/1970s record sleeves.

soulful, delicate cover of the Addrisi Brothers' 'Never My Love', made famous in the US by the Association in 1967.

Ran and Tuk pushed the mainstream as far as it could go, but while Ran especially enjoyed a great deal of fame and fortune, she was never alpha female. Her fellow Battambang native, a singer by the name of Ros Sereysothea would come to claim this prize as well as the hearts of a nation – both then, and now.

The same year the Association released 'Never My Love' Sinn Sisamouth convinced a nineteen-year-old Ros Sereysothea to move to Phnom Penh, and within a short time the pair were bringing a 'Tammi Terrell and Marvin Gaye' Motown vibe to Cambodia. Their romantic duets were so potent and prolific that many were convinced that the love they so often sang for each other was real. They were the king and queen of Cambodian rock and pop.

Reserved and softly spoken, Sereysothea's country-girl stage presence was not a patch on that of her rival, Pen Ran. Sereysothea played the romantic heroine to Ran's tomboy. They had studied together and had made it big in the same profession, but that is where the similarities ended. Unlike her ex-schoolmate, Sereysothea's beehive hairstyle was often paired with less provocative clothing; a-line dresses and buttoned-up-to-the-neck shirts, her upbeat, freewheeling melodies often at odds with her tragic, lovelorn lyrics. From traditional ballads to Latin rhythms to psych and garage-rock belters like her biggest hit 'Chnam Oun Dop-Pram Muy' ('I'm Sixteen') – to which Ran responded sarcastically with her own pop classic, 'I'm Thirty-One' – her back catalogue was not only varied, but prolific.

By 1970, as Sereysothea's star continued in its ascendance, anti-Sihanouk sentiment had long been growing among the intelligentsia and within the ranks of his own cabinet. The head of state's increasing focus on the arts – he had by now produced, directed and scripted nine of his own feature films and recorded many songs – and handling of the anti-communist, anti-monarchist guerrilla force, the Khmer Serei, and other rebel factions, had turned opinion against the once popular leader. Sihanouk's cabinet were far less concerned about the Khmer Serei than Sihanouk, who had taken on a personal – and in his cabinet's opinion, politically reckless and time consuming – vendetta against the Cambodian nationalist Khmer Serei (who'd accused Sihanouk of communist sympathies) and, frankly, anyone who dared smear or slander his good name. Some members of the government banded together in secret and busied themselves with preparations to overthrow Sihanouk and his Sangkum party.

On 18 March 1970 – while Norodom Sihanouk was on a state visit to Moscow – the Prince's cousin, Lieutenant General Sisowath Sirik Matak, and the premier, General Lon Nol, led a bloodless *coup d'état*, exiling Sihanouk from power and installing their own nationalist, right-wing military government in his place. The political leaning of the new power and its links to America – who were at war with North Vietnam – ended Cambodia's neutrality and plunged the country into almost five years of war. The Khmer Republic's troops were attacked on all sides by the North Vietnamese Army (PAVN) and the Communist Party of Kampuchea, who, in truth, Sihanouk had worked long and hard to keep at bay. They were by now known as the Khmer Rouge.

Since the mid-1960s the 'Red Khmers', led by Pol Pot, had been gaining support from farmers in Cambodia's countryside. When they suffered poverty and starvation resulting from the Sangkum's heavy taxes, or lost their crops, their land or their homes in American air raids meant for suspected PAVN and Viet Cong soldiers hiding in the Cambodian jungle, the Khmer Rouge were there with the rice bowl, at the bomb craters, ready to console and cajole distraught smallholders. They fanned the flames of government and military corruption, landowner greed and foreign exploitation, swaying vulnerable countrymen and women to their side. For life in the countryside was a world away from the film stars and glitterati traversing Phnom Penh's dancefloors, and the intellectuals debating in the city's lecture halls. From that distance, Phnom Penh seemed almost immune from the fighting, poverty and hardship tearing the rest of the country apart. The capital's inhabitants – deemed imperial by the anti-imperialist Khmer Rouge – were added to their enemy list, and the divide between countryside farmer and affluent urbanite grew.

With their royal champion in exile, Phnom Penh musicians under the new Lon Nol regime were given a choice: join us and work, or resist and don't. The new government effectively nationalized radio and TV for propaganda purposes, and while this was no different to what Prince Sihanouk had done in his time, or the French before him, there were many royalists and Sihanouk devotees who resisted the new regime, at least for a while. Sisamouth was one who held out the longest; his wife claiming he was out of work for as much as a year.

Members of the King's Guard Orchestra were sent away for a month of 're-education', musicians elsewhere were encouraged to don military garb for public performances, and the hippies and rockers were pressured to cut their long hair. They sang fewer songs about love, and began singing about the nationalist revolution and criticizing the monarchy. The 1970s brought newcomers; folk and heavy rock came to Cambodia with pioneers like Yol Aularong, Pou Vannary, the Drakkar band, and those who followed in their wake.

No band embodied 1970s Cambodian rock better than the Drakkar band. Trailblazers from the very first, their music ushered in a harder, more American rock influence, thanks to the sounds they emulated from US military radio and their own frontline experience playing for the troops in war-torn Vietnam. Their shows on the Phnom Penh party circuit were legendary.

Often antagonistic and sometimes quarrelsome, their drummer Ouk Sam Ath taunted the post-war establishment with his shirt-less appearance; and frontman Touch Tana picked fights with the audience and other bands on the concert roster. They were the second coming of the *yé-yé* bands of the 1960s. A hard rock group within an industry dominated, at the time, by solo musicians.

Their closest solo counterpart, Yol Aularong, was inspired by the Rolling Stones and the French folk singer/garage rocker Antoine. His frontman antics could parallel Iggy Pop on energy alone and his songs were often filled with humour and social commentary. He rebelled against the bourgeoisie establishment of his youth with hit songs he penned in the early 1970s; covers like '*Yuvajon Kouge Jet*' (a psych version of the punk anthem 'Gloria'), his fuzz guitar often sparring with a Hammond organ to ignite his go-go dancers. His stage presence was mettlesome; he'd lurch his skinny trouser-clad frame to and from the mic, throwing out heavy garage riffs and comedic lyrics the audience could get drunk and hurl themselves around the dancefloor to.

His antithesis, the folk songstress Pou Vannary, was also a fan of American music and had a natural ability for mimicking English and American accents, which was allowed under the Lon Nol regime but had been seen as a form of youth defiance under the previous Sangkum government and banned from the radio. The original Cambodian hippy, Vannary was the first Cambodian woman to play a guitar onstage – a vast, acoustic copy of a Hofner Congress – and became best known for her haunting vocals and the rock-lite cover songs that propelled her to stardom in 1969. Throughout the early 1970s she supplemented her recording career by entertaining Cambodia's troops, fronting the military band the 3rd D.I.

From March 1969 to May 1970, as the neighbouring Vietnam war escalated further, US National Security Adviser Henry Kissinger ordered Operation Menu, an apocalyptic bombing campaign of the areas surrounding the Ho Chi Minh trail, designed to cripple the routes that carried the Viet Cong's arms and food supplies from North to South Vietnam, and their sanctuaries and bases along the trail. This was followed soon after by Operation Freedom Deal which cast the net wider, carpeting at least half of Cambodia with bombs. That campaign lasted until 1973. Reports vary on the exact tonnage of explosives dropped by the US on Cambodia during the Vietnam War, but after President Clinton declassified military documents in 2000, historians Ben Kiernan and Taylor Owen uncovered a figure far exceeding two million tons: more than the UK and its allies dropped on Europe and the Pacific theatre during the whole of the Second World War.

The invasion of 'neutral' Cambodia by the US helped to fuel Khmer Rouge propaganda in rural Cambodia, as well as anti-war sentiment and widespread protesting in the USA. In a televised address to the nation on 20 April 1970 President Nixon emphasized the continued withdrawal of troops in Vietnam, insisting that the invasion of Cambodia would help achieve that goal by enabling him to bring back another 150,000 men. The same number of Cambodians were estimated to have been killed by US bombs during the Vietnam War. Clearly, the life of a US soldier was worth far more to the American government than that of a Cambodian civilian.

With the Khmer Rouge's propaganda wheel by now in full swing the 3,000-strong army gained some 37,000 extra recruits between 1970 and 1973, along with control of vast swathes of the country. Their first conquest – the north-western region of Cambodia – was handed to them by the North Vietnamese Army (PAVN), who had invaded in the summer of 1970 in an effort to protect the military bases they'd set up along Cambodia's eastern border which were central to the success of their Vietnam War effort. At the same time, growing tensions between Cambodia and

Vietnam were marked by widescale protest in Cambodia against North Vietnamese aggression and the neigbouring, escalating Vietnam War and US bombing. Earlier, in the spring of 1970, Cambodian military and civilians alike had massacred hundreds of migrant Vietnamese, sending their bodies back down the Mekong as a message to Vietnam. Enemy lines were formally initiated that summer between Lon Nol's US-backed Khmer Republic Army and the China/North Vietnam-backed Khmer Rouge, thus igniting civil war between government and Khmer Rouge insurgents. The Khmer Rouge gained ground fast and by 1972 their territory extended everywhere except the land routes connecting Phnom Penh and the north-western regions, the mining town of Pailin and the ports surrounding the Gulf of Thailand. By the following year only these ports, the jungles to the north-west, Pailin and a few cities and airports – Phnom Penh, Battambang, Kampong Thom, Kampong Chhnang, Kampong Cham and Siem Reap – remained in the hands of the Khmer Republic.

Lon Nol's Khmer Republic government was corrupt and disorganized, its army largely untrained, unpaid and outnumbered for months on end. Khmer Rouge fighters on the other hand were hardened radicals, skilled in guerrilla warfare; their leadership was a self-proclaimed brotherhood shrouded in mystery. Unlike many communist regimes, to begin with the Khmer Rouge lacked an idolized figurehead like Mao or Stalin. Many Cambodians didn't know who their leader was until the last year of the regime, when a human identity emerged by the name of 'Pol Pot'. Until then, Pol Pot and his brotherhood of senior officials were simply known collectively as 'the organization', or in Khmer, *Angkar*.

The founding members of the early 1950s incarnation of the Khmer Rouge were a mix of farmers, the anti-colonialist Khmer Issarak movement, the Indochinese Communist Party (ICP) – created in Vietnam – and nationalists drawn to the communist Marxist-Leninist revolution while travelling or studying abroad.

The latter – 'the Paris Set' as they would come to be known – saw peasants around the world as the repressed slaves of capitalism. They believed that applying the revolutionary theories of communists Karl Marx and Vladimir Lenin would lead to Cambodia's independence and, ultimately, salvation. By 1973 the party's leaders were the Paris Set: Brother Number 1: Saloth Sâr (who later renamed himself 'Pol Pot'); Brother Number 3: Ieng Sary; Brother Number 4: Khieu Samphan; and a veteran of the ICP, Brother Number 2: Nuon Chea.

The brotherhood began to collectivize villages, forcing countrymen, women and children who refused to join the regime into slave labour – or, if they escaped, into hiding. The civil war raged on for a further two years, and the death rate spiralled. In total, it's estimated that up to 300,000 Cambodians died during the five-year civil war.

The Khmer Rouge brotherhood. 1st row, l–r: Pol Pot, Vorn Vet.
2nd row, l–r: Nuon Chea, Ta Mok.

Meanwhile, as Phnom Penh held on, the fighting edging ever closer to the city limits, recording stars of the time like Pou Vannary, Yol Aularong and the Drakkar band somehow continued to record the soundtrack to 1970s Cambodia and were better off than some of their contemporaries who relied more on the nightclubs than the party circuit for their income. Between 1973 and 1974 the government cracked down on all entertainment establishments, threatening to close the cities' cinemas and nightclubs.

In response to the encroaching civil war – and the Khmer Rouge's practice of throwing grenades into nightclubs and cinemas – the plan was to protect buildings where large crowds of civilians were essentially defenceless sitting ducks. The film industry argued their case for the government benefiting from the increased military spend that replaced tax breaks on local production, which, by now, was almost at a standstill thanks to the war. The pillars of industry further argued that cinema closures would put an end to social life, thus capitulating to the Khmer Rouge. The nightclubs were not so persuasive, but they continued to open and close their doors on a temporary basis until their owners finally put the locks on themselves in the final days before the fall of Phnom Penh. Some artists waited out the storm, some – like Sisamouth – were offered work in Thailand. Some went to work in the clubs of Pailin city, which had heavy security to guard Cambodia's jewel mines. Needless to say, it was the beginning of the end for the careers of many Cambodian musicians.

As American forces pulled out from the Vietnam War and the US withdrew funding from the Khmer Republic's army, the Cambodian government grew ever weaker and more divided. Its leader, General Lon Nol, who had long been regarded by the US and Cambodians alike as a puppet, became further dependent on the counsel of Buddhist mystics. He was losing his mind, reportedly ordering his military helicopters to sprinkle a circular line of consecrated sand around Phnom Penh city to protect it from approaching Khmer Rouge forces. By early 1975 platoon after Khmer Republic platoon simply fell or fell back from their last remaining strongholds surrounding their military bases and cities.

On 17 April 1975 the Khmer Rouge army invaded the capital and overthrew Lon Nol's regime. They brought with them an extreme form of Maoist communism: a utopian dream of agrarian life, a classless society of Khmer equals who lived and ate together, a rewriting of history, a return to year zero. Anyone who resisted their way of life – who was not ethnically Khmer, or was found to favour ideologies of imperialism, modernism, elitism and Western society – was put to the sword.

Within hours of the takeover the army began rounding up the city's two million occupants to evacuate them, spreading the lie that the Americans were coming to bomb the city. Civilians were told that they would only be going two or three miles from the city and would return in a few days. Instead, the American bombs never came and the civilians walked for days, in some cases weeks, to forced labour camps. Many were forced into marriages or faced starvation, illness and death over the course of the next three years, eight months and twenty days. Families were torn apart, children brainwashed and armed by the regime. Men, women and children were forced to kill their fellow countrymen in what became Cambodia's autogenocide. In the evacuated cities, banks were dynamited and Phnom Penh's 20,000 hospital patients were turfed out to stagger and crawl to the countryside, the elderly and the infants stumbling side by side. Many died or starved en route, and so many more died in systematic purges and unimaginable cruelty and violence as the Khmer Rouge Brotherhood's vision imploded on itself.

The regime stripped the middle and upper classes of their positions, turning society upside down. Now the provincial lower classes held positions of leadership and authority, and the metropolitan middle and upper classes harvested rice and built dams. The Khmer Rouge believed in the old Khmer proverb: 'With water make rivers, with rice make armies.' But the harvests – farmed no longer by the traditional peasant class, but by untrained

Cambodians working on an irrigation project. 'January 1st' dam, Chinith River, Kampong Thom Province, 1976.

former accountants and shopkeepers – failed, and the district and regional leaders (former farmers and soldiers) under pressure to fulfil their rice quotas, grew evermore paranoid. They refused all outside aid, instead, instigating extensive searches for 'the enemy within', ordering widespread executions and filling mass graves that came to be known as the killing fields. Approximately 1.7 million people – over 20 per cent of the population – are estimated to have died from disease, exhaustion, murder and starvation in those few short years. Under the Khmer Rouge's Democratic Kampuchea, artists were targeted for their imperialist and Western influence. Those who were recognized were killed.

Much like their southern, Westernized neighbours fearing the Viet Cong, Cambodian musicians, fans and collectors of modern and Western-influenced music hid their identities and buried their music. Literally. Holes were dug, nooks were found, and records were poured into these hiding places. Their film industry counterparts were likewise muted, and much of their work was lost in the chaos of evacuations, deaths, squatting and unclaimed land titles that followed in the aftermath of genocide. I met a film buff called Rin Chhoum Virak who'd uncovered old documents detailing an output of 700 Cambodian movies before 1975. Since then, only 400 have been accounted for. The creative industries were devastated, an estimated 90 per cent of artists killed, and, even now, recovery and preservation cannot bring back some of the country's centuries-old traditions, arts and culture.

In one sense, the diaspora of artists and music fans fleeing the Khmer Rouge regime saved Cambodian music. But those who made it to the safety of other countries before or after the genocide, some taking their records with them, were now flung so far apart that they had little or no access to the music of the past, no national culture in which to create. Even in the 1980s and 1990s – when the reign of the Khmer Rouge had ended and the survivors made it back to Cambodia, their music resurfacing again – years of fighting between PAVN (the People's Army of Vietnam) and the rebel factors of the Khmer Rouge kept recovery at a snail's pace.

The return of independence and a working infrastructure to Cambodia at the end of the Cambodian-Vietnamese war in 1991 – and the support of collectors and the diaspora community – brought about a revival of Cambodia's golden age music. The politicization of Cambodian radio loosened, tourism returned, and the release of the *Cambodian Rocks* compilation in 1995 on the US label Parallel World heralded the start of a resurgence and global interest in this music.

Compiled by an English teacher named Paul Wheeler from six cassettes he bought in a market in Siem Reap, the songs had already been remixed in Long Beach, California, for the Chlangden label by a Cambodian refugee named Thoeung Son – who added electronic drums and keyboards to refresh his original cassette dubs – before these remixes made their way back to the markets of Siem Reap, and into Wheeler's hands.

Ethnomusicologist Professor David Novak and the Cambodian Vintage Music Archive's co-founder Nate Hun tried to track down Thoeung Son in 2019, only to find that they were too late: Son, the man responsible for the derivation of much of the Cambodian rock compilations in circulation, had died two years earlier.

Since the initial Parallel World collection, more than a dozen Cambodian rock compilations have been released, most notably by some renowned, independent reissue labels like Sublime Frequencies (*Cambodian Cassette Archives*), Dust for Digital (*Don't Think I've Forgotten* soundtrack), Lion Productions (*Groove Club* series), and specific album and single releases, from Metal Postcard's *Drakkar 74* album reissue to French label Akuphone's two Baksey Cham Krong singles.

I went back to Cambodia to uncover for myself the stories of the musicians who survived, and those who didn't. The quest took me not only to Cambodia but to Europe and the US in search of those who had lived to tell their story. There were thousands of miles of travel, years of research, too many phone calls and hours of interviews to count. But there were also friendships and madcap escapades along the way – from shaving buffalos to going on tour with a revivalist. In the wake of war and in the absence of records and books destroyed by the Khmer Rouge, of missing posters and newspaper clippings that once clung to walls bombed by American forces, I went back looking for answers. I entered into this voyage in the spirit of preservation, of culture, and memory; of adopting the same storytelling traditions that have preserved centuries of Cambodia's history, literature and proverbs, by listening to the voices of those who lived this story and committing their memories to paper for all time. I wanted to capture Cambodia's golden age of music before it was forever silenced by the deaths of its last remaining survivors, and maybe inspire a new listener or two along the way. This book tells of my adventures uncovering the treasure of Cambodian music, and those living treasures who played it.

The following chapters are their lives and their stories. They belong to the artists who survived not only the 1960s, but also genocide. More, even than them, this book belongs to those we lost along the way.

2

Palace Music

Svay Sor surveys his classroom.

'Hello and thank you for flying Cathay Pacific. Ladies and gen-
tlemen, we request your full attention as the flight attendants
demonstrate the safety features of this aircraft . . .' a saccharine,
Asian-American voice announced over the tannoy. Most of the
passengers remained defiantly disobedient, eyes down and

absorbed in their books, but I lay mine face down in my lap. I have always loved an aeroplane safety demonstration: the rush of anticipation, that amber light signalling the impending journey and the ensuing synchronized choreography of oscillating arms. The row of heavily made up, kitschy uniformed men and women fading back towards the first-class curtain, diminishing along with my selective hearing. I'd listen out for my favourite phrases like 'stow your tray table'.

'In the event of an emergency,' the voice continued, 'assume the bracing position.'

'What, no "BRACE, BRACE"? That's my favourite line,' I pouted at Kevin who hadn't so much as looked up from the duty-free magazine resting on the peaks of his tall, bent knees. Nothing tantalizes my Midwest American husband like a bargain, and he lurched powerlessly towards the red fonts and strikethrough numerals like a mule to a carrot and stick. As the demonstration was wrapping up, I looked beyond his downcast eyes to the oval window and the clouds that hung habitually over England. Knowing that the next time I'd see that sky, feel its heavy shadow and that sharp, cool breeze would be in six months' time, or perhaps even longer if the winds of destiny willed it so.

The date was 8 April 2014. Two days earlier I'd withdrawn all of our savings from the bank. With traveller's cheques and Kevin's TEFL teaching certificate in hand, we boarded a plane bound for Phnom Penh to uncover the Cambodian rock mystery. Touching down sixteen hours later, we made our way through the airport's sliding doors and into the frenzied bedlam of tuk tuk drivers on the other side, picking up the most persistent driver in the throng.

Phnom Penh is an assault on the senses. Motorbikes race in all directions across both roads and pavements, amplifiers compete, shouting over one another in Khmer; the smell of sweet spices, fermented fish and drains cling to the air – the thick, polluted air that slaps new arrivals in the face like a hot, heavy hand. I was born in an Asian city. I spent the first eight years of my life in Hong Kong. So in a sense every return to urban Asia feels like a homecoming. There's something in the heat, noise, pollution, chaos, the hustle and bustle, the freedom and lawlessness of some Asian cities that tells me 'this is where I belong'. Phnom Penh embodies it all.

Kevin and I sat in the back seat of our tuk tuk in silence, listening to the hum of motorbikes, flashes of car radios and snippets of Khmer conversations from mobile phones tucked into helmets at traffic lights. Accelerating alongside other tuk tuks and SUVs – driven by gangsters with Glocks in their glove compartments – familiar lush, green boulevards lined with palms and white champa magnolias flashed through gaps in the traffic, their crowns culminating just below the matted, tangled telephone and electrical wires that lined our route – communicative lifelines for the billboards and townhouses of central Phnom Penh.

After all the sacrifices, rounds of toast and 50 pence soups – the hours, days, weeks and months of planning and research – we were back in our beloved Cambodia revisiting these known sights, and a sense of fruition washed over me. Kevin and I turned to one another. I took in the colour and life returning to his olive skin and darting hazel eyes, the mass of sandy-coloured hair – that, after a sixteen-hour flight and a kilometre in a tuk tuk, now resembled less Ray Davies more Hendrix – and beamed. As the traffic grew thicker and the sights more persistent and familiar, we turned into the dimly lit narrow warren of Tonle Bassac Lanes where we stayed with a friend for a few days and worked on setting ourselves up in our new city.

No one walks in Phnom Penh, especially in its hottest, driest months of April or May, but, in an effort to save money, Kevin and I must have lumbered our pink, dehydrated bodies around every part of the city centre, wilting en route in air conditioned shops and bar stops, saved by coconuts and Royal-D rehydration sachets. It was on one particularly long walk back from a mobile phone shop that we stopped off at a Mexican bar, plonked our sunburned aching bodies down on a couple of bar stools, gasped 'two waters and one beer' to the waiter, and loudly gulped our icy water tumblers down like we'd crawled out of the Sahara. I watched as a runaway water droplet escaped, following the line of Kevin's strong, angular jaw, before settling among the sweat lines that ran down his neck.

'Ah,' we sighed, reinflating.

'OK, so just to recap on our first two weeks,' Kevin started. 'We've found a flat, set up a bank account, got sim cards, started a country band with a Filipino guitar player called Jun. You found a translator/fixer, we've probably walked around the entire city by now, lost about 20 lbs in sweat, confused and amused the locals . . . I think we've done OK so far.'

'And started learning Khmer,' I interjected.

The previous week, in Phnom Penh's red-light district, we'd begun our language learning alongside an American I'd met – an English teacher named Paul Eldred. The organization behind the classes administered just about the strangest dichotomy of an NGO you could ever hope to come across. It had two missions: the first was to teach Khmer to *barangs* – the Khmer word for French people and, furthermore, all foreigners – and the second was to provide a crèche for the children of local sex workers.

So, once a week, Paul, Kevin and I sat on child-size plastic chairs, gazing at a miniature whiteboard penned by our teacher Mr Lee, learning the Khmer words for every conceivable animal egg and making up nonsensical sentences about every type of moon. Behind our circle of miniature chairs, small gangs of giggling children ran out from the crèche divide every few minutes to refill their cups at the water cooler – a game they never tired of. The lessons became especially useful later when I finally got to grips with Khmer grammar and realized why the coconut seller had been looking at me so strangely every morning when I'd proudly requested a coconut.

'*Muy dong*,' I'd beam, only to be met with a quizzical look that bordered on repulsion. What I hadn't realized, until Mr Lee pointed it out, was that in Khmer grammar, the number goes *after* the noun. Putting the words in the wrong order could, at best, be confusing but, at worst, the subtle differences between many words compounded by rookie mispronunciations could lead perilously towards an altogether ulterior meaning. I could have been forgiven for a minor grammar mistake or mispronunciation if my mistake simply reverse-transformed to 'coconut one' but, according to Mr Lee, by reversing these two words they had taken on a completely different meaning, and I had in fact been asking the coconut man every morning to 'hit me'. I swiftly moved on from that mistake and onto other mispronunciation conundrums, like introducing Kevin not as 'my husband' but as the closely sounding 'my ladyboy'.

'Anyway . . . high five to our achievements so far,' I said to Kevin, smacking my hand against his, before he returned to his icy beer. 'What's next on the list?' I asked rhetorically, retrieving a sweaty ink-smudged paper from my pocket.

'So . . . I need to go to the Bophana Center to do some research, and you need to get your suit ironed for job hunting. And we need to set up a PO box.'

'Right. How about you go to the Bophana Center now,' Kevin suggested. 'And I'll get my suit ironed, and maybe we leave the PO box for tomorrow?'

'Sounds like a plan,' I said, slapping the beer money and a tip down on the bar, and bracing once more for the furnace outside.

A ten-minute walk away, the Bophana Center was an oasis of calm and culture. Founded by Rithy Panh, an Oscar-nominated Cambodian filmmaker, and veteran Cambodian filmmaker Ieu Pannaker in 2006, the research institute specializes in acquiring

Khmer film, photography, television and sound archives. A feat of modern and traditional Cambodian architecture, the building blends the contemporary Phnom Penh townhouse design with the city's modernist era, its balcony poles reminiscent of historic Khmer stilt houses. Beyond the crisp white exterior lies a traditional red and white ceramic floor, work spaces, ceiling fans, white walls brightened by open balconies, and a library of books housed in dark, heavy Khmer wood, the tops of which are strewn with lounging cats. A couple of blocks away from my apartment, the Bophana Center became something of a second home to me; my very own culture temple. While my fixer, Lim Sophorn, spent those first few weeks finding telephone numbers to set up interviews with musicians, I spent hours at Bophana copying information from books on Cambodian culture, my right hand writing, my left hand often stroking a sleeping cat, its ears twitching to the gentle birdsong carried in by May's emerging monsoon breeze.

It was on my walk home from Bophana one afternoon in early May that my fixer, Sophorn, called. I'd met him at the Center soon after I'd returned to Phnom Penh; it's where he'd worked his first job, fresh out of college. Undoubtedly the most innocent, honest and honourable person I'd ever met, Sophorn had some knowledge and appreciation of Cambodian 1960s rock music, a good grasp of the English language and a kind, gentle spirit. From the moment we met I knew that he was the one to take this journey with me. In retrospect, however, it's a wonder we ended up getting as far as we did, for Sophorn was a greenhorn to translation and fixing; as naive about the world then as I was about Cambodia and its culture, but therein, I believe, lay a lot of our subsequent good fortune.

That particular phone call in early May marked a milestone in our working relationship, for Sophorn had telephoned with the news that he'd set up an interview for the next day with a master musician called Svay Sor, aka 'White Mango'. It was to be our first interview together. We arranged to meet at Bophana the following morning and I hurried home excitedly to ready my questions and equipment.

In the shade of a tamarind tree within the grounds of a pagoda on the outskirts of Phnom Penh, Sophorn and I waited. We would come to learn that timekeeping was not one of Svay Sor's strong points. We stared across the grounds at the temple gates, willing Svay Sor to appear and, with nothing else to do, made small talk, and I got to know the young man who was to be my translator. We talked of families and of the family home Sophorn shared with his sister and mother; the home we'd passed en route. He showed me photos on his phone of their soft, kind faces so similar to his own, just more feline. A line of saffron robes flapped gently in the breeze behind us as I talked about my life in London, and Sophorn's usually wide, round eyes narrowed quizzically. Inevitably, the conversation turned back to work, and the Cambodian artists we had planned to track down. He showed me a photo of an ex-beauty queen and 1960s actress he offered to introduce me to, pointing to her photo before looking to me and saying, 'You know, in this photo, even though she is much older than you, she is much prettier,' and chuckling with an errant glimmer in his eye. This was the closest to 'daring' Sophorn ventured. And because of his pure heart – there wasn't a malicious bone in his body – I crumpled with laughter, embracing his frank candour in all its splendour.

Half an hour passed before we got through to Sor's phone, and around fifteen minutes later a man arrived at the temple gates in a maroon shirt sheltering a flash of gold medallions; his sunglasses hid eyes that perused the vicinity for us. With both legs planted firmly either side of his bike, one arm dropped at his side, Sor was every inch the action movie star. But before I could catch him, he shot off back down the red dirt road – and though running, for me, is practically an out of body experience, I took off after him like a bat out of hell, arms waving in all directions and shouting in Khmer, 'Uncle! Uncle! *Stop!*'

Glancing back, I could see that Sophorn's lanky limbs had barely moved four paces while I continued to flail and weave with all the grace of a hippo down a death-trap highway. Mercifully, Svay Sor must have seen me in his rearview mirror, for he eventually swung a 180 degrees back around for my rather breathless introduction, before I hopped back on Sophorn's scooter and Sor led us home.

We were at the city's drop-off point, a barren landscape of sparsely scattered houses, thick dry brush and a wide open dirt road. In the distance I could see yellow rice fields sucked dry by spring's unrelenting sun and desperately awaiting the life-giving monsoon season. They seemed to serve only to accentuate the contrast as we turned into Svay Sor's street. Lined with pastel-coloured houses, bougainvillea and palm trees, it was an oasis tucked behind a desolate desert. There was a large green swing seat in his front yard gently rocking a few children and a music school set up under an awning. Twenty red leather-bottomed fold-up chairs and keyboards faced a white board littered with musical notes; a PA system lay dormant in the corner. Hanging proud above the doorway a framed 'master' medal with a royal insignia caught my eye.

'Prime Minister Hun Sen awarded me with this medal of honour,' Sor smiled softly, following my gaze. 'And it was signed by Prince Ranariddh, for my musical talent.'

It was one of a number of medals he went on to show me, including one from China's former premier, Zhou Enlai, and another from Indonesia's former vice president. They recognized Sor's services to Cambodia's palace music and were a legacy to his life before the war – the life I wanted to learn about.

Crossing over the threshold, Sor invited us to sit and share the pineapple, mangosteens and bananas I'd brought him. Cambodia is steeped in ritual and ceremony derived from Buddhism; it's a place where a gift of fruit bears far greater meaning than simple gratitude. In the context of Svay Sor it's a *yok chett krou* which, translated literally, means to 'take the teacher's heart'. A symbolic offering, celebrating the high social status of Svay Sor as both teacher and master musician, it reflects the wider Buddhist ceremony of honouring teachers alive and dead through *sampeah krou* ceremonies. These take place before or after performances, in a time of need or before an important occasion. Whether he knew I knew it or not, I was performing my own *sampeah krou* ceremony for Sor, having read articles that, in their reverence, portrayed his almost mythical, masterly status. For a country founded in courtly dynasties and Buddhism, the path to enlightenment and the concept of a master – one highly skilled and trained in the art of religion, performance or traditional craftsmanship; and one who passes their knowledge on – comes hand in hand. This concept of enlightenment through the teaching of the masters is deep-rooted; as ancient as the bas-reliefs upon which they are celebrated.

Tucking into a mangosteen as Sophorn and Sor discussed the interview logistics, I studied the man they call 'White Mango'. With his soft white cloud of hair and face uncomplicated by its shallow lines, he was the vision of a Zen master. Beyond simply what I could see, it was what I could feel in his presence. Perhaps it was who he'd always been, or perhaps it was an aura nurtured while spending the better part of the 1990s in Japan, the place synonymous with Zen Buddhism. Whatever it was, my spinning, frantic world seemed to slow in his presence, the outside noise softened and time quickly became lost.

A stalwart of the Cambodian 1960s music scene, accomplished session player and a go-to for national TV music – then and now

– Svay Sor had originally piqued my interest in a short piece I'd read in Phnom Penh University magazine, *Dontrey*, about his career links with the Royal Palace in which he outlined how the palace provided a rich training ground for many Cambodian musicians of the 1960s. Svay Sor had to rise through the ranks of the disciplined and revered Royal Palace music training programme before earning his place in the company. Following a rigorous three-year training course – talented teenage musicians from all walks of life, from paupers to royals, were welcome to join the ranks – those who stayed the course achieved paid jobs at the palace and most respected universities and institutes of the time. The students learned within groups in the morning – from Cambodian styles such as the Royal Ballet's newly renovated *pinpeat* orchestra to a twenty-five- or thirty-strong Western marching band – with individual lessons taking place in the afternoons. Sessions were conducted on the Chanchhaya ('Moonlight') Pavilion or in music rooms onsite by Khmer masters and foreign teachers, both Filipino and French, and ranged from theory in both Sanskrit and Western notation to practical work. Sihanouk's mother, Queen Kossamak, known as the patron saint of Khmer dance, invested her personal fortune to house artists and their families within the royal compound and to educate them all, not only in music but in other subjects that would support their training – from the basics of reading and writing to history. The post Second World War era was an exciting time for Cambodian royal dance and music. Men were permitted to join the traditionally female *pinpeat* orchestra and dance troupe; the orchestras regained their strength after the turmoil of the colonial collapse; modern twists on ancient arts were invented and new forms of music and dance like the celestially inspired apsara dance were created.

Svay Sor joined the palace music programme at this time of great resurgence. But what set him apart for me was that he was also born at the Royal Palace in 1937 to one of the palace gardeners. He play-fought with the royal children, was close to the young princes, Naradipo and Ranariddh, and grew up there until the age of fourteen when his father struck out on his own, bought a small city plot to build a house, and moved the family away. Years later this pauper's son would rise to an honourable position in the king's close-knit inner musical circle. As Sor explained, his home would, in fact, come full circle, with the help of a Royal Palace bandleader, a Filipino called Denacio Saem.

Denacio's name would crop up in books and in conversation with a number of ex-palace students I interviewed. Charitable and revered by peers and scholars alike, it seemed the leader of the Royal Fanfare Band had taught just about every musician trained at the palace in the first half of the 1900s. Denacio's work was overseen by a Frenchman named François Perruchot, who led the palace music department from 1913 until 1952. Perruchot created Cambodia's first national anthem and brought written music notation to the kingdom. This meant that musicians could learn from other forms of music and, for the first time in centuries of oral learning, physically record their own music. His protégé, Denacio, shared his own Filipino musical culture with Cambodia and was instrumental in the continuation of *pleng Manil* or 'Manilla [marching band] music', which began as a music-training programme run by Filipino musicians at the Royal Palace as early as 1872 and ranged in style from Mozart concertos to swing jazz to all the fun of the military fanfare. By the early 1900s American jazz music had swept across the Philippines and the Filipino Constabulary Band based out of Cambodia's Royal Palace was shaking traditional Khmer folk music – the chime-tingling *mahori* and wining fiddle gourds that had entertained kings and queens for centuries – to the core with its trombone, horn-blasting brass and Western fanfare arrangements. By the 1940s, when Denacio was appointed the Royal Palace band leader – officially known in

French as *chef d'orchestre* – the marching band was in full swing. Its sonorous tuba rumbled against a cyclical clash of symbols, punctuating the thirty-piece reed, wind, horn and drum sections as they marched to John Philip Sousa songs like 'Semper Fidelis' and 'The Washington Post'.

Denacio was Svay Sor's neighbour and the pair became friends when Sor was around fifteen years old and had nothing much to offer but a little shared appreciation of the French language, a keen ear and a passion to learn and work. Denacio took Sor under his wing and helped him to secure a place in the Royal Palace training programme one year before Cambodia marked its independence from the French in 1953.

An outstanding student, Sor studied harmony and the clarinet under the celebrated French music teacher, Maurice Liébot, a former Jewish concentration camp survivor who lived to be a hundred years old and remained devoted to Cambodian music and Prince Sihanouk long after the Cambodian civil war. Training as a multi-instrumentalist, Svay Sor eventually specialized in the piano and accordion, fast tracking his way to a further scholarship within a year and a half, just half the time of a regular student. A year after being granted a further training scholarship, Sor was a paid palace musician earning a modest monthly salary provided by the civil service. He performed weekly, sometimes nightly, in the palace's great dancehall for royals and foreign dignitaries, honoured his ancestors in Cambodia's ancient temples, and played in Prince Norodom Sihanouk's troupe on ceremonial trips.

Sor soon caught the attention of Sihanouk, and in addition to his continued studies took on some official duties such as tuning the royal piano when the royal tuner and director of the distinguished l'Université des Beaux-Arts, Mam Bophani, was unavailable. Following Sihanouk to his various residencies around the country, Sor would eventually add another notch to his belt as an arranger on some of the prince's own musical compositions, which were mostly classical and bossanova instrumentals or sentimental ballads about women and Cambodian towns that would not have been out of place on the silver screen of Hollywood's golden age or, indeed, Cambodia's. After all, many of them did end up in Sihanouk's own movies. Its unclear how much collaboration was involved in his songwriting process, but as a multi-instrumentalist and as a staunch patriot of both Cambodia and France, Sihanouk wrote for both Western and Khmer instruments, sang in French, English, Khmer and Chinese, wrote largely in the pentatonic scale favoured by Cambodian composers and amassed a stack of protest songs throughout the 1960s and 1970s, often about his latest political adversity.

As Sor talked of pianos and palaces, a mysterious black box in the corner of the room caught my eye. Following my line of vision, he grabbed a hold of his knees, stood up from his armchair, walked over and picked up the black box off the floor. He unclipped the hinge, and inside was a beautiful old accordion, which he played, breathing life into the vinyl bellows and filling the room with sweet syncopated notes. I was lost in his music and all too soon it was time to go. I felt we'd only scratched the surface of what Svay Sor had to say, so before parting ways, we arranged to see each other again.

When I returned to Svay Sor's house the following week, he was finishing up with a class. The septuagenarian taught children in one-hour lessons, three times a day, seven days a week; some children travelling as far as ten kilometres to his school on foot. I recognized four of the students from the swing in his garden the last time we were there. The middle boy was shyly singing into a microphone, while the eldest boy accompanied him on keyboard, another on guitar, and the youngest – a girl who couldn't have been older than eleven – was staring at the floor, shuffling her feet, hands tucked in under her bottom. I remembered feeling unsettled by their demeanour the last time I was there. Both the girl and eldest boy couldn't look us in the eye, and the young girl's eyes were infinitely sad. Svay pointed each of them out in turn, and revealed their stories. 'I feed, house and take care of four of the children, and I send them all to school,' he told me. 'Two of them are brothers, and a sister, and they were orphaned in April this year. Their parents were drug users and died of AIDS. They all have HIV. The other is a child from the forest [from an ethnic minority tribe]. He could barely speak Khmer when I met him, but he liked music and so I helped him . . . music is like medicine. They're traumatized from what has happened to them, but the other day someone came – who had last seen them months ago – and noticed that the girl has put on weight. And they talk more than they did before, they seem happier.'

Cambodia's indigenous hill tribes have declined rapidly since the Khmer Rouge drove many of them into slavery in the early 1970s, though it also drove some members of the Kreung and Tampuon tribes deeper into hiding, only for them to emerge from the forest almost three decades later, convinced that the war was still going on. The picture for HIV and AIDS is becoming brighter, the number of cases having quartered since the virus reached epidemic proportions in the mid-1990s. However, both ethic minorities and HIV retain their stigmatic, individual marks on Cambodian society today, and in the case of these children I needed no more convincing that the man was a saint. But Sor's own family was still a mystery and I got a sense of something – or someone – missing within the walls of his home. Before I could ask, we got lost in some old photos of his very handsome younger self. One photo was clearly from the Sangkum Reastr Niyum years of Prince Sihanouk's political career; the rest from the life we had yet to talk about. Judging by the moustache, combat trousers and enlarged shirt collars of the Lon Nol era, these shots were taken after the Cambodian *coup d'état* of 1970.

*TVK network television, 1970. L–r: Svay Sor, Touch Chhattha, unidentified man,
Ly Tai Cheng, unidentified drummer, Huoy Meas, unidentified man.*

'This one is when I went to work for the Department of
Broadcasting at TVK television in 1970,' Sor said, handing me
a black and white photo of himself with the rest of the band all
in military garb, on what looked like a minimalist, monochrome
set decorated by the op-art painter Bridget Riley and 1960s
monochrome queen Mary Quant. He pointed out the famous
singer and broadcaster, Huoy Meas on vocals, Touch Chhattha of
the Drakkar band and Ly Tai Cheng of the Amara band on guitars.
Next, he showed me a photo of the famous singer Pen Ran's sister,
the fellow but lesser-known singer Pen Ram, with her backing
band, who played regularly at the Magetat nightclub in Phnom
Penh. Though no records survive to attest to any recording career,
Ram was said to be in demand as a nightclub singer, as well as her
other gigs fronting military bands and backing the likes of rocker
Yol Aularong. In the photo a freshly shaven Sor stands with Ram
and the rest of the band, who are wearing short 1960s ties and
Beatles hairstyles. I guessed from the attire that it must have been

a nightclub band shot, and Sor near enough confirmed it with words inspired by his gaze. 'I played in the Olympia nightclub,' he told me, fingering through more photos from the time. 'It was near Chroy Changvar Bridge [also known as the 'Cambodian–Japanese Friendship Bridge', in a north-western district of Phnom Penh]. As well as Cambodians there were many foreigners who came to play music in this nightclub. In fact, there were many foreign musicians from China, USA, Vietnam, the Philippines and France who came to play in the restaurants and dancing clubs at the time. We had Ben Goodman, a trumpet player from the Philippines, as well as Benny Goodman, a clarinettist from the USA.'

Svay Sor's time of suited supper club bands, playing clarinet at royal and ambassadorial ceremonies, of cleaning his beloved king's saxophones, came to an end with the 1970 *coup d'état*. Much like Sihanouk, the new regime's leader, Lon Nol, was keen to utilize popular culture to influence and coerce the people to his side. Within the walls of the Ministry of Propaganda, the songwriters' association – an official body run by the doyens of the music industry to effectively vet lyrics and the quality of releases – was given a new mandate. Lyrics that degraded Sihanouk and roused age-old hostilities against their neighbouring Vietnamese were encouraged (in particular, the Viet Cong and North Vietnam's army, PAVN, who at the time were supporting Lon Nol's enemy, the Khmer Rouge, by passing Cambodian territory they had invaded over to the insurgents). So too were lyrics that promoted the ideology of the new Lon Nol regime: a mix of chauvinist nationalism and mysticism, or 'Neo-Khmerism' as Lon Nol himself described it. Military garb was prescribed to musicians, although, as with the new lyrics, it was all controlled in a rather haphazard way, and these new practices were not enforced with an iron rod. However, some musicians who remained outwardly loyal to Sihanouk, or who opposed the new regime, did get caught in the political crossfire and were subsequently ousted from their roles. In the reshuffle many jobs were changed. Sor was one musician who needed to continue working – he had nothing else to fall back on. Fortunately, his talent and strong connections in the palace and wider music world presented him with an opportunity. Sor was offered a new role as a talent scout and composer for the RNK radio and the Télévision Nationale Khmère (TVK) network, which fell under the watchful eyes of the Ministry of Propaganda.

'It was my job to advise the director of RNK radio and TVK to select musicians from the Royal Palace, but it was not me that directly employed them,' Sor told me. 'I would give the names to the director and he would then approach them. Names like Pen Ran, Pen Ram, [and guitarist] Ly Tai Cheng . . .'

Though he missed Sihanouk and the palace, the early 1970s were, for the most part, a fairly free and happy time for Sor and many of his colleagues. That is, until around 1973, when the Khmer Rouge escalated their grenade attacks on mass gatherings in Phnom Penh.

On my last visit to interview Sor we talked more about his days at Kosnaka, which began life as Radiodiffusion Nationale Khmère (RNK), Cambodia's first national, state-owned radio station in the forties. Originally intended as a mouthpiece on public events and current, national and international affairs – foreign language songs were initially banned from regular national programming – it also created a platform for music and aired the Cambodian big band orchestras of the time, often live. By the time Sor started working for the station, 1970s rock and pop dominated and Kosnaka was rehashing much of its content from old broadcasts as it approached the mid-1970s and civil war surrounded the capital.

At one point I caught Sor lost in a faraway gaze, and asked if he was comfortable to tell me what happened to him after the Lon Nol period. I chose my words carefully to offer Sor the chance to skip over the Khmer Rouge genocide if he wanted to. But without pause he continued with the events of 17 April 1975, when Phnom Penh fell to the communist army and its inhabitants were swiftly evacuated into the countryside to slave labour camps. Sor was separated from his wife and children in the mêlée and walked thirty to forty kilometres from Phnom Penh to a small village called Tarun (at the time). Sor thought he would be there for a month but ended up staying for a year, before being moved on to work in Battambang, the north-western province otherwise known as Cambodia's rice bowl, famed for its rice production and paddies as far as the eye can see.

'I always hid my identity,' he told me, 'because if Angkar [the Khmer Rouge] knew that I was a musician or worked for Lon Nol they would kill me. What saved me was that they didn't know me . . . not like they did the singer, Sinn Sisamouth, for example. I didn't play music during the Khmer Rouge period. I followed the orders from Angkar and did everything they asked me to do. If they asked me to work in the rice fields, I would work in the rice fields, and if they asked me to dig a ditch, I would dig a ditch.'

Sor stayed in Battambang until the People's Army of Vietnam (PAVN) invaded Cambodia in January 1979 and the Cambodian people were freed from their life of deadly servitude. When the fighting between the PAVN and the Khmer Rouge died down and people were allowed to leave the camps and rural villages and return to their original homes, many ended up seeking refuge in the Thai refugee camps on the border instead. There lay better hope of food and safety than in the land the Khmer Rouge had left behind. But the first thought on Sor's mind was his missing wife and children, so he returned to his old home in Phnom Penh in search of them. Shattered in rubble, the city was barely recognizable. Its abandoned buildings, cars, and ghost gardens the only signs of life from the time before Angkar. After less than four years of power, Pol Pot's agrarian dream to return the land to Year Zero had decimated the Cambodian economy and all its infrastructure. A disastrous harvest in 1979 and years of fighting to follow between PAVN and Khmer Rouge rebels only exacerbated the poverty, starvation and disease and stymied the country's economic return.

As more and more civilians returned to Phnom Penh in 1979 to reclaim their former lives, a number of desperate musicians banded together to reform the state military band under the command of Cambodia's newly installed, Vietnam-backed government, the Kampuchean People's Revolutionary Party. Sor had work and food, but he was alone, not knowing what had happened to the wife and young children he'd been separated from during the evacuation. Many organizations like the Red Cross were working hard to connect the families who'd been separated during the war and genocide and, in 1982, Sor received word from his sister-in-law that she and the rest of his family had been relocated to Japan from a refugee camp. After all he'd survived, there was good news at last.

By then, smuggling and illegal entry to Khao-I-Dang, the oldest refugee camp on the Thai border, was rife. As a result, Thailand was no longer operating an open-door policy and the deaths of desperate illegals trying to get into the camp were rising. In an effort to quell the death toll, the Red Cross loosened restrictions on entries and the UN transferred and redistributed large numbers of refugees to other Cambodian refugee camps along the border. Sor knew the risks involved in crossing the minefields and getting into Khao-I-Dang, but this camp was also his best hope of a relocation to join his family in Japan. After travelling 500 kilometres to the camp, against the odds, he made it in.

'At that time we were told people could stay in the camp for up to three years, but I ended up staying for five years because they loved me for playing music to the refugees in the different camps,' Sor told me, smiling. 'They had Christian songs in their songbook and I didn't have a problem playing Christian songs, so long as I got to play music. One of my best memories from that time was around 1986 when I was given funds by the Thai people to organize a concert to celebrate their king's birthday.'

With that, Sor's eyes glinted, and I watched as he hurriedly retrieved a stack of papers from beside me. I'd presumed he was going to fish out a photo taken at the event, but, instead, he pulled out a tattered book that was wedged into the pile. Opening it, he showed me some handwritten French scrawled on the inside cover. The talk of the Thai king must have made Sor think about his own, beloved Cambodian 'king', Prince Sihanouk – who after his abdication of the throne in 1955 was still referred to as 'King' by his friends and loyal subjects. Since the 1970 *coup d'état* Sihanouk had been living in exile, first in Beijing, and, later, under house arrest in Phnom Penh under the Khmer Rouge, the army he'd pledged his support to shortly after the coup. Sihanouk flew to Beijing on 6 January 1979, the day before the Vietnamese army ransacked Phnom Penh and seized power from the Khmer Rouge. There he sought asylum and, by the time Sor made it to the refugee camp, Sihanouk had established a resistance movement of royalists called Front uni national pour un Cambodge independant, neuter, pacifique, et coopératif (FUNCINPEC for short) and was begrudgingly holding coalition talks with the Khmer Rouge in order to oust the Vietnam-backed government, the PRK. In spite of the politics, he was still the 'People's Father' and loved by many. As Sor handed me the book, I gazed at the romantic curves of French handwriting on the inside front cover and read:

Dear Svay Sor,
Khao-I-Dang Camp, Thailand
With love very deep,
Norodom Sihanouk, 18th June 1986

When Sor heard that Sihanouk was coming to the camp he went to find him. The book Sihanouk gave his former piano tuner and arranger remains one of Sor's most treasured possessions; the memory of their reunion one of his most cherished. It was the memory of an unsevered bond between two kindred spirits who had shared so much history together; Sor had been childhood playmate to the king's children, loyal servant and musical peer. Divided by a war and then reunited in the most unlikely of places. 'Had Sihanouk heard that Sor would be there? Had he brought the songbook especially, or was it already Sor's?' I wondered. Before I could ask, Svay Sor had moved on through the pile to some photographs of his wife and children in Japan. Naturally all his children were photographed with instruments in their hands, and the sight of them prompted the finale to his memoirs. He flashed through this final chapter of his life telling me he'd left the camp in late 1986 and, having finally located his family and fearing for his life in his war-torn homeland, reunited with his wife and children in Japan, before eventually returning to Cambodia in 2000.

We looked out on his wards in the yard, swinging quietly on the great green carriage swing. Sor glanced at me and paused before looking back at the children and opening his mouth for one final tale about the early days of Cambodia's first rock 'n' roll nightclub, the Kbal Thnal, named after its surrounding area in south-east Phnom Penh.

'Kbal Thnal helped start the careers of the singer Sinn Sisamouth, the famous violinist Hass Salan . . . and Peou Vanchon [the little brother of the famous composer, Peou Sipho] who played piano there. There were no walls, just curtains made from leaves. People were so honest back then that you never had to worry about stealing or security. It was special because it was the first nightclub in Phnom Penh. I often cleaned instruments for the musicians, and when I was around fifteen or sixteen years old, I also arranged some music for them.

'Before it became Kbal Thnal, it was called Simoeun's Restaurant; this was around 1950. Simoeun was a French Viet-namese lady and she was like an adoptive mother to me. She bought me a bicycle and books, and gave me some money now and then. I was poor so she took me into her heart. When I couldn't find a job, she sold her restaurant to the man who turned it into the Kbal Thnal nightclub, gave me some money and moved to Vietnam. She did this to help me. Because of this memory, I took in these four children to study in my school and live with me. My adoptive mother, Simoeun, loved me so much. That is why I follow her example with these children.'

It struck me then that Sor had both created, and been a part of, many families throughout his life – biological parents, biological children, adoptive parents and adoptive children – and no doubt endless reams of friends along the way. He had attracted good karma and brought out the goodness in people because of the positivity he exuded. Kindness and talent had opened up the many doors of his extraordinary life, and the teachers, parents, kings and common folk he befriended had undoubtedly shaped the gentle and giving man he was, and still is.

I never did get to the bottom of why he'd returned from Japan to his motherland, leaving his wife and some children behind for a time, but by 2014 his daughter and her children lived close by. He saw them regularly, and his phonebook certainly seemed full. When I last saw him in 2019, his wife had returned from Japan, his school was full and I had the honour of playing music with Sor and his eldest adopted son (one of the boys from the swing). In the interim years, Sor had also befriended the one-time Miles Davis Quintet piano player, American jazz musician Herbie Hancock. Having first visited Cambodia as a UNESCO goodwill ambassador in 2011, the pair met on one of Herbie's many visits, and a friendship based in music that transcended language barriers ensued. Sor was full of surprises like this. He'd drop a bomb in a conversation without a speck of grandiosity or expectation. It was one of the characteristics I so admired in him and, as I was leaving, I was touched to find a photo from the first time we met framed within a collage next to Herbie.

I was sad to say goodbye for what I feared could be the last time, even though Sor – who in 2019 was eighty-two years old – showed no signs of slowing down. It was clear that he'd followed a karmic path, passing on the legacies of Denacio and Mme Simoeun, and he relished the teaching more than anything. Swinging my leg over Sophorn's moped, I watched a flurry of children enter the yard, each readying themselves for class. As Sophorn and I pulled away I spun around to wave, but by now Svay Sor had turned towards the whiteboard, his right hand bending into the curve of a treble clef.

Svay Sor had touched on the rites of passage for Cambodia's golden age of music: musicians originating from the palace, the radio station, the music schools and the church. In a predominantly Buddhist country, it was this final origin, *the church*, that piqued my interest and led me to the brother of the royal piano tuner Svay Sor had sometimes filled in for, another palace musician called Mam Bophani. I'd come across Bophani's name in books and would come to hear it peppered across many conversations I'd have with other artists who came up through the palace and the most prestigious music school of the time, the Royal University of Fine Arts (or what was then called l'Université des Beaux-Arts, or UBA for short). Students graduated there as multi-instrumentalists, the UBA rivalling only the equally vigorous palace training programme in producing the finest musicians in Cambodia. Bophani was the school's director in the golden Sangkum period of the 1950s and 1960s when it was staffed by an impressive roster of Cambodian teachers – including the prominent composer Mer Bun – and a number of international teachers, mainly French and Russian.

Bophani and his equally musical brother, Boutnaray, were legends of the Cambodian music establishment, revered by many who followed them in both time and training – and yet the brothers were shrouded in mystery. Bophani had died long before my own investigation, and those who remembered him couldn't tell me what had happened to him. Before his death, he had been a composer, a director at UBA, a piano master and revered multi-instrumentalist who was deeply influential in shaping the universal education of many musicians in mid-twentieth century Cambodia. I did eventually come across his obituary. He died a devoted layperson and a martyr to his Catholic faith in 1975, the year the Khmer Rouge won the war, and five years after Lon Nol's Vietnam War retaliation and subsequent mass deportations and killings of the Vietnamese. Before then, the Vietnamese accounted for around 92 per cent of Cambodia's 61,000 Catholics.

Bophani's younger brother, on the other hand, was still alive but elderly and reclusive, and if Bophani was a man of mystery then Boutnaray was an absolute enigma. A well-respected palace multi-instrumentalist, teacher and master in his own right, the full details of his story were as elusive as the tales were intriguing. During the Vietnamese occupation from January 1979 to May 1993, when Boutnaray, I'd been told, was a young and bold activist, he'd spoken out and was shot in the leg. His leg recovered but his pride didn't, and he recoiled from the regime and the world outside, which grew more frightening with each passing day – or so went the stories I'd heard from those who knew him. I'd been briefed by a number of people that this story would be off limits, that he will take the words that got him shot to his grave, so the truth is still out there on this one. I'd also been warned that, try as I might, I'd never be granted an audience. Many had tried and failed to do so but my translator and fixer, Sophorn, was an indefatigable optimist and tried every which way to sway Boutnaray's wife. She was chary over the phone, so Sophorn suggested we should go in person to their house in Phnom Penh and give it one last shot. Given that Mam Boutnaray was renowned for having never agreed to an interview with anyone, we weren't expecting to pull it off, but it was worth a go.

After some detours and a few more phone calls, we found the rough location of his house and parked Sophorn's moped outside a nearby hairdressers to wait for Mrs Mam. A few moments later, a short elderly lady arrived and querulously made her way through the parked motorbikes with the maximum of fuss. She continued straight past us without so much as a glance, sharply motioning us to follow her down the side street. It was at this point I twigged that she was Mrs Mam, instinctively braced myself and fell in line.

There was construction going on in the neighbouring house and we all had to climb over a sand hill half a storey high to get into the Mam residence. Mrs Mam went first, scaling the mound like an emperor penguin chick shuffling over a snow dune. Inside, the man in question was seated in his chair, walking stick in hand, and I was immediately struck by his smiling face – so at odds with his wife's world-weary frown. His old irises were rimmed with blue, and dark strands of thinning hair look liked they'd been stretched like strings on a loom, then freed to bounce back over his crown. Mrs Mam and her daughter hurried in and out of the floor-to-ceiling tiled lounge like bluebottles, Sophorn snatching their collective attention in precious moments of stillness. After fifteen minutes of this routine, our gentle reassurances paid off and we were granted thirty minutes of their time to ask our 'non-political' questions. I'm not sure exactly how Sophorn had managed to swing it – already we'd gone further than our predecessors – but I didn't ask. We were on a strict timeframe and there was no time to lose.

Born in 1930, seven years after his brother Bophani, Boutnaray's first instrument was the mandolin. The son of a doctor who loved to sing and play violin, Boutnaray talked to me about the catalyst for his musical destiny, found not in Cambodia, but, in fact, in France.

'I was sixteen or seventeen years old when I went to France to study journalism,' he told me candidly. 'But I ending up transferring to music and I was taught by a Moroccan teacher called Mr Joe and a French teacher called Maurice Liébot. I later studied again with Mr Liébot when he came to teach in Cambodia.'

Boutnaray had spent only a handful of years in France with Svay Sor's same music teacher, the concentration camp survivor, Maurice Liébot, before returning to Cambodia. And yet, some seventy years on, his French was still impeccable.

'It was a private school,' he continued, slipping back from French into Khmer, 'where I studied for six years before I came back to Cambodia. I must have been around twenty-two years old then.'

Convinced he was older than that, Mrs Mam suddenly piped up from the corner with a flurry of angry Khmer words, but the disagreement was terminated by their daughter as quickly as it had escalated. Mr Mam 1 Mrs Mam 0. Disgruntled, Mrs Mam folded her stocky arms as a conversely gaunt but gratified Mr Mam continued to talk about his return to Cambodia. Upon his homecoming, Boutnaray traded piano singalongs and jazz renditions at Parisian parties for an organ and hymns in a Phnom Penh church alongside his brother, Bophani. He was, by then, an accomplished multi-instrumentalist, able to turn his hand to the mandolin, piano, guitar, accordion and church organ, and he marked his return to the motherland with a new name, an artist's name: Mono Cakey.

Throughout their twenties and thirties, the brothers spread their musical branches across the Royal Palace, the nightclubs, the university and radio, but Bophani and Boutnaray remained rooted in the Catholic church. It was what separated them from their peers, what defined them, and, ultimately, what, along with their talent, venerated them.

By his late twenties Boutnaray was composing his own music. His training in France and Cambodia gave him both worldliness and a homegrown heritage for songwriting that spanned many genres – bolero, bossa nova, pop – all tinged with traditional Cambodian music and lyrical themes. Slipping naturally back into French he began, 'I played Andalusian, American and French songs in the Cambodian nightclubs of the time—'

'*Khmer!*' Mrs Mam ordered with another eruption from the corner.

'Speak Khmer!' their daughter echoed, in English, from the other side of the room, our heads swivelling as both women tutted and muttered their frustration to understand what was being said. Score change: tie.

Perhaps it was the era we were talking about that brought his French tongue to the fore, or perhaps he had convinced himself that I was French. In any case, it wasn't long before he slipped back into the language, but for brief exacerbated interruptions by his daughter in English and his wife truculently shouting at him in Khmer, so that she too could understand what was being said. Boutnaray would fleetingly obey their requests to speak in Khmer before reflexively diverting back to French, and yet more frustrated sighs and more multilingual shouting would follow from the two women. It certainly put Sophorn through his paces and remains the most chaotic interview we have ever done, but I basked in Boutnaray's serene smile, seemingly unaffected for the most part by the spontaneous eruptions from his wife and daughter. We soldiered on listening to – and diffusing – the family's feuds.

We discussed Bophani and the school where he worked for a short time, but regrettably, in no great depth. However, in time, the many conversations I had with musicians about the roots of 1960s Cambodian rock only enforced the three main groups of origin for musicians of the era: those who were trained at the royal palace; those who were trained at schools – the best of which was universally considered to be L'Université des Beaux-Arts; and the *yé-yé* guitar groups, who were most often self taught or privately taught. For those who qualified to study at UBA – Bophani's school – the aim was to safeguard the musical traditions of Cambodia; the school cited in its 1947 manifesto that musicians and composers must be of 'good morals' and of 'intellectual culture and scope' so that they might reinvigorate Khmer music with original compositions. I found as I spoke to more and more people, this principle threaded through the very heart of Sangkum musical society. Traditions were upheld but music was also open to progressive moulding and reshaping with influences from across the globe. And it was in this vein that I was brought back to Boutnaray's songwriting ideology, and the place where I gave my heart to the music of the era.

Classical Cambodian string instruments like the *tro* – a kind of spike fiddle – and the *chapei* – a cross between a sitar and a lute – infused with electric Vox guitars and Hammond organs in the most effortless way. Western and Eastern instruments converged to impersonate each other – an electric guitar mimicking a Cambodian floor zither called a *takhe* in the Drakkar song 'Sarawan Chhan Penh Boromei' ('Dancing Saravan Under the Full Moon') or brass chimes replacing a high hat on Sisamouth's 'Sat Stiang Heur Stouy' ('Stingray'). They do it in a way that only Cambodian musicians capable of not only playing but embodying the sounds of both their ancient ancestral home and their modern, wider world could do. Rocker Pen Ran made a departure from her usual go-go dance repertoire when she covered Dick Burnett's 1913 bluegrass ditty, 'Farewell Song' (later recorded by a number of artists including Dylan under the name 'Man of Constant

Sorrow'). In Ran's version the Appalachian violins of the Stanley Brothers' 1951 B-side are replaced by a three-sting *tro*, and Ran's note-bending warble harks back to the songs of her ancestors, lending it a distinctly Cambodian sound. The song structures of mid-20th century Cambodia were by and large cyclical and modern, following the Western intro/verse/chorus pattern; the lyrics of Western pop songs altered to reflect Cambodian life. No one else could interpret and then blend these cultures so masterfully, because it was in the Cambodian musicians' blood. The rhythms they created were as inherent as heartbeats, the melodies they constructed, as intuitive as speech.

From UBA Boutnaray moved swiftly onto the subject of his and Bophani's film careers, slipping once again into French. He talked about playing the piano – with Bophani on accordion – in Norodom Sihanouk's 1966 classic movie *Apsara*, the pair swapping instruments two years later in Sihanouk's *Shadow Over Angkor* while dressed in the pink and green silks of the royal court. A departure from the love-triangle plot and ballet dancing of *Apsara*, the political drama *Shadow Over Angkor* was about a state-run coup backed by the CIA. Two years later the American-backed coup that overthrew Sihanouk was a case of life imitating art, an eerie echo of a plot he'd himself written.

Just as soon as we were finding our rhythm, another multilingual argument began, and our short half-hour was up. Sophorn and I left a tired, smiling Boutnaray and his quarrelling family, grateful for their time and the whole mad experience of the day. The early evening traffic took on an almost meditative calm after the lively but endearing frequencies of the Mam household.

That night I played out my homecoming ritual of immediately clicking on both wall-mounted fans, stripping off my clothes, soaking a bedsheet in cold water and wrapping my naked, sweating body in the wet sheet while standing with arms outstretched like a mottled, pink biblical figure at the mercy of the rotating fans. Once cool, I sat down, still wrapped in my fast-drying sheet, and trawled the internet until I found the movie *Apsara*. Set in Phnom Penh, the film is a love story within a love story. On the surface there's the plot – a love triangle between a military commander, a ballet star and a pilot – and beneath that there's the director's love for his country, or at the very least his aspirations for Cambodia: a bold and well-oiled air force, a suave display of political manoeuvring and wide-angle views of glamorous locations and people. There, in the middle of it all, were the Mam brothers, both dressed in white and playing their instruments with such discipline and focus, save the odd timid glance from Boutnaray at the singers Sieng Dy and Sinn Sisamouth. It was hard to reconcile the rumours of the latter-day resistance fighter and recluse with the smiling, peaceful man I met today and watched perform almost bashfully all those years ago.

Catholicism has never been a prominent religion in Cambodia, but after centuries of ebbing and flowing in influence, it reached near extinction after the mass deportations of Vietnamese Catholics in 1970 and religious persecution by the Khmer Rouge in the latter part of the decade. The *Phnom Penh Post* reported that the 10,000-capacity Notre Dame Cathedral on Monivong Boulevard was dynamited by Pol Pot's cadres in 1976, and after the war, all that was left of Phnom Penh's oldest church, Preah Meada ('Sacred Mother') was a small section of wall and a gatepost. On the other side of town, UBA was closed after the evacuation, and many of its students were killed for their 'imperialist attitudes' or forced to play propaganda music about Angkar and its glorious rice fields.

Every society in the world has a history of artistic and religious persecution, often balanced with slivers of hope, stories of resurgence and triumph over adversity. In Cambodia, both the church and Khmer arts made a comeback in the 1990s, with the country now home to around 66,800 Catholics.

The present location of UBA has had a faculty of music there since 1965. It's still standing just as it was when it was built in 1918 and is currently one of only a few Cambodian arts institutes to obtain government support. It enjoys an influx of new talent each year and proudly celebrated its centenary in 2017. If the tales of the Vietnamese occupation and subsequent bullet to the leg are true, Mam Boutnaray never did make a musical comeback, but like his faith and his brother's school, he survived against all odds to tell his tale. In both French and Khmer.

The time I spent with palace players, Svay Sor and Mam Boutnaray, left me even more fascinated by the rites of passage for the golden age musicians and the relationship between their different worlds. 'Were the palace players ever at war with the university musicians?' I wondered. 'Did the *yé-yé* bands ever mix with the palace players?'

It was a chance meeting with a young reporter from the national (now extinct) *Cambodia Daily* newspaper that led me to some answers. *Daily* reporter Mech Dara put me in touch with someone who worked deep within the Royal Palace. All he gave me was a phone number and a name: Thomico.

3

Royal Rock 'n' Roll

For me, without music I would die. My heart is music.
Why? Because when we have music, we have peace.
When we listen to music, conflict goes away inside.
The music can kill the fire of anger and war. It looks
like a dry land that becomes green and fresh when
I hear music.

MINH SOTHIVANN, MUSICIAN

Apsara dancers (Princess Norodom Bopha Devi, centre),
Royal Palace, 1960s.

Diminutive and beautifully turned out, Thomico arrived at our riverside brasserie in smart white slacks and a crisp white mandarin-collared shirt with a fine brooch of royal insignia pinned to his breast pocket. He looked both regal and pure all in white, and seemed to inhabit his ceremonial attire like a banker does a suit. I simply couldn't imagine him wearing anything else. I gave the man in white a polite *sampeah* (Buddhist bow) and clumsily mumbled a formal Khmer greeting.

'*Jum Re-ap . . . Sor*,' I stuttered as he bowed in unison and responded in perfect English, 'Hello, you must be Dee. *Enchanté*,' he smiled, with all the poise I was so clearly lacking, his soft, chic accent befitting his style, honed thousands of miles away and a lifetime ago in the city of lights.

Cambodia Daily reporter Mech Dara had informed me of Thomico's first name and advised that he was *the* man to speak to about palace music but, beyond that, I knew nothing about the man in front of me. I motioned for him to sit down in my quiet leather booth and wasted no time digging around for clues. It was only when I asked Thomico for his surname that his palace links became clear. It turned out that the street we were sitting on, Sisowath Quay, was his namesake and Thomico was, in fact, not only a royal aide but Prince Sisowath Thomico, the nephew of the late Prince Sihanouk. He was the first prince I'd ever met and when I tried – and failed – to hide my embarrassment Thomico responded only with the utmost humility. He was hesitant to talk about himself but he did talk a little, and with deep reverence, for the late Prince Sihanouk, to whom he was a personal secretary for over thirty years until Sihanouk's death in 2012. He remained in active service to the family in the years to follow, serving both Sihanouk's widow, Monique, and heir, Sihamoni, alongside his own campaigning work for the Cambodian National Rescue Party (CNRP).

In recent years the CNRP has been the only political party in serious opposition to Cambodia's reigning Cambodian People's Party (CPP), led by ex-Khmer Rouge cadre and military dictator, Prime Minister Hun Sen (currently his official title is: 'Princely Exalted Supreme Great Commander of Gloriously Victorious Troops'). In 2013 the CNRP came close to halting Hun Sen's thirty-year autocracy but, unsurprisingly, the rightwing CPP 'won' this election, as it had all others before then. Left-leaning in their policies, the CNRP captured the imagination of young city dwellers and the south, and while I was living in Phnom Penh, a year after their most recent election failure, there were often protests in the streets quashed by military thuggery. Rolls of tank-sprung razor wire were a common and foreboding sight in the city – their curling barbs often threaded with lotus flowers in peaceful protest.

As part of his efforts to support the CNRP campaign, Thomico had staged a hunger strike with monks at Wat Phnom to take a stand against the government's handling of the 2013 elections – and when I later watched his rally cries at well-attended, filmed demos and got to know him better, I was impressed by his dynamism. Here was a man who could wear many faces well: a distinguished royal courtier; a gentle but effective political figure; a diehard campaigner; a doting husband and father; and, for now, my royal fixer. He seemed to flit effortlessly and authentically between these various hats, and became somewhat of a father figure to me in the months that followed our introduction.

The first person Thomico put me in touch with was his cousin, the musician, Sisowath Panara Sirivudh, who went by the nickname 'Nong Neang' in the 1960s when he was the lead singer of the Apsara band – one of the first rock 'n' roll guitar bands to emerge in Cambodia. Continuing my search into the origins of Cambodia's 1960s musicians and having already dipped my toe into the palace training ground and music schools, I was now ready to dive into the wild and wonderful world of Cambodia's *yé-yé* guitar bands, to meet the *enfant terrible* of Cambodian rock.

Named after the heavenly nymphs of Hindu cosmology that inspired and share their name with Cambodia's Royal Ballet, apsaras are carved into Cambodia's famous temples, and their anatomy-defying dance narrates the Buddhist and Hindu myths of the temples' bas-reliefs. So important is the dance to Cambodians, it is an emblem of Khmer culture, listed globally by UNESCO as an 'Intangible Culture of Heritage and Humanity', and, legend has it, the word 'Khmer' was derived, in part, by Mera, one of two mythical founders of the nation – an apsara. Prince Norodom Sihanouk's mother, Queen Kossamak, tasked her court dance masters to create the dance in the 1940s, integrating both knowledge and practice of Khmer dance dating back as far as the 6th century AD. Much like their forerunners, Kossamak's dancers were recruited before their young bodies had fully formed, so they could train their fingers to bend almost back to the wrist, their backs to arch and the bridge of their feet to flatten to communicate the unnatural, celestial gestures of the dance. Twenty years after Kossamak's resurgence of Khmer traditional dance, as it was hitting its peak in popularity, the Apsara band emerged, honouring the dance by naming themselves after both the dance and the Apsara Award – Cambodia's own Mercury Prize – they won early in their career. The awards, founded in the early 1960s by Prince Sihanouk, celebrated emerging talent, their statuettes modelled on heavenly apsara nymphs. At that time, apsara dancing was more than just a symbol of ancient Khmer cultural heritage. It not only invoked a sense of nationalist pride, its resurgence – led by the 'it girl' of the time, Princess Bopha Devi – elicited the glamour of Phnom Penh in the 1960s and the rebirth of Khmer arts after centuries of decline.

When it came to interview fixers and translators, I knew I couldn't rely on Sophorn's services alone twenty-four hours a day. He was tied up with a film job in a distant province when my interview with Panara came through, so I contacted a guy I'd met with a special interest in – and possibly the greatest knowledge of – Cambodian 1960s music; a knowledge that went far beyond mine, indeed it went far beyond that of anyone who hadn't themselves lived through those times. A United Nations worker by day and archivist by night, Oum Rattanak Oudam was known by everyone as 'Oro'. We shared the same birth year and a passion for Cambodian rock music, which swiftly cemented our friendship. Oro devoted all of his spare time to a project he'd co-founded with a Cambodian-American, Nate Hun, called the Cambodian Vintage Music Archive, celebrating the music his parents introduced him to early on in his life. Digging for buried treasure, hunting down treasure hoarders, combing for answers . . . he has spent his adulthood searching for a lost past.

To date, the archive has collected hundreds of Cambodian rock records and digitized around a thousand vinyl records; records collected from just about every continent in the world; records that have become masters in their own right given that the war decimated master tapes and most recording equipment inside Cambodia. The 45s, 78s and 33-and-a-thirds that did survive are a drop in the ocean compared to the number they once tallied, and many of them are so rare that there may be only one of their kind remaining in existence. Oro was very much a part of my own Cambodian music quest and I am eternally grateful to him not only for his fixing and translation skills, but for letting me witness his unwavering dedication to the preservation of Cambodian music.

Oro contributed research and Nate compiled the *Don't Think I've Forgotten* soundtrack, alongside director John Pirozzi, and together they have uploaded many original recordings to the archive's YouTube channel as well as historical information to the audio recordings logging site, discogs.com. When I mentioned to Oro that I was going to meet Panara and needed a translator,

I knew he'd jump at the chance to meet the singer. We straddled a borrowed motorbike early one morning, our traditional chequered Cambodian *krama* scarves blowing in the breeze, and set off for BKK1, the land of NGOs, expats and young tourists. This wealthy corner of the city had come up in recent years and now housed a multitude of restaurants and guesthouses, where once hordes of NGO workers lived. Known as Phnom Penh's foreign quarter, rents here are to Phnom Penh what Upper Manhattan is to New York City. By the time I arrived in 2014 rents were hovering around $500 a month for a two-bedroom apartment; easily a full monthly salary for a middle-class Cambodian, or half of a foreign teacher's monthly earnings. Rising rents had driven out many of the foreign NGOs, but the tourists still flock to its lively bars and boutique hotels, wealthier expats learn to meditate at Langka temple, and its resident middle-aged American diplomats can be spotted riding their Segways to work on Street 240 – much to the bemusement of my regular tuk tuk driver, Horn.

Panara lived in a large, slightly rundown house on the corner of one of BKK1's most popular tamarind-tree-lined streets. Nestled between the tourist zone and the grand houses of the Segway brigade, he was sitting on some prime real estate. As we arrived, a large electronic gate swung open and an elderly Panara shuffled out to greet Oro and me, yelling excitedly, a harem of young female staff in tow. Still unsure of how to greet royalty after I'd undoubtedly cocked it up with Thomico, I tried in vain to mimic Oro's low *sampeah*, half curtseying up and down like an awkward yo-yo, until Panara put me out of my misery. 'Enough, enough, come inside,' he chuckled warmly, motioning us to follow.

Inside, Panara's home had been moved to ground level. His half-made bed was littered with mobile phones on lanyards from different mobile networks which would intermittently go off during our interview and we'd all scramble madly to find the ringing phone. The unkept bed was surrounded by more formal décor: official-looking photos sparsely adorned the walls, and traditional heavy Khmer wood furniture decorated the floors. I later mused at the juxtaposition between the bed and its surroundings: a metaphor for Panara's inner tensions – the teenage rocker and, later in life, the grown-up government official.

He wore oversized 1970s glasses that swamped *The Golden Girls*'s Sophia Petrillo's and an arm brace, and had a limp that had been caused by a stroke a couple of years prior. Extremely jovial, welcoming and just a little eccentric, I studied him babble excitedly on a call from the palace and could barely keep up with the pace. If I'd had a decibel meter to measure the volume of his speech, or could heatmap his brain activity, the graphs would be seismic, the visualizations psychedelic.

With the palace eventually ringing off and the tape rolling, Panara didn't miss a beat, launching into fluent English – much to my relief – about the details of his early life. A seasoned raconteur, the first thing he unabashedly and earnestly announced was that he was born with a passion and talent for music. Panara entered the world in January 1946 – the same year as Cambodia's first general election – and started singing and playing the piano and guitar when he was just a pre-schooler. By the time he was a pre-teen, he was learning to play the saxophone. In the dawn of rock 'n' roll – and unlike the palace players and university musicians – his young soprano was honed not by notes or words on a classroom chalkboard, but by listening to rock and pop records. Soul, rhythm and blues and rock 'n' roll all hugely influenced his young mind.

'I learned to sing from listening to black music,' Panara grinned. 'Artists like Ray Charles and Little Richard. He was very hard to imitate but I'd try and then I wouldn't be able to speak after – I'd lose my voice! I can sing so many styles; rock 'n' roll, disco, even rap, and I sang a lot of Platters songs when I was very young. And Gerry and the Pacemakers!'

This prompted a sudden burst of song, a finger from his brace-free hand wagging the rhythm in the air like an old metronome, his faint lisp somehow becoming more prominent when he sang, 'How do you do what you do to me . . . ?'

I was quickly warming to Panara. Not only for his spontaneous, melodic outbursts, but his unextinguishable, frenetic energy. He could change verbal tack faster than a roadrunner on steroids, his infectious chuckle the only thing to break his stride. Without warning, Panara had moved on to the subject of Cambodian songwriters who shaped his early love of music. Chum Kem – the king of Cambodian twist – had introduced Panara to American rock 'n' roll artists, but it was homegrown composers like Kem's occasional bandmate, Peou Sipho, who inspired the Cambodian influence in his own music.

Arguably the most famous composer of the time and a pro-genitor of modern Cambodian music, Peou Sipho rose through the ranks of the colonial police force in early adulthood and on to a career of distinguished musical notoriety in the early forties. He was a friend to all, even the Japanese, whose top brass he befriended during the Second World War by writing songs for them. He was the first to pen songs for Sisamouth and was lauded, both as a master of his songwriting craft and as a highly gifted music teacher at the Conservatoire de Paris; his raw talent, prolific output and hard-working ethics setting the bar high for the Cambodian writers to come. Alongside his own work composing mostly traditional music for crooners and solo musicians, he led the first RNK radio band and was a leading member of the songwriters' association (a body run by the most famous writers of the time to vet song lyrics and scrutinize the quality of releases). He had his tentacles in every aspect of the Cambodian music industry for a long and sustained career, incorporating the timeless, poetic ballads, *romvong* and bolero songs he was known best for, but also, later, the sounds of the 1960s. Needless to say, traditionalists would argue that Sipho was untouchable – he was to Cambodia what Gershwin and Bernstein were to the 20th century American music establishment – and no other composer came close to achieving the quality of his work, not even Sinn Sisamouth. For Panara, Peou Sipho's influence ran deep: 'He could take away your spirit with a song. He is immortal; he lives forever in your mind,' he uttered wistfully.

As Panara talked and the wisps of French romance and charm unfurled from his lips, I found myself drawn to his expressions and language, much in the same way I had been drawn to his energy and the passion in his pitch-perfect singing voice. He studied in both French and Khmer at the Sisowath Lycée high school, where Saloth Sâr, the boy who would later become the Khmer Rouge leader, Pol Pot, was also a student. By the mid-century, the Sisowath Lycée and the Lycée René Descartes had become the fashionable choices for schooling the children of wealthy and royal families, and remain so to this day. Saloth Sâr, for instance, was the son of a prosperous farmer. Other alumni include famous musicians and members of the Khmer Rouge, including Saloth Sâr's future wife, Khieu Ponnary, who was the first woman to receive a bachelor's degree in Cambodia. She taught at the school in the 1950s. She may have even taught Panara, though he couldn't recall.

The young prince signed himself up to play in the school's youth orchestra, and it was here that he formed his band, Apsara, in 1961. They began as nearly all bands do, in the bedroom. But unlike Britain, where a working-class background was often a prerequisite for a rock 'n' roll band in the 1960s, in Cambodia it was the upper classes, with their connections, access to society parties and the money to buy expensive instruments that made them rulers of the rock world. The members of both Apsara and

Baksey Cham Krong all came from wealthy families and led the dawn charge of the *yé-yé* band movement in the early 1960s.

By 1963 the five-piece band was wielding its vox-amplified Fenders, Gibsons and Hofners publicly, performing at talent contests, high schools and the parties of the rich. They rehearsed at the home of bass player Minh Prahul. Making up the rest of the group was lead guitarist Hour Lonh – who often experimented in alternative tunings and arranged much of the music – drummer Tong Sany, Panara on lead vocals and rhythm guitar, and Hin Kraven, whose signature late-1950s finger-picking style was unmistakable.

Apsara in 1964. L–r: Prahul, Kraven, Panara, Lonh, Sany.

Their sound and that of other Cambodian surf rock bands – a mix of doo wop, surf pop and rock 'n' roll – was heavily inspired by the Ventures and the Shadows and the other latest French,

English and American chart toppers transported back from European destinations in the luggage of their teenage friends. Panara himself visited Britain annually with his family, but the source of most of his records came from his cousin, Prince Sisowath Sirirath, who sent 45 rpm singles home from his English boarding school. It was the luck of the draw whether the hotly anticipated records would land at their destination – weeks after release – intact, or in broken pieces.

Panara's home life was unconventional, for it was not his parents, but his aunt – the wife of a governor who was often out of town – who raised him. Brought up in the trappings of a wealthy family, the cousin to the king never wanted for anything and had three loves in his young life: music, politics and horses. He collected horses like records, and at one point had so many polo ponies stabled in the suburbs that his biological mother nicknamed him 'Crazy Horse'. As Panara spoke about his childhood, I wondered about their expectations of their son, and was curious to find out how his guardians felt about his music. He responded by smacking his cheek then shaking his thick, right hand. 'Oh, don't talk about it!' he chuckled and, rising an octave, imitated his aunt, '"Oh, what is that music? Saxophone! Too noisy!" What did *I* do? Turn up the amplifier! Every time I think about my aunt, oh my God . . . they suffered a lot.'

When I asked him what it was like, being in a band in Cambodia in the 1960s, the French charm returned and he replied wistfully, 'Oh, possibilities . . . No problems; it was the golden age.'

In 1962, at the tender age of sixteen, Panara wrote and recorded his first song with Apsara. At that time, everything recorded for radio was recorded live and there was no margin for error, no re-run. Panara recalled in horror, the Stasi prison-like tiles and soviet era sage green and Bakelite machinery at the Ministry of Information's recording studio. Built to record voice broadcasts and classical music, it resembled the set design of a 1950s sci-fi flick, the studio's moon crater-like soundproofing doing nothing to dampen the untameable echo of electrified rock 'n' roll. As a result, many of their early performances here sounded more like a warped, muddy soup of electronic instruments than harmonious pieces of music.

When Apsara eventually cut their first 45 (released on the Wat-Phnom label), it was in the popular Van Chann Studios on a two-track reel-to-reel. But despite the band's growing popularity, their early records didn't fly off the shelves, mainly because the expense exceeded the piggy banks of their teenage fanbase. They did, however, get a lot of airplay with songs like 'Anny' – penned by Panara – with its Mancini-like melody, Panara's sweet, lovelorn lyrics interspersed between Hour Lonh's epic guitar solos. 'Anny' offset Hin Kraven's hard-edged writing style on surf hits like 'Bat Oun' ('Missing You') and 'Tepoabsaar Krongkeb' ('Kep Fairy'), and preceded the band's lighter, calypso influences on songs like their cover of 'Yellow Bird', originally made famous by the Arthur Lyman Group in 1961, with it's intricate guitar phrasings and light percussive beat. Sadly much of their music didn't survive the war, and of the few vinyl records that did, the sound quality isn't great.

In their mid-1960s heyday Apsara played a lot of parties for the wealthy elite, but it was always the writing that Panara gravitated to, and he wrote for a number of other singers, including Sinn Sisamouth, Pen Ran and Ros Sereysothea. The financial security and social status of his background afforded him a modesty that bordered on nonchalance. He took no pride in writing credits, and while he loved to party at nightclubs like Raja Palace and the Magetat, Panara had no interest in performing there; it was only band members Hour Lonh and Minh Prahul who played the clubs for the extra cash. With the start of regular transmissions of Cambodia's national television network, TVK, in 1966 Apsara made frequent televised appearances, their fame reaching its pinnacle before coming to an impasse a year later when Panara, aged twenty-one, emigrated to France.

The band continued with a new singer, an architecture student from Belgium called Tan Kdompi. However, Apsara never did reach the heights of their earlier days. The next generation of bands was coming up around them, and one by one the band members moved on to more serious jobs as their childhoods were ending, and Apsara eventually dissolved.

Tan Kdompi left to form the band Wise Hippies, Hour Lonh went on to study architecture in Paris and Tong Sany left the band in 1969 to study in East Berlin. Neither Lonh nor Sany ever returned to Cambodia. During the civil war, Hin Kraven became a helicopter pilot for Lon Nol's Khmer Republic Army and, according to Panara, died when the Khmer Rouge came to power in 1975. Minh Prahul also died at the hands of the regime. Panara, meanwhile, was living a very different life in Paris. He became a polymath of the sciences, from medicine to sociology to politics, but he never gave up music entirely. In his spare time he played the cafés of Paris with musicians from every corner of the globe, both Parisians and nomadic troubadours passing through town.

In 1991, after more than two decades of living in France while civil war and genocide tore his country apart, Panara returned to his homeland. I grappled with imagining what it must have been like to not recognize the place you grew up, to piece together a jigsaw puzzle of whispered years; to stand back and behold the full extent of its horror. Broken tanks – remnants of war – lay dormant on roads, cities were reduced to rubble, their household taps no longer released running water; starvation and disease were rife. Those Cambodians who were lucky enough to escape their country before the genocide still had to come to terms with survivor's guilt, the deaths and disappearances of loved ones, and the decimation of their lives, their homes and their country.

The Paris Peace Agreements signed on 23 October 1991 aimed to expel foreign, partisan interference from Cambodia, and to transform the conflict from a military one to a political one; in short to end the war between the Khmer Rouge and the Vietnamese-backed PRK government. Spurred on by the hope of the agreement, Panara returned to Cambodia, only to find it was still very much a country at war: the Khmer Rouge taking their last stand against the Vietnamese army. Cambodia had lost its economy, its production and currency, as well as its infrastructure – and those who had managed to survive in this wilderness were trapped and starving. It would be years before the fighting finally stopped in the Khmer Rouge strongholds of north-west Cambodia, and the many who'd escaped could return. Having a strong social conscience, Panara did what he could. He went first to the camps along the Thai border to help the refugees, and, a year later, worked at a radio station in Thailand's Surin province, transmitting messages for FUNCINPEC, the royalist political party that stood for peace and a free Cambodia, founded by exiled Prince Norodom Sihanouk in 1981. What began as a resistance movement against the post-war Vietnamese-backed de facto government, the People's Republic of Kampuchea (PRK), formally became a political party in 1992. A year later FUNCINPEC formed a coalition with Prime Minister Hun Sen's Cambodia's People's Party (CPP) in the first general election to be held since the Khmer Rouge were ousted from power.

In addition to deploying his political studies, Panara put his musical background to good use, taking up a position as the Secretary of State for Culture within the government in 1993, and alongside his fledgling counterparts, helped to rebuild his broken country. 'That is what I did to revive my culture,' he told me earnestly. 'For me, culture is the only way to show people who you are, your identity. Music, art, theatre is one part of culture, the way you live, the way you are; how your ancestors lived is the other.' Panara held senior roles as a minister and as Secretary of State for Culture for thirteen years, before a stroke prompted his resignation. But in his time at the ministry he went to great lengths to preserve and further Cambodian culture.

Panara talked at length about the differences in the music industry of his time and the industry now, especially in regards to copying songs and abusing copyright. While Apsara were inspired by and often covered Western songs, they respected intellectual property laws, and he insisted they were not just 'copying' songs like writers do these days. He told me that the writers of the 1960s took all these influences and fused them into their own writing styles, sometimes covering songs by rewriting the lyrics in Cambodian, changing the sound, the instrumentation and the feel; effectively putting their own stamp on these songs, much in the way that Mam Boutnaray had explained to me. The academic term, I believe, is 'contrafactum'. I was curious to hear Panara's views on how we could better preserve Cambodia's music, given that the laws around copyright are so loose and the industry so corrupt. He looked at me forlornly and explained, 'It is a shame for me to tell you. You are a foreigner. We don't do anything for our culture. What we do every day, is we take the Chinese, the Korean songs, Thai songs, sometimes Vietnamese, and we take out the words, recreate them as karaoke records. I think, "How can our ancestors have built Angkor Wat?" We are creative people, the Khmer – look at our civilization, our culture. How can we do this now? When I was Minister of Culture, I worked hard to collaborate, to liberate the intellectual properties for the songs. But I left this job and nobody can do anything. They need to have the political will to challenge it. It's only money, money, money, because the producer doesn't want to spend money. They are gangsters. They don't encourage – they kill – Cambodian culture. I can't explain the fatigue . . .' he sighed and Oro nodded in agreement. Numerous times in conversation, Oro impressed on me his scorn for the copyright thievery of artists and record reissue compilers. In some cases this was just a matter of their disregard for correctly referencing the music on the artwork, but what really irked him was their exploitation of Cambodia's flawed copyright system and the poor remix quality – paramount to sabotage – of the original music Oro prized. He bemoaned the poor quality of mixtapes sold in their droves on the stalls of Phnom Penh's Russian market, berated the reverb-overloaded remixes of the California-based Chlangden label, and the overdubbed *Cambodian Rocks* album released on Parallel World. But while Oro is right, like many others, *Cambodian Rocks* provided me with a portal into the world of Cambodian rock music.

'They want to make money easily,' Panara continued, referencing the copyright exploitation by some producers working now. He likened their popular practice of copying songs with loose or no copyright and pawning them off as their own to glorified karaoke, devoid of creativity, honour or, indeed, any shame.

Karaoke is a booming industry in Southeast Asia. Phnom Penh is littered with dimly lit bars lined with sad karaoke girls looking to show the male patrons a good time. Social and mainstream media has been homogenized by churning out generic, pasteurized tat, and piracy is so rife that you're hard pressed to find a DVD or CD that is licensed in Cambodia. Copyright law was introduced to Cambodia in 2003, and for the princely sum of $7 to the Ministry of Culture and Fine Arts – or an agreement with the original composer if still alive and traceable – a production company could purchase the rights to cover a song. It's no money-maker for the ministry or the artist, and the resources to enforce the copyright law or indeed invest in obtaining copyright for old songs – much of which are missing songwriting credits – remains minimal. These copyright problems, the popularity of the karaoke movement and the scale of piracy in Southeast Asia make the current issues insurmountable. As Panara stated, it begins with political will.

Asia-Pacific piracy costs the US motion picture industry alone an estimated loss in potential revenue of hundreds of millions of dollars a year. So for Cambodian producers and music industry executives with political influence there is no motivation for change – while big bucks continue to be earned from the current system. As the Cambodian saying goes: 'Do good, get good. Do bad, get money.'

Preservation societies like Oro's Cambodian Vintage Music Archive (CVMA) struggle for funding and, more often than not, are propelled instead by passion. They are lone warriors fighting insurmountable wars; in the case of CVMA their enemies are piracy and the fallout from Cambodia's history. Outnumbered but dutybound they soldier on, locating, cleaning and digitizing original records, while providing evidence in landmark legal copyright cases. They've had some wins, particularly in the support they've lent to the Ros and Sisamouth families' successful court claims for copyright, so not all hope for change is lost. But with so many master tapes and original records missing, so little copyright information on surviving record sleeves, and so many pirate tapes out there, the mountain can seem impassable.

As our conversation on copyright came to a gradual close, I asked Panara whether or not there was anything else that he wanted to say about Cambodia's musical golden age and he responded in his very French and romantic way: 'No, I have nothing left to say now, only nostalgia . . .'

Oro and I left him to his reverie, and I made my way home to make sense of the hours of Panara's breathless stream of consciousness. I still had questions about the Apsara band and was keen to hear from another voice in the group, but the only other surviving members lived in Europe. However, my fixer, Sophorn, had managed to track down Apsara bassist Minh Prahul's younger brother, Sothivann, and arranged an interview.

Sothivann worked not far from Panara's house, and one

morning in August 2014 Sophorn and I rode over the bridges and past the pastel-coloured houses, washing lines and palms that lined a canal in the BKK2 and BKK3 districts of central Phnom Penh. Despite the overpowering smell of drains it had become my favourite city route for its beauty, lackadaisical vibes and the sensation of stomach flips and arms-outstretched-freedom experienced flying over those small bridges on a motorbike. Somewhere between Venice, the Caribbean and Santorini – in its uniformed minimalism and cleanliness – there was nowhere else like it in Phnom Penh. The light hitting the soft hues of family homes, the spikes of warm chatter that broke through our motorbike's rumble, the sun that raced alongside us and danced on the water seemed to penetrate my cells and made me feel radiant every time I passed through.

In recent years Minh Sothivann had stepped out of his brother's shadow and had become a successful music industry figure in his own right. If you asked around, many Cambodians would recognize the famous songwriter by his smooth, round, bespectacled face and his kindly, humble manner – and they might even reel off his multitude of talents and achievements. But, what few know about Minh Sothivann is that he is also – at least in my opinion – a poet. When we arrived at his studio – a serious grey and black box tucked behind the array of bright colours, sequins and frills of his wife's wedding shop – I was immediately put at ease by his welcoming smile and warm handshake. He spoke impeccable English in a soft, high pitch and, despite a lucrative singing career, a successful recording business and a televised judging spot on Cambodia's version of *Pop Idol*, he was all modesty, humility and hospitality, eagerly gesturing for us to sit, fetching us bottles of water and making small talk.

Being born the younger brother of Apsara bass player Minh Prahul meant there was no escaping music. His older brother encouraged Sothivann to learn to play the guitar and spurred him on with records by the Beatles, the Stones and, later, Grand Funk Railroad, Black Sabbath, Santana and Deep Purple. By the end of 1974 the talented teenager had built up some interest within the community of composers and musicians he had grown up with but, just as his career was taking off, it was quashed by the Khmer Rouge.

Up to this point I had spoken to musicians who were old enough to have established a career and a life for themselves before such things were stolen by the communist takeover. I wondered what it was like for one born in 1958, whose life and musical path were just beginning then.

'I don't want to talk about politics, but this is my real story . . .' Sothivann began, solemnly, the gentle smile dissolving from his lips. 'After the evacuation,' he continued, 'my family was moved to three different places and, in 1977, we were somewhere between Battambang and Pursat. It was there that my brother, Prahul, died from malnutrition. He got oedema and his whole body swelled from his legs to his torso then head. Before he died he wanted to sing a harmony song, and that night he sang "Let It Be Me" [by the Everly Brothers] with me. I loved to sing harmony. We sang together and then he went to sleep, and died.

'After my brother died, it was my turn to face death. I got diarrhoea and there was no medicine [bar "traditional medicine" produced by the Khmer Rouge, served to everyone for every kind of illness]. Because I saw many dead bodies around me, I believed that I would die by the morning because I was seriously sick and I couldn't eat anything. That night there was heavy rain, and I thought Tevada would come and take me with the rain.*

---

* A Tevada is a Khmer synonym for a 'Deva'. A Deva [Sanskrit meaning 'radiant' or 'shining'] refers to a god or deity found in both Vedic Hinduism and Buddhism.

I saw associates of the Khmer Rouge who came to stay in my house to shelter from the rain, and I was afraid because they had a lot of guns. It was a stilted house with space underneath and I wanted to stay underneath the house out of the way, but the Khmer Rouge insisted it was OK for me to stay inside because it was flooded underneath the house. The Khmer Rouge cadres slept in their hammocks inside my house. They kept their guns with them, but one of them, he had a small mandolin.'

The sight of a modern instrument instantly energized the sick nineteen-year-old. I remember myself at that age: the finger callouses my guitar built up never had time to soften. The excitement Sothivann must have felt, even in that desperate moment, having been starved of the ability to play music for almost two years, must have been overwhelming. Believing this could be his last night alive, Sothivann threw all caution to the wind and asked his friend to make a request to the cadres on his behalf.

'I wanted to hold this instrument before I died. This Khmer Rouge [cadre] asked loudly to everyone in the room, "Who is it that wants to hold this instrument?" I was afraid. Normally the Khmer Rouge did not allow us to play modern music. It was the first time in a long time that I had seen a modern instrument. This man then walked over to me and said, "Was it you?" And I replied, "Yes, it was me." Then he asked if I could play. Mandolin and guitar are different and I didn't know how to play mandolin, I only knew how to play the guitar, but I decided to answer "yes" because I desperately wanted to hold the mandolin.' The cadre handed the mandolin to Sothivann, who gently caressed its strings. 'Even though I'd never played a mandolin before, I played it in a guitar style and I could play! It was a miracle. I played Khmer Rouge music, and nobody believed that I could play, so they were really listening. The rain stopped and the Khmer Rouge changed their attitude and they were good to us. All the people around me could not believe it, and we were very happy. This one cadre had never heard the voice of the mandolin before. In the forest they never heard music, so the "new people"* and the Khmer Rouge were both surprised to hear music, and we were happy together, the music brought us together.'

In a candlelit wooden hut, in what Sothivann thought might be his last night on this earth, I could all but see this brief moment of harmony in a place of such discord. As I pictured that huddled collection of victims and perpetrators and their momentary ceasefire I was reminded of the filmmaker John Pirozzi's vision for his 2015 music documentary *Don't Think I've Forgotten: Cambodia's Lost Rock and Roll*. In a press interview with the *New York Times* John told reporter Ben Sisario, 'I wanted to show that the music would endure beyond everything it had been put through.' With nothing left to lose, Sothivann and his music had brought about a stalemate between both sides but, sadly, it was not to last. With encouragement from the cadres, Sothivann launched into his second song, but that brief burst of energy had depleted his reserves. Exhausted and somewhat disorientated, he dropped the mandolin.

'The Khmer Rouge [cadre] asked other people what sickness I had. They told him that I had diarrhoea, and he said, "I have some medicine." Then he took the medicine from his bag. It looked like it had gone bad – the packaging was broken and wet – and he didn't know what the medicine was for. But, because I was hopeless, I decided to take this medicine, and, besides, I could not refuse the Khmer Rouge.' To Sothivann's disbelief, the medicine worked and within a matter of hours he was on the

---

* 'New people' was a term the Khmer Rouge coined to refer to city people and those who (unwillingly) joined the regime after their victory on 17 April 1975. They were treated far worse than the 'old people'.

mend: 'I stopped having a stomach-ache and I could sleep well! When I woke up I had energy and I didn't hurt in my stomach any more. The Khmer Rouge leader stayed with me, he didn't leave the house. After that I stayed with him and I worked for him. There was lots of work in this village but he changed my job to just playing music for him each time he returned home ... Music saved my life.'

Sothivann never knew what happened to his saviour/captor, because the following year, 1978, he was moved on to another village to dig the land. He had no shoes and his hands were destroyed by the relentless hoeing he was forced to do. He felt hopeless again, but everything would change the following year, when the Vietnamese invaded Cambodia and overthrew the Khmer Rouge.

'In 1979, after the invasion, I found the road to Phnom Penh. In Svay Daun Keo village [between Battambang and Pursat provinces] I saw Vietnamese military soldiers playing music. A soldier put his gun down and picked up a guitar next to him. Then when I saw it I immediately ran to them and listened to their music. They could tell that I really wanted to play that guitar! They gave me the guitar and I was very happy and I embraced the guitar because I had not seen one in over three years. I wanted to sing a Grand Funk Railroad song, "I'm Your Captain (Closer to Home)", but my hands were so destroyed that they couldn't play the song like before, and I thought I would never be able to play guitar again like I used to.'

When Sothivann arrived back in Phnom Penh, he stayed with his sister in the Muncipal Apartments, a building that was known to all as 'the White Building'. Designed by Lu Ban Hap and Vladimir Bodiansky, and overseen by the legendary Cambodian architect Vann Molyvann, the building was originally created to house people of moderate incomes. Artists flocked to the residence. Built during the most exciting period of architecture since the Angkorian temples, it was part of a large civic house building project along the Bassac River and left an impressive mark on the capital's skyline. Much like the music of the time, Vann Molyvann masterfully merged traditional Khmer design with Western influence, particularly that of the modernist architect Le Corbusier. Molyvann's output was so prolific and admired that Phnom Penh was transformed into 'the Pearl of Asia', influencing the built environment of some of the region's major states, such as Singapore. But then came the civil war, the evacuation of Phnom Penh and the genocide. Much like Cambodia's music, construction stopped and many of Vann's proud buildings were destroyed or fell into disrepair.

When displaced former residents and others returned to the city, the White Building came out of hibernation. Large parts were squatted and crime was rife, but the building never stopped evolving, growing and decaying, with art constantly coursing through its veins. Local collectives and artists returned to once more pump the building's beating heart. Surrounded by dancers and artists, Sothivann's sister – a former Royal Palace dancer herself – and her musical brother fitted right in. Despite the hardship of living in a war-torn city in the process of rebuilding itself, Sothivann looked back on this time with fond memories: 'In 1979 the White Building was full of artists. I became a security guard for the building. Some nights, when I worked on the street, I would hear some music from under the houses, and sometimes the people above peed on me because they didn't know that I was under their house guarding it! I had a friend who found an old guitar – it was repaired many times and one of the five remaining strings was a bicycle brake wire. There were other parts of the guitar that were also replaced with other makeshift objects. The musicians who played during the Sangkum Reastr Niyum and Lon Nol periods asked me to play Beatles songs, and I tried to play the song "Let It Be". As they were talking, I would pick up words and be reminded of song lyrics and I would start playing the songs. I couldn't believe it; I could play again. That old guitar helped me play again.'

As Sothivann was rediscovering his musical feet, the country was starting to rise again from the ashes. Sothivann was asked to join the Ministry of Culture and Fine Arts band, to play lead guitar in exchange for rice, alongside fellow musicians Yin Dykan, Yil Chathou and the composer Ell Bunna, who had all known Sothivann's brother Prahul.

Sothivann was taken into the post-war bosom of his brother's peers. They would share stories about Prahul and the world they lived in before the evacuation, and I got the impression that Ell Bunna, in particular, took the younger Sothivann under his wing. Before the genocide, Sothivann's style had been influenced heavily by the West, but with the help of the aforementioned more traditional Cambodian artists he learned to retrace his steps back to his roots and an altogether more Cambodian mid-century style. His usual rocking repertoire became infused with the marching band music and the bolero ballads of his youth – a fusion of Cuban and swing beats; a blend of both jazz and traditional Cambodian reed and percussion instruments. Surrounded by professionally trained musicians the young rock 'n' roller went on to play for the Ministry of Interior band, where he began composing and further honed the talent that would jet-rocket him to stardom in the mid-1980s.

When it came to the end of our time together, I didn't want to go. I left with huge respect for the man, if not a little muted by sadness for his harrowing past. After the sun had set I lit a cigarette and swung alone on my balcony hammock, listening to the Everly Brothers singing their song 'Let It Be Me'. The words hit me hard. I thought of the Minh brothers singing these words together in Prahul's dying moments – the lyrics a heart-wrenching tribute to a brother's deep love – and I cried alone in the dark. I'd left that morning expecting to uncover more of the Apsara story, but Sothivann showed me, before I knew it, just what this book would become. I'd grappled with the challenge of capturing the history of Cambodia's rock 'n' roll story as one whole, linear tale. Months had turned into years before I realized the lesson Sothivann taught me that day – that I'd had it backwards all that time. The individual stories didn't slot into the narrative – they led the narrative. I'd been looking for pieces of a jigsaw that didn't appear the same to Sothivann or Panara or Svay Sor or Mam Boutnaray or anyone else. My puzzle had holes, and my assumptions were challenged by a lack of surviving documentation and by cultural divisions. I was learning that truth is subjective: one person's version of history is different from another's. I was learning that memories often had holes.

4

Jivin' Jitterbugs 'n' the King of Cambodian Swing

Even though the composers of those songs have died, their songs still live, they're beautiful in your ear. You can follow the music, imagine the situation, you can feel the spirit and that is why they live forever.

Lay Mealea, singer

Lay Mealea (centre) and Joe Wrigley (right) perform with their band, Miss Sarawan.

Joe Wrigley was a rockabilly from Stoke-on-Trent with a corkscrew quiff and a stronger work ethic than anyone in Phnom Penh showbusiness. In 2012 he closed the door on his life as a player and dealer on the London poker scene. He travelled the world, landed up in Cambodia the following year, and never left. Here, Joe made a living solely from playing live music, and by the time I met him in 2014, his yearly gig count must have rivalled Bob Dylan's. He was in at least four bands, including the Cambodian rock revival band Miss Sarawan with his gifted wife, Lay Mealea.

I first saw them perform at a smoky pool bar called Slur's in Phnom Penh's red-light district, and it was outside this bar a few weeks later that Kevin and I loaded our rucksacks into a van and took off on tour with six musicians, their entourage and a yappy Pomeranian called Bing, for a rollicking, rough-and-tumble ride. By then, I had toured in the UK and Europe with some different bands, mostly playing rock and pop music to empty houses, mad drunk Europeans and soulless city hipsters. Off the road, I'd spent my early to mid-twenties eeking out a pittance playing regular covers gigs in depressing bars in suburban towns. Glamorous it was not, but I was staving off the inevitable 'proper job' as long as I could, and somehow I always scraped by on the rent. By the time I met Kevin in 2004 – on a European tour for his 1960s jangle pop band the Waxwings, and my lo-fi pop band Jack Adaptor – Kevin had toured the States alone fourteen times and at one stage had spent the best part of five years on the road. But touring in Cambodia was, without a doubt, new and unfamiliar ground for us both.

When Joe mentioned there were two empty seats in the van and asked if Kevin and I wanted to come along for the ride, we jumped at the chance. I wanted to visit the towns and cities I'd heard about in songs, to experience touring in modern day Cambodia with a 1960s revivalist band as if it might open a portal to the past. I hoped, perhaps, that a van packed with musicians and their gear, navigating Cambodia's rotten roads and playing its dark bars to a soundtrack of 1960s Cambodia might bring the past to life.

Our motley crew included friends of the band: a reserved

Canadian Bitcoin enthusiast called Josh Bouw and a crazy Russian with jet-black Betty Boop-style hair called Kristina Yanko. No dancefloor was safe from her whimsical prancing. She brought the fun and was to the group what Joel Gion is to the Brian Jonestown Massacre; what Keith Richards was to the Gram Parsons band. The tour's headlining band, Joe and the Jumping Jacks, was a rockabilly act of European and South African descent starring Joe Wrigley on rhythm guitar and lead vocals, a dry-humoured Englishman, Andy Potter, on drums, a Swedish software engineer of 1980s musical fame, Jan Fex, on lead guitar, and a 6 foot 8 inch burly South African teacher, Andre Schwartz, on bass. 'Andre the Giant', as he was sometimes called, swamped the female entourage: Jan's quiet and serious wife, Sokheng, and Andy's jocund wife, Rattana. But Sokheng, Rattana and Kristina were practically Amazonian compared to the support act's star, 1960s Cambodian revivalist Lay Mealea, or Miss Sarawan, and the effect of Mealea standing next to Andre was both farcical and endearing.

She was, to me, my Cambodian Dolly Parton: a 'Little Sparrow', pure of heart, true to her roots and diminutive in stature yet large in personality, not to mention lung capacity. She captivated with her raw talent and canary-like song. The first time I heard her sing she not only resurrected Cambodia's most famous songstress, Ros Sereysothea, from the grave, she floored me. Every note was so rich and beautiful in tone, so controlled and yet so natural. She was an audio incarnation of an apsara dancer performing her moves: precision and utter perfection, and had an interesting backstory to boot.

Born in 1989 Mealea and her identical twin, Lay Mealai, grew up in the countryside, in Kampong Cham province, central Cambodia. Their father was a musician, their mother a singer, their grandmother a theatre actress. Singing as far back as she can remember, Mealea spent much of her early life on the back of her beloved water buffalo, spurring on her fellow villagers as they toiled in the fields. The radio and her mother's songs were great influences, and at Khmer New Year her village – lacking the funds to buy instruments – would collect pots and woks and make music from dawn to dusk.

In her teens Mealea moved to Phnom Penh and spent five years living in a working monastery called Wat Saravan, cleaning clothes for the monks in exchange for room and board. She sung while she worked and it wasn't long before her voice caught the ear of a kind-hearted monk. Taken aback by the live voice he'd mistaken for a voice on the radio, he asked her why she looked sad, to which she solemnly replied, 'I have no money to go to study.' The monk pondered her quandary for a moment, then, stroking his chin, made a proposal: 'Come, come here!' he motioned. 'Sing a song for me and I'll give you five thousand *riel*.' (The equivalent of $1.5 USD around 2005.) The regularity of these singing sessions became a ritual for Mealea and the monk, and, as time went on, she took part in the vocalizations for Buddhist festivals like Pchum Ben.

The Mexicans have Día de Muertos, the Taiwanese have the Ghost Festival, and the Cambodian Buddhists have Pchum Ben ('Ancestor's Day'). It's a fifteen-day ritual, where the living family transfer karma to their dead relatives in order to alleviate the suffering of those souls trapped in the hells of Buddhist cosmology. Mealea's participation in such festivals grew alongside her religious fanbase, and her impromptu acapella performances in the temple grounds attracted increasingly larger crowds of *riel*-paying monks. Eventually she earned enough money to study *mahori* and other types of Cambodian folk music under an ageing and hidebound singing teacher called Mme Malis. Under Malis's instruction, Mealea learned age-old techniques to warm up her vocal chords (such as eating spicy malou leaves) and, over time, honed in on the skills of her idols, singers like Ros Sereysothea,

Huoy Meas and Pen Ran. She met Joe in 2013; the pair fell in love and Mealea joined Joe in the life of a working musician in modern day Cambodia. I met them the following year, and watching them nuzzle into one another in the tour van, Mealea coddling Joe at every possible turn, they appeared very much in their first throes of love.

The first stop on the tour was Kampot, a sleepy river town famed for its surrounding pepper plantations, a few hours' drive south from Phnom Penh. A backpacker's haven and weekend getaway for Phnom Penh-based ex-pats, it boasted hotels, Western and Khmer restaurants, crumbling colonial architecture, wild swimming, kayaking, jungle trekking and a cleaner, slower alternative to the miasma and sensory overload of Phnom Penh.

'Here at last!' Andre sighed, stretching and decompressing his long limbs outside and straightening his neck for the first time in hours. The rest of us followed suit, tumbling out of the van one by one – all but Bing, who'd yapped incessantly all the way from Phnom Penh and, left alone in his dog carrier, had by now reached fever pitch.

'Bing! Bing! Oi . . . shut up!' Jan called to the Pomeranian as he hurriedly retrieved the dog carrier from the car's boot.

We'd arrived at Bodhi Villa, which would be both our stage and bed for the night. A crusty but much-loved hippy paradise, tanned bodies in crocheted bikinis and hemp shorts lounged on a floating pontoon by day, and swished their dreadlocks to Bodhi's live music by night. The music – anything raucous, from pub rock to ska – could be heard a mile downriver and often went long into the early hours.

That night, Miss Sarawan held the swelling crowd of Bodhi guests and local Cambodians in spellbound suspension for a full half-hour before closing out their set with a Pen Ran song aptly named 'Hippy Men'. Joe then donned a Stetson and took to the stage with the Jumping Jacks in their matching red western shirts and black jeans. They kicked off their set with a zestful cover of the Hank Williams song 'Hey, Good Lookin''. The barflies howled, the hippies looked momentarily confused, and Kristina fired up the dancefloor. Within five minutes the place was a mass of happy, heaving hippies and drunks, and it was a miracle no one fell in the river.

The following night in Sihanoukville was an altogether different show entirely. The bands played to a crowd outnumbered by their own entourage in a bar so lacking in atmosphere it would have made a brutalist building look like a fairground. By the time everyone returned to the hotel late that night it was a blessing they were good and drunk. Almost deserted, the damp could be smelt from down the street and the rooms were like teal-coloured prison cells. A three-hour drive west of Kampot and a five-hour drive south of Phnom Penh, the city named after its founder, Sihanouk, took Cambodia's international seaport mantle from Kampot in 1955. It was also drawn into both the civil and Vietnam wars within fifteen years of its founding.

By 1967 Sihanouk's faith in the USA and South Vietnam winning the Vietnam War was dwindling. He'd broken off diplomatic relations with the USA a few years earlier when he suspected the CIA of having ties with the anti-monarchy rebels, the Khmer Serei. And while the head of state wanted to portray an impression of neutrality to the world, he also wanted to stay in favour of the winning side and keep Cambodia out of the war. So he secretly opened Sihanoukville's port to South Vietnam *and* the USA's enemies, the North Vietnam Army (PAVN) and the Viet Cong. The port acted as an extension of the Ho Chi Minh trail during the Vietnam War; a 16,000-kilometre supply line for the communist Viet Cong and PAVN, hidden deep in the forested borders between Vietnam, Laos and Cambodia. The trail's extension to Sihanoukville became known as 'the Sihanouk

Trail', until it was snuffed out by escalating American bombs in the early 1970s.

The wars decimated Sihanoukville. Once a jewel in Sihanouk's crown, the seaside hotspot and playground to the rich and famous of the 1960s came to be deserted. Its modernist hotels and large buildings fell empty and into disrepair, and any traces of its glamorous past were tarnished by conflict. After decades of political turmoil, it stabilized again in the mid-1990s, and by the early 2000s investment flooded in and the resort began to reclaim some of its former allure. But Sihanoukville became a victim of its own success, falling into decline a decade later. One by one, the European and American tourists left and the Chinese gamblers moved in. Over time its already fading natural beauty was buried in yet more rubbish, its coastline concealed by imposing, Chinese-owned casinos, the local casino workers paid a pittance and priced out of their own city. Downtown rapidly declined into something that resembled a depressed Cambodian border town – despite lying some 400 miles east of Thailand.

Still drunk from the night before, the first thing Kevin did the morning after the Sihanoukville show was to sneak into the closed hotel bar. A sign blazing the words 'Black Grouper Bar' in slanted yellow scrawl hung behind the counter. When the off-duty barmaid sauntered in to check on things, she glanced quizzically at Kevin behind the bar. He pulled out every trick in the book – a charming smile, drunken, exaggerated doe eyes, submissive pleading – and some money, and she eventually cracked a smile, put the cash in the till, and walked back to her room seemingly non-plussed and pococurante in the same breath. As soon as we heard her door click shut, Kevin swivelled on his feet and pointed both hands at Kristina. 'What can I get for you? Hair of the dog?' he winked.

'But, of course!' Kristina roared in her thick Russian accent, still sheltering from the sun behind dark glasses.

'Aha!' he exclaimed, grabbing a daiquiri glass before pausing then reaching for another, 'Let's make it two . . .' I wasn't drinking and, instead, rolled my eyes. Yes, Kristina was sorely hungover, but when Kevin reached for that second glass I knew his ulterior motive was to stave off his own impending hangover for as long as possible.

'Vodka is a good morning drink. I'll make a Dangerbird. That work for you?' Kevin asked, lining up a bottle and referencing the name of a cocktail he'd created himself that basically involved anything alcoholic to hand.

'Nothing to lose this morning!' Kristina quipped, rubbing her hands together in anticipation.

'Now, let's see . . . a little bit of this . . . and a little bit of that . . . a drop of this . . . a drop of that,' he hummed, pouring what looked like a shot from just about every conceivable bottle behind the well-stocked bar. The finished result lived up to its name. I was convinced Kristina would reflexively bring the contents of that glass back up, but she took a sip and nodded sincere approval, 'Not bad,' and clinked her giant glass against Kevin's.

The radio, Kristina, Kevin and Bing were the only noises heard on the first leg of our van trip back to Phnom Penh. They sang and laughed and yapped as the rest of the previous night's roisterers slept off their hangovers. All but Jan who, head in hands with green eyes firmly shut, occasionally opened his mouth to groan, 'Bing, shut up!' to no avail.

As we passed a cluster of wooden stilt houses, a Ros Sereysothea song came on the radio and Mealea began softly singing along. The symmetry of their voices was uncanny and I closed my eyes for a moment to bathe in the sound. When the song finished I asked Mealea why she felt this music was important after all this time. She told me, 'When I sing, I feel like their spirits are all around me . . . and they are happy with what I am doing. I want us to remember, Dee . . . not forget. Even though the composers of those songs have died, their songs still live, they're beautiful in your ear. You can follow the music, imagine the situation, you can feel the spirit and that is why they live forever.'

With her words still ringing in my ears and her song renewed with another track from the past, I turned back to the window, to the arid fields and drying riverbeds. As we rolled past towns that Sisamouth and other 1960s songwriters had romanticized in song, I thought about what Mealea had said, what this tour with a revivalist band had meant to her audience and to me, how its soundtrack had evoked the past and, somehow brought it into our present. I thought of the 1960s musicians shuttling from shows between Sihanoukville and Phnom Penh. I thought of the present day radio stations and karaoke pubs so often blasting out the oldies, and the other Cambodian rock revivalists in Miss Sarawan's corner.

The late Kak Channthy – also known as Srey Thy – and her psychedelic band, CSP (Cambodian Space Project), are one such example. Their sound, a *mélange* of 1960s Cambodian and Western rock, psych and soul is just one part of the whimsical, wonderful world the band inhabits. Hailing from Prey Veng province, Channthy grew up below the poverty line, working as a hostess in the karaoke bars of Phnom Penh before meeting her future husband and bandmate, Tasmanian Julien Poulson, and finding salvation in their group. In a career spanning more than a decade, five albums, one documentary, a rock opera and numerous creative hubs and other trippy visions – from the 1960s to the space age and beyond – the band has collaborated with Cambodian musicians and Westerners alike, including Motown Funk Brother Dennis Coffey and the Bad Seeds' Mick Harvey. Poulson was – and remains – the band's visionary, continuously evolving the Space Project through his boundless creativity, panache and off-the-wall imagination.

Another popular, mixed-heritage revival band is based across the Pacific, in LA, California, where the largest Cambodian diaspora exists. Chhom Nimol is the frontwoman of Dengue Fever. Bringing both the world and indie music communities together with their brand of psychedelic Cambodian garage rock, the band formed in 2001, cut their first record in 2003 – the self-titled *Dengue Fever* – and since then the six-piece has released ten more albums and featured on a number of movie soundtracks, documentary films and even a theatrical play.

But it's not just bands behind the arts revival. There are countless individuals and individual acts that are both reviving and preserving memory. In Phnom Penh I'd met a film-set makeup artist named Ok Silyauth who talked at length about dancing in the clubs and parties of the free love era and flashing his 'jerk' dance moves on the dancefloor. Created by American rhythm and blues band, the Larks, for their 1964 hit, 'The Jerk', it's a dance that consists of swinging your arms up and down in a jerky motion, like a drunken monkey taking aim. After the genocide, Ok told me he felt dutybound to pass on his jerk dance moves to the students of renowned 1960s actress and film producer Dy Saveth taking singing, dancing and acting classes at the private stage school she runs. He talked about it with such gravity it was as if he were bringing back the dodo.

Turning my attention back to the road, Sihanoukville and its surrounding landscape still whispered of a time long ago. The modernist seaside buildings that revealed a voguish riviera were now far behind us; in Sihanoukville's surrounding Kampong Som province occasional bomb craters – inverted mounds filled with brush – were gravestones to lost villages, while overgrown orchards masked their bygone yields. Elsewhere in the countryside much seemed unchanged for millennia. Wet-rice farming and lontar palm sugar production continued, but with fewer forests and animals, and more people.

Some of the musicians I admired most had written songs about the places that lined our route. Sinn Sisamouth had sung about

'Kampot From the Bottom of my Heart' and yodelled – possibly the only Khmer yodelling song ever recorded – the chorus of 'Kandal Goddess', about an 'Earth Angel' in Phnom Penh's surrounding Kandal province. Ros Sereysothea had sung about the 'Memory of Kampong Som' backed by an orchestral band playing a slow rumba. I'd learned from my talks with Panara and Svay Sor of the marching bands that paraded the countryside, and, as I looked out on village thoroughfares, I could almost hear the feet of drummers as they marched, their hands beating drums, the horn sections fingering trumpets and horns in jubilation.

My thoughts turned finally to Chariya, the man at the nucleus of all that was glamorous and ceremonial about Cambodia's musical golden age. Sihanouk's cousin and once booker at the Magetat, he was a prince I'd first caught sight of in a dark, river-side watering hole in Phnom Penh earlier that year. Frail and hunched over the bar, he wore a faded brown baseball cap and was sucking on a cigarette, a single blue plastic bag at his feet. Spotting my waving hand, Chariya slowly gathered up his things and sauntered over to greet me with a wide, sad smile that instantly put me at ease, yet lay heavy on my heart forever.

In the 1960s he'd been the king of Cambodian swing. He'd led one of the most famous marching bands of the time, was a booker for the most fashionable nightclub of the era and had married a leading 1960s film star. No one elicited the spirit and glamour of the golden age better than him. Over time, as I got to know and love Chariya, his initial unassuming demeanour transcended into an air of *savoir-faire*: a sophisticated, worldly quality I found intrinsic to Cambodian royals.

Born in the dawn of swing – the era of Duke Ellington, Cab Calloway and Glenn Miller – and a cousin of both Sihanouk and Thomico, Prince Sisowath Chariya's love of music began here, and he saw many jazz bands pass through Phnom Penh in his teenage years: artists like Italy's Giancarlo Barigozzi and America's most beloved contralto, Marian Anderson, shortly before she sang the American national anthem at John F. Kennedy's inauguration in January 1961. The first concert he saw was the Benny Goodman Orchestra, who played at the Royal Palace in 1956 when Benny was touring the Far East. Chariya was by then learning to play the saxophone, piano, clarinet and trumpet at the Royal Palace under its bandleader, the Filipino Denacio Saem. Five years later, fluent in multiple instruments and the basics of songwriting, he flew to France to complete his training under the celebrated Cambodian composer Peou Sipho at the prestigious Conservatoire de Paris. In his downtime Chariya took in shows at London's Ronnie Scott's – still in its infancy then – and legendary concerts like the Beatles during their eighteen-day residence at the Paris Olympia in 1964, alongside Trini Lopez and Sylvie Vartan. A few months later, with his training complete, Chariya felt the call of home and returned to Cambodia to embark on his music career.

Not long after his homecoming, he met his future wife at a wedding; a leading singer and film star called Sieng Dy. Chariya was instantly mesmerized by her voice and aptitude for singing in French, and his life, as he knew it, was forever changed. Dy was nineteen when she married Chariya but by then already a seasoned performer with a successful solo career, having grafted her way up the ranks of the military band, Yothea Phirum, since 1959. She went on to reach her apex in the late 1960s, starring in two of Prince Sihanouk's most popular feature films, *Apsara* in 1966 and *La Joie de Vivre* in 1969.

Her biggest hit featured on *La Joie de Vivre*'s soundtrack. A Santo and Johnny-meets-Broadway number, 'Jum Reay Assom Kum' ('A Song of Hopelessness') was also performed by Dy in the movie. I have a photograph of the nightclub where the scene was filmed, recovered from the University of Phnom Penh's archives. Many times I've gazed at the Magetat's rouged curtain Dy performed in front of, imagining the club's red vinyl booths

Sieng Dy performing at the Magetat.

Exterior of the Magetat.

and chairs filling up with patrons drinking and wearing out its chequered floor. Military men jived with their wives as American and French journalists languorously stirred their drinks and put the country to rights, and embassy workers chased hostess girls – known then as 'taxi girls' – and shook off their day. Prince Sihanouk was often in the crowd, and Chariya was the club's promoter during its heyday from 1965 to 1970. After long hours at the club he'd crawl into bed at his apartment in the fashionable White Building, where Sothivann had also lived after the war.

To listen to Chariya and others talk, I got the sense that Phnom Penh nightlife in their time seemed far more glamorous and sophisticated than the Phnom Penh of mine. As he and others regaled me with tales of the nightclubs and opium dens of the 1960s, it was hard not to draw disparaging comparisons with the hostess bars and 'Happy Herb Pizza(s)' of my time, where you could buy a marijuana-sprinkled pizza along with an ounce of weed. That was when I first arrived in 2012. Since then, the government has cracked down on the pizza joints but the hostess bars have proliferated, with more and more beautiful young women working more and more rooms, looking for their kid's next meal and a ticket out of poverty by way of a fat gullible geriatric foreigner. The allure of the floating supper clubs of the 1950s and 1960s has more recently been reduced to drunken river cruises, the dancing bars succeeded by neon-lit karaoke bars lined with rows of sad-looking taxi girls in gold lamé minidresses. None of the 1960s bars survived beyond the war, but one of the oldest city bars existed back then under another guise; its current name, Sharky's, is in honour of its working women – its taxi girls. Women whose profession goes back as far as that of the ancient kings' concubines are still called taxi girls by Cambodians today, just as they were when they collected men in their cyclo carriages in the 1960s. As the *Khmer Times* reported in a 2016 article 'Remembering "Big Mike"', Sharky's patrons called them 'sharks – women who would stalk the bar hunting for male prey'.

Sharky's founder was a barrel-chested Chinese-American with a Fu Manchu beard, called Michael 'Big Mike' Hsu. A former Hell's Angel, bartender and assistant music manager of New York's CBGB's and Max's Kansas City, Mike opened Sharky's in the mid-1990s when there were only a couple of other infamously debauched bars in the neighbourhood – the late Maxine's and the Heart of Darkness, where gang warfare shoot-outs were par for the course. The quintessential dive bar, Sharky's is, and was, Phnom Penh's rock and punk mecca, a place of outright libertinism and lawlessness; of dimly lit pool tables, historic dancefloor murders and gun-drawn sieges. It's been home to a revolving door of bands, and drinking gimmicks, like the 'Golden Tequila Mile' – where contestants must crawl, hands tied, beneath a tunnel of barfly legs while drinking tequila. (Or the 'Mortar Round': a cocktail served in a mortar shell, placed inside a Vietnamese army helmet. As the patron dons the helmet and starts to drink their cocktail, the bar staff grab sticks from behind the bar and beat the poor soul's head with them. I've seen the spectacle first hand on wild nights spent with friends at Sharky's and have vivid memories of ducking the incoming sticks as they engaged with the heads of bodies perched on neighbouring barstools.)

There is something in the seedy underbelly of the capital's nightlife that still feels refreshingly free spirited. Long gone are Sharky's lawless bordello days, when UN soldiers had to check their AK-47s at the door, and the infamous Walkabout pub brothel was a stubborn stain on Rue Pasteur. Yet, there is still that element of unfettered hedonism and danger in the red-light district. One day I had to pay off a furious sex worker who'd brought a mob to intimidate my wayward, penniless friend. We had just sat down to eat lunch when, from out of nowhere, she stormed over and accused my friend of not paying her for a past dalliance. It's a common trick – one that relies on the punter being unable to recall whether he paid the sex worker or not after emerging from a drunken blackout. Things escalated to fever pitch quickly, and the only way out of a lynching was to pay up quick. But on the same corner, on another night, I remember the whole of the red-light district's Rue Pasteur street – a crowd of fifty tourists, locals, punters and sex workers – all howling and hooting with joy to the words of the Righteous Brothers' 'Unchained Melody' outside the Black Cat bar. Such a spirited place could turn on a half-penny, from the heart of darkness to . . . light.

In Chariya's time the brothels, bars and clubs were scattered all across town, from Wat Phnom in the north to BKK3 in the south; some even floated along the Mekong River. In the 1950s

Sharky's was a fusion restaurant called Le Noveau Tricon, which specialized in Chinese food but also had sections for French, Cambodian and Vietnamese cuisine. Its history with taxi girls dates back to then, when they could be seen working the tables, flirting with the last of the French Foreign Legionnaires as they sipped their aperitifs and clung desperately to vestiges of their vanishing empire.

For many of her residents and visitors – for the avant-garde and the bohemians – Phnom Penh in the 1960s was intoxicating. Even opium dens like the infamous Madame Chum's *fumerie* – reported to be one of the largest brothels in Southeast Asia – was seen as more of an upmarket bordello, a welcome ritual for the visiting high-ranking French officials and a place of business for Europeans and Asians, where friends bonded over a shared pipe while being massaged by one of Madame Chum's girls. The warm glow of kerosene lamps illuminated its bamboo-reed partitions and window blinds and set the tone for the relaxed atmosphere inside. In fact, the powerful and popular Madame Chum herself – who provided every pleasure a patron could want, including a rather gruesome act of bestiality they called the 'Cholon Duck', as detailed in Steven Boswell's fascinating book *King Norodom's Head* – reportedly drew the line at admitting Americans on account of their 'boisterous nature'. Elsewhere, in the daylight, the last vestiges of the French protectorate could be found upon white tablecloths, played out by suited waiters serving food from the homeland in restaurants like La Taverne and Café de Paris.

Naturally, Chariya's *savoir-faire* leant itself well to the nightlife of 1960s Phnom Penh. He was at home among the movers and shakers of various professions and industries, all of whom converged to form the rich framework of Phnom Penh's social scene. Both Chariya's talent and connections helped expand his role beyond the Magetat, and cemented his puissant status within Cambodia's music industry. At the height of his career, he spent his nights running the Magetat's music programme and his days rooted in the jazz *fons et origo* of his early marching-band training, leading the thirty-piece state-run SKD (Société Khmer des Distilleries) band. The orchestra represented a powerful alcohol distillery that was staffed by around 3,000 workers. They dealt with Cambodia's imports and, from 1965, its exports, including SKD's (still) popular brew Angkor beer. The band played almost anything from fanfare to swing to rock 'n' roll; their days spent practising, playing ceremonial events or recording at RNK radio, their nights playing parties and weddings. When Phnom Penh hosted Asia's continental version of the Olympics, the GANEFO Games, in 1966, SKD had the honour of opening the ceremony.

Chariya was what the French might call *l'éminence grise*, for he possessed no airs or graces, was modest to a fault and seemed uninterested in the limelight and the glory, but was nevertheless a powerful operator behind the scenes – or, in his line of work, the curtains. But the glamour and enchantment of Chariya's golden age came to an end when his world fell apart in 1970. It began with the unexpected closure of the Magetat on 17 March 1970.

'The military were coming to get us,' he told me. 'We were just told to pack our bags and leave the Magetat immediately!'

From 11 March large-scale city protests and riots had been mounting almost daily in opposition to the Vietnamese forces and their war. The US bombing of the Ho Chi Minh trail had claimed too many Cambodian lives. Young people gathered in their thousands to demonstrate outside the National Assembly in Phnom Penh, and the senior nationalists in government did little to counter the protests.

The Cambodian civil war soon followed the uprising. When Lon Nol's demands to the North Vietnamese army – to leave their hidden bases within Cambodia – were not met, fighting broke out, first in the north-west between North Vietnam, their new allies, the Khmer Rouge guerrilla army, and their common enemy the Cambodian army. In the years to follow, persistent heavy bombing across Cambodia as well as explosives detonated in Phnom Penh's public places by the Khmer Rouge meant that city nightlife shut down. Some venues reopened for a time during the early 1970s but the Magetat never did, and its closing kickstarted a chain of events that would put an end to the life Chariya and Sieng Dy had built in Phnom Penh.

The day after the Magetat shut its doors, on 18 March 1970, the political unrest reached breaking point when Prince Norodom Sihanouk was removed from power in the bloodless coup by Prime Minister Lon Nol and his supporters. That is what was widely reported – however it was, in fact, Chariya's own father, Deputy Prime Minister Prince Sisowath Sirik Matak who, alongside the Americans, was said to be the puppeteer controlling Lon Nol's strings. Matak was reported to have swayed Lon Nol to remove Sihanouk from government, some say at gunpoint, though this hearsay has never been proven. I never did ask Chariya about this, or whether Sihanouk's brainchild, the state-owned Magetat, was a pawn swept up in this – whether it was the case his father's administration had inadvertently sacked his own son. Chariya never talked about his family in the course of our conversations. His silence on the matter spoke volumes. I suspected later, through piecing together dates and facts Chariya had given me, that he may have severed relations with his father. Certainly his actions suggested he stood by Sihanouk instead.

Chariya's SKD band was renamed Infantry Brigade 13. Under the Lon Nol regime it was a military band tasked with extolling the virtues of the new regime and damning Sihanouk and the Sangkum. Chariya remained tight-lipped about his views on this, but he did blame the economic and military situation for his eventual emigration to Thailand with Sieng Dy later that year. By late 1970 much of the countryside was controlled by the Khmer Rouge and the roads outside Phnom Penh were fraught with danger, but the couple found a way to get across the country and into neighbouring Thailand where they fled to the capital Bangkok. Here they stayed with a cousin who worked at the UN, and to make ends meet Chariya played the organ with a popular Thai band in a beer garden on the Phet Buri Road. They had a son, Charidy, in 1971, and later a daughter called Dita, and spent the next twenty years playing music and living nomadically between Paris, Long Beach and Beijing, where Chariya helped campaign for his cousin in exile, Prince Sihanouk.

Chariya in the 1980s.

The first Cambodian election since the 1960s prompted the family's return to their homeland in 1993, and in 2004, after forty years of marriage, Cháriya and Sieng Dy parted ways. In spite of this, and Dy's reported diva antics – so at odds with Chariya's character – Chariya only ever spoke of his estranged wife with respect and warmth. His reverent, romantic, parting words for Dy stayed with me long after he spoke them. He told me earnestly, 'She dedicated all of herself to the music.'

Sieng Dy passed away in Lakewood, California, following complications from a fall in 2019, two years on from Chariya's own passing from ill health – he left behind a second wife and two young children in Siem Reap, Cambodia. When I learned of Chariya's death I was crestfallen. Humble and kind to a fault, he'd left an imprint on my heart. His handful of trips from Siem Reap to Phnom Penh to see me often coincided with medical appointments, the abscess on his chest growing larger each time. As I helped him into a taxi that last time in 2014, and felt his kind, sad smile bore into my heart, I wondered if I would see him again. Sophorn had grown fond of him too and they spoke often in the intervening years. Sophorn was never one to hold a grudge: even when confronted, insulted or shot down, he remained stoically silent and brushed off conflict with resilience and an untarnished belief in humanity I could only dream of. He was simply the best barometer for judging people; he only ever commented on the good he saw, and by this definition always had much to say about Chariya.

Sisowath Chariya had lived – really lived – his seventy-seven years. Many of the musicians I tracked down were of a similar age and readying themselves to move from this life into their next, and the hourglass of time was never far from my mind. I wondered – beyond the work of Cambodian rock revivalists – how else was the musical legacy of Cambodia's golden age being preserved? What will happen to it when they all die?

On 10 October 2017, the seventh day following Prince Sisowath Chariya's death, the Sacred Dancers of Angkor gathered under the thatched roof of their open-walled practice space to pay their respects with a Buddhist passing rite. An unintentionally metaphoric stairway to heaven, the altar was constructed from some stage stairs and decorated in candles and incense, with lotus petals scattered on the wooden floor and a smiling portrait of Chariya framed by lotus flowers resting on the fifth step. It sat beneath another portrait, that of the troupe's de facto leader, the royal dancer and Sihanouk's daughter, Princess Norodom Bopha

Devi. Fourteen apsara dancers dressed in white knelt in front of a traditional *pinpeat* orchestra, while their principal dancer, wrapped in a white gossamer veil, moved exquisitely before the altar to a hypnotic backing of hand drums, cymbals and wooden xylophones, bridging the gap between the prince and the spirit realm just as apsaras had done for centuries.

5

Buried Treasure

Whenever the bombs came, I ran with my records and the clothes on my back. I didn't care about saving anything else, I had to save my records.

Keo Sinan

Thach Soly.

Grandeur and a certain louche sophistication may have been synonymous with clubs like the Magetat, but this club was just one part of a larger scene. There were many other clubs, each one hosting different clientele and lesser-known artists; the royals and their friends were not the only ones hitting the stages of Phnom

Penh. I wanted to learn more about the wider scene, and to hear if the passion and sweat inside Kbal Thnal had trickled down into the smaller, more basic clubs where less famous house bands carved out a living bringing *romvong, saravan*, the twist and the tango to dancefloors. And what of the fans, I wondered? The collectors? The hard-working house-band players?

I met someone who would shed a light on some of this: a session drummer and record collector by the name of Keo Sinan, from Kampong Thom province in central Cambodia. He was close to my friend Oro, and when Oro told me Sinan was visiting him in Phnom Penh, I took the opportunity to set up a meeting.

As I waited early that morning at the entrance to Oro's alley near the riverside, I could feel eyes on me. As if staring down the barrel of a rifle my vision became almost telescopic. I saw past the vibrant street colours and the blurring, rushing locals and locked eyes with a mysterious man across the street, leaning cross-limbed against a parked car. He wore his brown button-down shirt with Clint Eastwood cool, his age disguised by a full head of jet-black hair but betrayed by the blue ring around his ethereal, maroon irises. He seemed invisible to all but me, and, in that split thunderbolt second in time we looked at each other, the street sellers were silenced and bicycles, mopeds and cars became hushed flashes.

Our strange, momentary astral plane was abruptly shattered when Oro bounded up to me and motioned over my mystery man from across the street, and it all slotted into place. I was duly introduced to 'Oum Non' ('Uncle Non'), as Oro affectionately called him, and we made our way over to a quiet café at the north end of the riverside, ordered a round of iced coffees and got to talking.

Sinan was born on a small farm in Kampong Thom, a hundred miles from Phnom Penh. Life in the province itself was a world away from the glamour of the capital and a far cry from the luxury

Panara and Chariya were born into. Situated on the flood plains of Cambodia's largest lake, the Tonlé Sap, rice harvests yield high in the dry season, and are replaced by fishing in the wet season when the lake and rivers break their banks, flood the plains, and people swap bicycles and motorbikes for boats to get around.

Sinan's passion for music came from the folk band in his village and lessons at school, where he first encountered the trumpet and a drum set. His primary school sponsored out musical instruments and Sinan immediately signed up to the initiative; an opportunity that might otherwise have been beyond the reach of his family's modest means. When Sinan left school, paid work in Kampong Thom was limited mostly to rice growing or fishing, but Sinan had other ambitions. He started out working in a cement factory in Kampot, southern Cambodia. It was here that he met Nop Noeun – the brother of the famous actor Nop Nem – whom Sinan referred to as 'a master of music'. And it was with Nop Noeun that Sinan's musical career began.

He spent two years learning all he could from Noeun before he left for Phnom Penh with his own trumpet and drumsticks in hand, to look for work. But the road to fame and glory was not paved in gold, and Sinan subsidized his meagre musical income with construction work, splitting his time between Phnom Penh and Kampong Thom, which, by the mid 1960s, was developing. In 1965 his fortunes changed when he met the husband of singer and radio broadcaster Huoy Meas, a drummer called Yel Om Sophanarak, known simply by all as 'Mr Yel'. Mr Yel helped Sinan refine his craft and eventually the young drummer landed a gig drumming in a small club called La Melodie, and another in a larger, 300-capacity bar called Sovanmancha ('the Mermaid Bar').

'It was like a neighbourhood,' Sinan shrugged with a smile, habitually stirring his iced coffee. Outside, a *chapei* busker had pitched up, the bluesy twangs of his nylon strings punctuating the city sounds. We all turned our heads towards the music and took a moment to drink in the notes, Sinan's gaze remaining fixed on the player as he continued to unfurl, 'There were lots of musicians in the scene . . . old timers and newcomers, musicians from RNK radio and record company session bands. The manager of the bar or club you were playing at would give the performing band a setlist of songs that you had to play and from six o'clock to ten o'clock we would play traditional (*romvong*, *saravan*) slow, circle dance music; from ten o' clock to two in the morning we would play international styles (rock 'n' roll, twist, tango). The audience was made up of a mix of people, from foreigners to military officers to actors and actresses, and when we started playing the international music later in the night, everyone would dance.'

The scene at La Melodie and Sovanmancha differed little from the more expensive clubs like the Magetat. Their music programmes were similar. The same off-duty military men frequented them, all to jive the night away with their wives; others chased taxi girls and shook off their troubles on the dancefloor. However, the main differences were the price of drinks – the clientele of La Melodie and Sovanmancha was less mixed and more middle class and Cambodian – and, of course, the talent roster: the patrons of the Magetat were paying for the big-name stars of the time.

We discussed the music industry layout back then – from studios like Van Chann to popular labels like Hang Meas and Chanchhaya, Cambodia, Angkor, Bayon, Wat-Phnom and more classical labels like M'kotpich – alongside his influences, which were mostly on the mainstream, romantic end of the Cambodian pop spectrum. Songwriters like Peou Sipho, Svay Sor, Mam Boutnaray and lyricist Ma Lopy spilled out of his mouth, along with the odd rocker like 1970s studio sensation, writer and producer Voy Ho, Cambodia's answer to the West's Quincy Jones. La Melodie's house drummer started collecting music around 1965, primarily to memorize the hits of the time for his nightclub setlists, and born from this a burgeoning – and now famous – collection of Cambodian music blossomed. Sinan collected stacks of 45s: from film music like Ros Sereysothea's blues title track of the Cambodian blockbuster *Tomorrow I Will Leave You* to her duet with Sinn Sisamouth called 'Karma' (from the 1968 movie *One Thousand Memories*). The collection ran the gamut from jive singles like Sereysothea and Sisamouth's 1973 release, 'I'm Ticklish! I'm Ticklish!' to bossa nova tracks like Sinn Sisamouth's 1966 number 'Malavy's Tears'.

'Between 1975 and 1979 it was too dangerous to have records,' Sinan confided, his voice taking on an altogether more serious tone. 'People who were found with records were killed, because they didn't allow people to listen to popular music any more. So, I had techniques: I hid them to keep them safe. It would have been dangerous if anyone had caught me with even one or two records. I would have been killed.

'First, after the coup in 1970, I entrusted my records to a monk in a Buddhist temple, until 1971. During the civil war, when the clubs closed, I was forced to move from the city to the farms and then back again to the city to find work, taking my records with me each time. Whenever the bombs came, I ran with my 45 rpm records and the clothes on my back. I didn't care about saving anything else, I had to save my records.'

As early as 1970 the Khmer Rouge cut off the land routes in and out of Kampong Thom, leaving the Mekong River slightly to the south and east as the only connection between the province and the capital city, eighty miles away. The severing of Kampong Thom – where Pol Pot's family home was burned to the ground in a bombing raid by American forces in 1970 – was a strategic victory for the Khmer Rouge. As one by one their army gained control of rice-growing areas, they localized production and effectively drove the refugee-swelled capital Phnom Penh and the Khmer Republic army into slow starvation. As the Khmer

Rouge party slogan goes, 'If we have water we can have rice, and if we have rice, we have everything.' For the Khmer Rouge, rice was not only a currency to starve their enemies and to ration their work collectives, but to sell to other countries, like China, in exchange for military supplies to arm their soldiers with.

In 1974 Sinan was living in Kampong Thom, forced to work as a vegetable farmer for the Khmer Rouge regime. That year, Sinan's village leader held a meeting: 'Our village leader asked everyone to bring any music records to them to be destroyed. At the time, I had been put in charge of planting vegetables, so I hid my records in metal boxes in an abandoned outhouse near my home. I didn't bury them, as they would have been destroyed with no air getting to them. So, I put them in loose plastic bags inside metal boxes so that the air could get to them inside the boxes and they wouldn't decompose in the ground. The outhouse contained chemical fertilizer and, because of all the poisonous chemicals and pesticides, people were reluctant to go near it. I visited the outhouse once a week to check on the records, always around noon, when most people stayed indoors to escape the heat. One time, a Khmer Rouge officer summoned me to tell me that he had heard that I was in possession of old records, and that if I did have these records I should not have them as they were prohibited. I told him that all my records were lost when my [old] house burned down after being bombed. But two officers kept visiting my house and investigating. I guess I was frightened so I gave them both two watches as a gift. There was constant danger. I loved those records more than anything.'

From Sisamouth's first twist release, 'Dance with Me', on the Angkor label, to dance hits like his 'When You Dance the Monkey' and Pen Ran's 'Ha! Ha! Monkeys', Sinan's extensive collection spanned the breadth of both artists' careers and musical genres as well as those of their peers.

Sinan, alongside anyone captured or brainwashed by the Khmer

Rouge before 1975, was considered by the regime to be an 'old person' (those who 'joined' the regime after the 1975 takeover of Phnom Penh being the 'new people'). The old people were generally regarded to have been treated better than the new people. They tended to be rural peasants, whereas the urban new people – Lon Nol supporters, the intelligentsia, free thinkers, city folk – represented the enemy of the Khmer Rouge's ideology. Their utopian dream was a classless society and a return to the land.

Sinan had straddled both worlds throughout the mid- to late 1960s and it took every ounce of tenacity and luck for someone in his position to survive almost a decade under Khmer Rouge rule. Just like the vegetables he tended to and nurtured, so did he routinely and opportunistically tend to the maintenance of his hidden collection in deadly secret.

When his village was taken over by the Vietnamese army in the early days of 1979, the first thing Sinan did was uncover his collection. I marvelled at what it must have been like for him to reclaim his 'buried treasure' after the years of war and genocide, after all the horrors he'd seen, the torments and the suffering he'd endured, and the equally merciless conditions his records had withstood, and yet remained, miraculously intact. What a reunion that must have been. Before I had a chance to ask him, he was scrolling on his smart phone for old black and white photos of himself aged around twenty years old in classic house band suits and pristine tuxs.

Time passed before Sinan got hold of a record player and brought his treasured records back to life, to sing once more. How it must have felt, hearing his music once again after all he – and his collection – had been through. That's when the miracle of it all struck me. After the genocide, there were thirteen years of Vietnamese 'liberation' – or 'occupation', depending on who you talk to. Those who survived the genocide were still facing war zones, famine and often the loss of their homes.

The Khmer Rouge had taken the country back to year zero – a place of no economic infrastructure in the capitalist sense. If people found vinyl records, there often wasn't a record player to play them on. I'd heard stories of children tossing vinyl records into rivers like frisbees. And among all this chaos, in a small village in Kampong Thom, a music lover took treasures in plastic bags from patinated metal boxes, carefully examined those that survived, and played them once more. To this day, Sinan still has those boxes, as a reminder of the lengths he went to to protect his collection. An undertaking many have benefited from. We owe him a great debt.

*Sinan digitising his collection
at CVMA.*

The Cambodian Vintage Music Archive has been slowly digitizing Sinan's collection of rock, bossa nova and *romvong* songs from the likes of Sinn Sisamouth, Ros Sereysothea and Pen Ran. Additionally, Sinan has made himself available as an oral archive and memory bank to the organization on a number of occasions. He's also participated in events showcasing Cambodian music, including an exhibition of vintage Asian music in Korea in 2016. When I thought of my own experience with music – how my love of music from an early age had shaped me and remained the one constant thread of my life through all the twists and turns – I could relate to why Sinan still dedicates much of his time to music. How could he do otherwise?

Music transcends time and space, peace and war. I may not be the person I was when I first discovered music, but I will always remember the passion I felt and the person I was when I made those early discoveries. Music transports. A song can capture a moment in time we can revisit simply by playing it. It can live forever in each of us, and sometimes there comes along a generous soul brave enough to pass it on, at all cost. Keo Sinan still lives in Kampong Thom and collects to this day.

Two days before the Cambodian Buddhist festival of Pchum Ben ('Ancestor's Day'), the mass exodus of Phnom Penh was well underway. Migrant workers gathered by their hundreds at the small bus station by Central Market to clamber onto buses bound for their ancestral homes in the provinces. Sophorn, Kevin and I scrambled through the sea of waiting travellers and boarded a bus bound for Kampong Chhnang, a province about a three-hour bus ride from the capital. The karaoke was blasting, the snacks were being passed around, and we were embarking on an adventure to track down the long-lost guitar legend Thach Soly.

It was late September 2014, the rainy season was coming to an end and in a matter of months the rice paddies en route had been transformed from muddy pools to soft sheets of the most vibrant green. Enraptured children splashed and torpedoed into rivers. Bony cows ambled along the roadsides, unimpressed by the passing traffic. Garlands of sausages hung from a rod on a roadside shop and a woman in pyjamas defended them with frantic arms, charging at mangey mutts and waving off persistent flies. Gone were the stone and brick houses of Phnom Penh and its bustling streets, the thinning crowds on dust-coated suburban corners, the vast palm oil plantations, roadside restaurants and neon beer signs that lined the highways. The road narrowed, traditional wooden stilt houses – built to withstand the floods – sprung up around us and I could almost breathe the cleaner air outside. It felt good to break away from the city once more.

Until then, I had merely passed through Kampong Chhnang province on my way to Battambang or Siem Reap. Lying fifty miles north of Phnom Penh, with its mountain vantage points and close proximity to the capital, it made an excellent military base. So thought the French during the protectorate, and the Khmer Rouge during their rule. Both built barracks in the province, and the Khmer Rouge built an airport using slave labour. The estimates of those who died during its construction range from 100,000 to 350,000 on Cambodia's own 'road of bones'. Now, these buildings lie vacant, claimed by nature, their secrets kept and silent.

Our bus reached Kampong Chhnang city within four short and uneventful hours. Kevin had booked us into a guesthouse in the centre of town and, as we made our way there on foot, Phnom Penh's crowds seemed a world away, for there was hardly a soul in sight. The formal monuments and clean, grassy boulevard of the city centre slipped from view, giving way to kerbsides covered in weeds, roads littered with potholes and roof upon roof of rust-streaked corrugated iron. Once a port city for the Tonlé Sap lake (the province's name literally translates to 'Clay Pot Port'), the condition of the roads signified that their desertion could not have solely been down to the Pchum Ben holiday. Our street was either underdeveloped or had undergone the same fate as Kevin's native Detroit, with more empty lots in sight than occupied ones. Derelict homes stooped like mausoleums in what was once a booming commercial centre with thriving citizenry. The dilapidation and silence paid proof to what can happen to a place lacking in natural wonders and the tourist potential of, say, Siem Reap or Cambodia's coastline. Beyond that, it's testimony to what happens, primarily, when a river changes course, as the Tonlé Sap had done centuries before. Many of Kampong Chhnang's inhabitants deserted and followed the new course south.

Our guesthouse neighboured a makeshift boule pit situated on a burned-out plot where a charred, wooden stilt house would have once stood pretty and proud. It was now leaning so far sideways it was a wonder it had not collapsed already. In front, naked children skipped and played in the sandy pit with pieces of rope, blissfully unaware of the danger looming overhead. 'Well, at least some community spirit has risen out of the ashes,' I thought. Next to the debris, the grounds of our Little Garden Guesthouse lived up to its name: a lush jungle of orchids, yellow padauk blossoms and rumdul flowers fragranced the evening air in Kampong Chhnang's ghost town.

The following morning we discovered that locating a couple of mopeds for hire on a national holiday was almost impossible but, eventually, we managed to find the last two sorriest-looking hire bikes in town. Armed with the best salt fish Kampong Chhnang had to offer we mounted our trusty and battered steeds and hit the 30-kilometre highway to Thach Soly's home in a small town called Baribour. I can still see Kevin now in my backwards glances, gripping the handles with all his might, his oversized helmet sliding down in the breeze, a look of terror plastered across his face. He later told me with a sigh and every ounce of drama he could muster, 'There were times when the big rigs came by I wasn't sure I was going to make it.'

He was referring to the large freight trucks that shot past every few minutes or so, creating gusts of wind so strong that we almost wobbled off the road each time. While Kevin rode and suffered

alone, I had lucked out with the safe seat on Sophorn's moped.
I clung to him and took in some of the most spectacular scenery
I'd encountered in Cambodia. As we left the clay pot stalls of the
city behind, I got that sense of moving back in time again, the
stilt houses towering over their seasonal floods, becoming more
basic and spread-out by the dozen. The vibrant green paddies
were dotted with palm trees and the Baribo River shadowed us
on our journey, winding, thinning and widening into tributaries,
hosting fisheries, birds and boats. With every mile we covered,
the adrenalin in my veins pumped harder just knowing that we
were a mile closer to meeting the legend revered by so many
musicians I had spoken to. After a few double-backs and phone
calls, we passed our final landmark – an ominous, grey military
barracks – and peeled off the highway, onto the dirt track leading
to Thach Soly's farmhouse.

Peeking past the blue shutters and geranium pots that lined
its timber walls, the dark heart of the home came into focus. The
charming, house-proud exterior contained an open-plan space
with little in the way of belongings, and a dirt floor packed and
buffed by the heavy footfall of bare feet. Mango trees, brush and
farmland surrounded us, and to the side was a large concrete
foundation covered by a thatched awning. Out from under it
strode a beautiful man of mid-height, with the same blue-rimmed
irises as Keo Sinan and Mam Boutnaray. He bore two long, deep,
wrinkle lines from the corners of each eye but otherwise his
smooth face belied his years. His eyes were kind, his hair and
clothing well kept, and he possessed an air of distinguished and
calm authenticity in every gesture, mannerism and word uttered
from his lips. He took in Kevin, and with his lips curling into a
smile, waggled his finger and said knowingly, 'Ah, Noel Redding
haircut.' An instant bond was established.

After a round of *sampeahs*, Madame Thach emerged to receive
the salt fish we'd brought, and Soly summoned us to meet the

rest of his inter-generational family who, silently poised, had decorated themselves around the many plastic chairs and tables under the awning. So obviously proud of their patriarch, they hung onto his every word.

A recluse for many years, the legend of Thach Soly came up in conversation with many people I interviewed. Both Svay Sor and Mam Boutnaray labelled him a guitar virtuoso and praised his innate ability as a session player to play any style of music – and play it better than anyone else, be it folk rock on a barrel-bodied acoustic, or dirty rock 'n' roll on a Stratocaster. The ex-guitarist and teacher had gained an almost mythical status as one who had transcended the social borders of his ethnic minority background to go on to master his craft and inspire the playing of many up and coming 1960s musicians – and who had then disappeared from view during the civil war, never to return. In many ways a provincial Mam Boutnaray.

Soly pointed out his place of birth, Kampuchea Krom, almost immediately. Kampuchea Krom is a place situated on a large swathe of the Mekong Delta in South Vietnam, occupied mainly by an ethnic minority group of Khmer people called the Khmer Krom. The victims of land grabs from the Vietnamese and colonial land traders, the Khmer Krom have been persecuted for centuries. They refuse to conform to Vietnamese culture, to send their children to learn in Vietnamese schools, and, fighting for their cultural identity and way of life are locked in a life of purgatory in a land no longer their own. The Vietnamese authorities are no longer killing the Khmer Krom in vast numbers, but they are breeding them out – jobs for young Khmer Krom men in Vietnamese companies often come with a catch: they have to take a Vietnamese wife – and silencing their voice. Buddhist monks have been arrested and defrocked, Khmer language is banned from being spoken publicly, and Vietnamese customs and values are enforced. The words 'social cleansing' and 'human rights' are synonymous with their fate. It's a silent genocide. Tied to their land, they are displaced: too Vietnamese for Cambodia, too Cambodian for Vietnam.

Soly's family moved from Kampuchea Krom to Phnom Penh when he was just one year old, and while they no longer faced the threat of death and violence from the Vietnamese authorities, they were treated as second-class citizens by their own fellow Cambodians. To countenance this, Soly found salvation in music early on. He joined a French exchange programme at his school and his French exchange student would write musical notes and name the corresponding notes in letters he'd send to Soly, who was only too eager to learn but had no instrument with which to exercise his knowledge. At seventeen, Soly saw a guitar in a Vietnamese theatre show, then bought some wood and bicycle brake wire and fashioned his own acoustic guitar based on what he'd seen in the show. American rock 'n' rollers like Bill Haley and Chubby Checker and, later, Englishmen the Beatles and the Stones, were big influences. However, it was poverty that first inspired him to pick up an instrument. He wanted to prove that even a poor boy from Kampuchea Krom could play music and make it onto RNK radio.

'I had to create my own knowledge with the music,' he told me. 'No one else was going to teach me, so I had to teach myself how to play.' Soly practised every day, and within a year had entered a song into a music competition at National Congress.

In the days of Sihanouk's one-party rule National Congress took place every six months near the Royal Palace in Phnom Penh. A large covered stage was erected in Veal Preah Man Park in front of the National Museum of Cambodia. It was an opportunity for the people to hear the government's record in a public forum and to celebrate Khmer arts. Delegates from the communes, cities and province capitals gathered to discuss and share new policies and legislation, and many famous and emerging artists followed the proceedings with a concert, attracting a crowd of thousands. A great cross section of society, people of all ages and backgrounds attended. For those who couldn't afford records and nightclub entrance fees, this was their opportunity to watch their radio idols perform, and for one day, twice a year, music brought everyone – princes and paupers – together.

The competition Soly took part in in 1960 was judged by Cambodia's finest: Maurice Liébot, the revered teacher of the Université des Beaux-Arts, and Denacio Saem, the bandleader for the Royal Palace. Sihanouk encouraged such competitions, as they promoted his vision of a modernized Cambodia and acted as an effective recruitment drive for new talent. That year, the monsoon rains came but the people stayed – the men taking off their shirts and wearing them on their heads as makeshift shelters. Soly's performance won him first place in the competition, which cemented his career path and within two years he was playing rock 'n'roll sessions regularly for RNK radio.

From what I'd learned already about songwriting associations and musical school training at the time, Soly's path was unusual. Although a number of singers were discovered through music competitions, not many songwriters and instrumental musicians were. Soly bucked tradition by not pursuing the restricted – and often military and bureaucratic – pathway that musicians of mid-century Cambodia were expected to follow, through the palace training ground or music schools like UBA. When I heard others talk of Thach Soly, there was always this hint of reverence, partly for his talent, and partly because their teacher flouted convention, stepped outside the box and succeeded, in spite of the odds.

After the National Congress competition, Soly started a rock 'n' roll band called Sophoan Dontrey (roughly translated: 'the Good Band') and he selected his finest students – a revolving door of great and promising musicians – to play with him.

Soly was also Cambodia's original home recording producer, having hired some recording equipment from a private company to record at home, before taking the tapes to the engineers at RNK radio to mix. The five-piece band – rhythm guitar, lead guitar, bass guitar, drums and vocals – divided the house up with partitions, each member having their own tablature and a room mic. Heavy sheets decorated the walls and dampened the sound and many of Soly's pioneering techniques on early recordings were replicated later by his students in their own garage recordings.

In the early 1960s other bands were breaking through – some made it onto RNK radio, others didn't. But Soly told me of the

Thach Soly (2nd from left) and his band, Sophoan.

emergence of a couple of young bands who did make the airwaves in those early years who joined him on the circuit: 'Baksey Cham Krong was created before the Sophoan band, but they weren't really a guitar band until later. Back then they were a folk outfit, playing violin, accordion and slow music. So, you could say that Sophoan was the first [guitar] band, even though we weren't as well known. Then came Apsara, then the Bayon band, Majura, and others. Most of the guitar bands at that time didn't compose their own songs, they just covered songs.'

And this is where, again, Thach Soly bucked the trend. He did write his own songs, but perhaps like much of the world at this time, Cambodia wasn't ready for it – or perhaps it was his social status that held him back. Whatever the reason, the Sophoan band never received the acclaim that Apsara or Baksey Cham Krong did, and no Sophoan band records exist as their recording career was limited to live radio shows. Instead, Soly supplemented his income from radio and live shows with teaching work from 1963 to 1970, and his teachings became almost a rite of passage for the guitarists of *yé-yé* bands to come, like Drakkar guitarist Touch Chhattha as well as mainstream artists such as the singers Chea Savoeun and Long Soda, who later became a fixture on the Long Beach music scene.

Having recorded around 120 songs and having spent a decade playing the party circuit, the Sophoan band dissolved with the changing times in 1970. Their career highlight, Soly told me, was playing a show aboard the Lotus D'Or floating supper club with French film star Charles Aznavour present in the crowd. Aznavour was in Cambodia shooting his movie *Le Facteur s'en va-t-en Guerre* (*The Postman Goes to War*), and the milestone also marked a time in Sophoan's career when the band were fast reaching their peak years of Beatles-inspired guitar music, between 1966 and 1968. Their dusk marked the dawn of Cambodia's civil war, when the music scene became more politically charged than ever before.

'The government wanted songs about the war but the people didn't want these, they wanted to hear romantic songs,' Soly told me plainly. 'The music style was still the same but the lyrics of the songs changed; they weren't catchy like before. For example [singer] Liev Tuk was inspired by Vinny Taylor, his music was still rock 'n' roll but his lyrics were all of a sudden about *Chenla* [a military operation named after the ancient dynasty] and winning the war . . .'

Riotous and extroverted, Tuk was Cambodia's godfather of proto-punk – no doubt a kindred spirit for Soly. He lived, breathed and screamed rock 'n' roll and his back catalogue of originals and covers tore the seams off Booker T. & the MG's 'Green Onions' and injected adrenaline into the Association's 'Never My Love'. According to Soly, Tuk died of a heart attack during the civil war, around the age of thirty, and though I heard the same sentiment echoed in conversations I had with other musicians, I was unable to corroborate this with any documentation from the time.

Lost in Soly's tales, I glanced down for a second to see my laptop fast running out of battery. The family was rousing around us and it was looking like we'd need to return the next morning to capture the rest of the story.

One by one Soly's family members were moving off to prepare for the night's celebration, and our still waters became tidal for the first time in hours. As I was packing up, a generator and PA system were being carried out and placed under the awning, and the tables and chairs were moved aside to reveal a dancefloor. Thach Soly stood off to the side, surveying and organizing the hive of activity, before turning to me to ask if his family could perform for us. We were touched and politely welcomed the kind offering, not knowing quite what was coming.

With the click of the power button the PA surged to life. The microphone screeched in protest, Soly jumped backwards, and we all winced before some kind soul flicked the volume down and tamed the console. Moments later Soly could barely be heard summoning his family above a roaring *romvong* backing track, and around fifteen family members of differing ages formed a circle, entrancing us all with graceful hand gestures and shuffling feet in the late evening light.

There is a Khmer saying: 'a bunch of sticks cannot break'. Family is the cornerstone of Asian life, and in Cambodia it's the glue of society. It was deeply touching to see them all together – some serious, some smiling, some young, some old – music and harmony at the centre of Thach family life. A proud grin spread across Soly's face as he looked on.

We left them to their dancing, and returned to the Little Garden Guesthouse, where we were rudely awakened to the pitfalls of staying in what was effectively a rainforest. The first attack came from a pair of bright blue tarantula-like arachnids that crept undetected into the hallway where Sophorn and I were working that evening. It wasn't until they scuttled ten feet from the door towards us at full pelt that I saw them and yelled, 'Sophorn, get your feet up . . . giant spiders coming!' Sophorn turned slowly to look, chuckling insouciantly as he picked his feet up at the last second and said, 'Dee, nothing to worry about,' as if I were certifiably insane.

'But look at the size of them,' I shot back. 'They're as big as my hand and they were coming right at us.'

'Not poisonous, I tell you. They're harmless,' he tittered. But I wasn't convinced by the city boy's knowledge of venomous spiders. I did, in fact, find out through another close encounter some time later that they were one of the most poisonous spiders in Cambodia.

The second attack came from red ants in our bed. Kevin was even more squeamish than I about such things, so it was my job to divert their path around the bed, just as it had been my job to flush a giant centipede down a plug hole with a jet-powered 'bum gun' – a Cambodian transmogrification of a French bidet – in Sihanoukville, and remove the occasional cockroach from our apartment. Needless to say, the dreaded return of the spiders and ants at the Little Garden Guesthouse haunted us, and neither of us got much sleep that night.

The next morning, we returned at first light to Baribour and waited under the awning for Soly. Dazed and still half asleep, Kevin and I gazed across at the next door neighbour's lot to see a loin-clothed man casually shaving the rump of his buffalo with a Bic razor. Sophorn followed our line of vision, and we must have all stared at this scene for seconds but it felt like minutes, a look of silent puzzlement mirrored on each of our weary faces. When I later returned to Phnom Penh, I turned to the oracle (Google) as I had done before for all manner of strange Cambodian mysteries, but nothing doing. I asked my friend Mealea, the self-proclaimed 'buffalo kid', who'd spent half her childhood on the back of a buffalo – but no answers there either. The strange loin-clothed buffalo-shaving incident remains an unsolved mystery, yet forever etched on my mind.

Just as the buffalo was being led out to pasture, Soly emerged from his house in smart grey slacks and a pressed purple shirt. He proceeded to give us a quick tour of his mango orchard and tilapia fishpond, before settling down with the family audience once more to pick up where we had left off yesterday – 1970: the start of the Cambodian civil war.

'After 1970 I was [in the] military,' Soly imparted. 'I played music for a military band called 43 B1, supervised by Deang Dell ... he also came from Kampuchea Krom. We played like a mobile unit, playing concerts everywhere. For example, if the soldiers went to this province we played in that province; we followed them around.'

The band played all manner of styles that were popular at the time, from the twist to the *romvong*, the traditional Khmer circle dance where men and women shuffle behind one another while gesticulating their hands gracefully. The eight-piece band included a couple of female singers, their sole purpose to keep spirits raised among the ranks and hammer Lon Nol's propaganda machine home. Soly continued to write songs during this time, but his lyrical focus had now turned to battle and to preserving the memory of fallen soldiers so that their widows, upon receiving the news, might find some comfort in their loss.

Soly was in Phnom Penh and out of uniform when the capital fell, which was fortunate, as anyone found wearing Lon Nol military garb was executed or sent for 're-education', as the Khmer Rouge put it.

'On 17 April 1975 I was with my general, Tep Mam, near Ponhea Hok School, which was close to the American Embassy at that time. I walked [and hid] from the general's house to my house, which was near the Olympic Stadium. I was evacuated to Takéo [province] where I stayed for two months before I was sent to Moung Russey District in Battambang. I stayed there until the end of the Khmer Rouge. When I was evacuated I didn't see any musicians, but when I worked in the rice fields I saw [singer and broadcaster] Huoy Meas. We couldn't speak to each other; we weren't allowed. During the Khmer Rouge we hid our identity.'

Soly went on to tell me of the tragic fate of singer and radio broadcaster Huoy Meas. She was a national treasure, Cambodia's very own Billie Holiday, known for her melancholic songs and wearing her heart on her sleeve. Prince Sihanouk was a fan and drew comparisons between her singing and that of Édith Piaf, whom his mother, Kossamak adored. Though reserved and unassuming in nature, the relatability and courageous honesty of her lyrics made Huoy Meas a feminine icon and a comfort to many other Cambodian women of the time. She started out training at UBA and went on to launch a successful singing career releasing hit songs like her haunting organ waltz 'Unique Child' and 'Samros Borey Tioulong', a romantic ode to a fashionable and modernist town built for public servants – and now abandoned – in the middle of Kirirom National Park. She was a firm favourite of composer Peou Sipho, and her style ranged from fronting his sentimental pop and slow swing arrangements – serenading supper clubs and ballrooms with a sound that harked back to the musicals of Hollywood's golden age – to belting out rhythm and blues hits like 'Leaving My Feelings With You' and a cover of the Vibrations hit 'My Girl [Hang On] Sloopy'. Alongside building a reputation as a prolific live performer, thanks to her dancefloor repetoire, Meas became one of the most popular voices of RNK radio, where she broadcast the hits of the 1960s and early 1970s. Her show was to Cambodian teenagers of the era what Radio Caroline was to England, and they tuned in religiously for a chance to hear the hottest new sounds and its host interviewing their idols between song plays. She was well liked within the music community and maintained strong links to her Battambang soul sisters, Ros Sereysothea and Pen Ran; the trio recording the popular go-go song 'We Three Virgins' in the late 1960s – a big hit for the song's writer, Voy Ho. Following the Khmer Rouge's evacuation of Phnom Penh in 1975, Huoy Meas was sent to her native Battambang to work the fields.

This was where Soly caught sight of her but, as he noted, they never dared speak. He heard from others in his collective that, after a time spent building a dam, she had fallen ill and had been sent to hospital. Sadly, by the time Soly arrived at the local hospital with some concealed palm sugar for Meas, he was told she had been sent away to be 're-educated'. Her second husband was a proud and jealous man called Kes Sarol, and many in their collective assumed it was his reckless and rebellious behaviour that revealed his wife's identity and got them both killed. Soly heard that Huoy Meas was raped by Khmer Rouge cadres before she was executed, making her monstrous end all the more tragic. The dam Meas worked on is still there but broken now. It lies near an airfield for T-28 aeroplanes that was the site of the last battle between the Khmer Rouge and Lon Nol soldiers in April 1975. Today, it's a quiet commune with a school.

Fortunately for Soly, his own fate took a turn for the better and music once again became his salvation. One day, he was handed a guitar by some cadres and asked if he could play. Soly knew that Western, modern influences were punishable by death so, unsure whether this was a test or not, he pretended to play the guitar like a traditional Cambodian string instrument called a *takhe* (a large, violin-shaped floor zither). The leader of his collective played the *tro* (the fiddle-like folk instrument) and took a liking to Soly: a fellow musician. When Soly wasn't busy with his job spreading fertilizer in the rice fields and farms, he was put to work recording Khmer Rouge propaganda songs in a vast oven – ordinarily used to create charcoal – due to the natural reverb the cavern created.

Soly managed to last it out until the Vietnamese invasion, and survived to play music more freely once more. Under the new Vietnamese state, the PRK (People's Republic of Kampuchea), Soly was given a job working in a laboratory, checking for viruses. At first he was focused on recovering from all he had endured, and the job helped him get back on his feet. In those early years of the PRK Soly received numerous invitations to play music, all of which he declined. He told me that the Khmer Rouge had left him depressed and traumatized and he had no desire to return to what once gave him joy.

However, when an invitation to join the Ministry of Industry band came from high up in government, he couldn't refuse, and Soly ended up playing in the ministry band from the early 1980s until the general election of 1993, when the band was retired. A few years later, he left Phnom Penh for a more peaceful life, turning his back on music and making Baribour his home. 'I came here to Baribour in 1996 or 1997. There were still Khmer Rouge around here then. Where the military camp is over there' – he pointed to a cement block a mere 300 yards away – 'they always passed through here.'

The Baribo River, which had snaked our journey north from Kampong Chhnang, had begun life in the Cardamom Mountains and flowed into not only the Tonlé Sap lake but also the small fishing communities that live along its tributaries. Apart from the neighbouring farm, the military camp was the only other building in sight. As I turned my head towards the camp – its appearance taking on an altogether more ominous guise – a flash of red caught my eye. Nestled against the nearby bamboo forest was an electric guitar modelled on a Fender Stratocaster, presumably left there from last night's exploits. Following my gaze, our host asked if we wanted to hear him play and we responded immediately with a collective and resounding, 'YES!'

After a quick tune up, Soly began strumming fast on the unplugged electric guitar – a two-minute, forty-second rendition of the Beatles' hit song, 'I Saw Her Standing There'. There was no flashy solo, no fancy frills – just the song played right and laid bare, with a strong unfaltering rhythm. After hearing all the rumours of Thach Soly's guitar prowess, I'd be lying if I didn't fess up to expecting to hear fast solos and flashy additions; the spirit of Jimmy Page to leap out from his nimble fingers to a backing section of trumpeting buffalo and a metronome of cicadas. But there was something so raw and honest about Soly's playing, and remnants of the young rock 'n' roller were still there in the vein bulging from his craned neck, the strain in his stance, and the passion in his voice.

Next, he took it down a notch, singing one of Kevin's childhood favourites, the Sinatra classic 'Three Coins in a Fountain'. He flicked at the strings as if he were playing a harp, his head dreamily bobbing from side to side. When the song had finished I felt like I'd just drifted out of a meditation, the background noises of shouting children, moaning buffalos and busy mothers having faded out during the performance, came to once more. Soly paused for a moment, looking down at his hands and the red

Stratocaster before smiling apologetically: 'I still love the guitar but I abandoned it for twenty years because my hands cannot play it any more and they hurt when I play. Music was my skill and my destiny. I wanted to play music for life, but I traitored music when I abandoned it at the end of my life. When I play music to young people they don't want me to play because they think I am conservative and old fashioned, but in my head and my heart, I am keeping the spirit of Cambodia alive. I don't begrudge the new generation – they can play anything they want to play – but I worry that we will lose this spirit.'

I'd been warned I'd find a recluse who'd turned his back on music and was just a simple farmer now, but I discovered that Soly's love of music hadn't diminished, even if his practice had. His kindness and humility had far exceeded any expectations I had of the character I would find at the end of that dirt track.

It's true, his hands had lost their flash, his voice was missing a few notes in range, and the glamorous times spent playing high society parties and floating supper clubs on the Mekong were a lifetime away from his current occupation as a farmer in deepest Baribour. But he was rich in all the things missing from his youth; he was now the patriarch of a large and loving family with a wealth of knowledge and life experience. He'd weathered the front line of the civil war, and used his spare time to give comfort to grieving widows by immortalizing their husbands in song. He'd battled the rigid caste and educational system of Cambodia to strike out alone, defy the rules, flout convention and succeed to become a legend. He'd survived the Khmer Rouge, when, all around, his peers had fallen.

Thach Soly hadn't allowed his impoverished Khmer Krom background to define and shackle him, instead he used it as fuel for the talent and courage that would shape his legacy and open up the possibilities that laid waste to such boundaries. And in the process, he'd helped jump start and shape the careers of many of the Cambodian guitarists of his time. Inspired by his courage, wishful working-class guitar players first touched a guitar in his classroom, struck by his playing, while 1970s guitarists like Touch Chhattha from the Drakkar band emanated his 1960s overdriven tone – not dissimilar to Jeff Beck's – on songs like Drakkar's 'Boer Bang Min Mayta?' ('Have You No Mercy?').

'Thank you, Dee,' Soly declared sincerely when it came time for me to leave. I was caught off guard and uncomfortable with the apparent role reversal, and found myself cutting him off before he could finish. I showered him with a lengthy, clumsy speech proclaiming why it should be me thanking *him*, and when my words finally dried up we looked each other deep in the eyes and I felt a weight lifted in Soly, a renewed sense of peace, as if he were somehow lighter than I'd found him the day before. I got the sense that his family knew little of his life before the war – that in divulging his lifestory to them at long last there was a release in that – as if he'd made peace with the man he was, the career he'd lost and, more importantly, with the man he'd become. His final words will remain with me always. We met each other's hands in a mirrored *sampeah*, and with a newfound resolute clarity, Soly confessed, 'I have hidden this inside for a long time.'

6

The Blind Master

Everything has evolution; everything evolves. If we don't have evolution we have dead art.

Panara Sirivudh, Apsara

Master Kong Nay.

One bright August day in 2014, my routine walk from our apartment in central Phnom Penh to the riverside was unexpectedly interrupted by the hum of spectators, musicians and their instruments emanating from the Royal University of Fine Arts (RUFA, what was once called UBA). As I walked past the low red stone wall I saw people of all ages, shapes and colours scurry through the zigzag walkways between RUFA's iconic imperial buildings, magnolia trees and manicured terraces. An eager young ticket vendor thrust a programme for the Amatak ('Eternal') Festival in my hands, and after a brief scan of the text I decided to suspend my errand and return her eager smile with a sale. I spent the day dipping in and out of small performances by old masters – seemingly brought back from obscurity from the farthest flung corners of Cambodia – fledgling school orchestras and traditional dance workshops where I voluntarily flailed my arms around and bumped into Oro and our mutual friend, Borey Pen. Borey was easily the most natural dancer in the city, and the most affable man in the country. So much so, that Kevin once told me in all earnestness that if he were to suddenly drop down dead, I should know I had his blessing to marry Borey.

The festival embodied the spirit of its producer, Cambodian Living Arts; easily the largest Khmer arts preservation society in the world. By encouraging the young student troupes to create their own original performances of traditional *mahori, pinpeat* and rare indigenous music alongside performances by Cambodia's master musicians, they were collectively carrying the torch for Cambodia's artistic heritage. As I traversed the signature red and white Khmer tiles that had once supported members from Cambodia's rock 'n' roll hall of fame, thoughts of the past hit me. I imagined the architect and ex-rector, Vann Molyvann, blueprints in hand, taking meetings at a heavy teak desk within the compound. In 1965 the buildings surrounding me changed from UBA's Faculty of Design, to its Faculty of Fine Arts, and, for a time, incorporated students from the Royal Palace too. I imagined ex-students of both departments tuning up together, filling the surrounding classrooms with wandering musical notes. Had Sisamouth played his mandolin in these halls, Svay Sor his piano, Chariya his clarinet, I wondered? Were the buildings painted the same red and orange hues then, as they are now?

Did the sparrows fly so brazenly in and out of the classroom air vents when the building was newer, the sparrow population presumably smaller then? Had the sounds of music – of wooden gongs and whistling flutes – changed much in sixty years?

I parted ways with Oro and Borey and made my way across the compound to catch the final performance. It was scheduled to take place on a temporary bandstand, erected outside the neighbouring National Museum. I hadn't arrived early enough to get a seat, so I joined the queue of latecomers outside. At that moment, a man was ushered past by who I assumed were the organizers; on his arm, perhaps, was his wife. The couple took their seats at the end of a row overlooking my queue; the man wearing black wraparound shades and leaning over the rails to chain-smoke, looking every inch the blues man. He had this star quality – captivated, I couldn't take my eyes off him.

On 23 September 1930 a baby was born in Albany, Georgia, USA. At the age of four he started to go blind, but he nonetheless went on to master his instrument, the piano, pioneering the crossover between white-dominated country music and black-dominated blues, rhythm & blues and jazz. His name was Ray Charles Robinson, and his formative years were shaped by his mother's pride and resilience. She was determined that her blind son would never beg or 'carry a cup', so she taught Ray how to scrub floors and chop wood. Her death in the spring of 1945 devastated her fourteen-year-old son. But that outpouring of grief also catalysed the career of one of the most important artists of the twenty-first century.

In the autumn of that same year, 1945, in the village of Duang, a small rural commune in southern Cambodia, another child was born. He also started going blind at the age of four, and had a resilient and tough-talking mother who taught him how to take care of himself. She, too, died when he was just fourteen years old, and, like with Ray, his mother's death inspired him to succeed. He was a skilled player of the *chapei dang veng* (a two-stringed Cambodian folk instrument, a cross between a lute and a sitar), and it was not only his skill people recognized but his pioneering efforts to bring about the *chapei*'s return to his countrymen, and its introduction to the world. For all of these reasons, and for bearing an uncanny resemblance to his American peer, he has been dubbed 'the Ray Charles of Cambodia'. But he is, in fact, Kong Nay, the bluesman I first saw in the bandstand at the Amatak Festival.

Not long after the festival, in the autumn of 2014, a Cambodian songwriter, Panara, he of Apsara and the oversized 1970s glasses, set my inquisitive cogs turning. He'd told me: 'We tried to make our music perfectly Cambodian, but we had so many influences from America, England and France at that time. Everything has evolution; everything evolves. If we don't have evolution we have dead art. We cannot stay where we are, we cannot copy, you have to improve, evolve . . . We picked some American and English – even some Italian – songs, and we would take the song and make it Cambodian.'

This relationship between the popular, often Western-influenced songs of the 1960s, and the traditional music of Cambodia had fascinated me from the beginning, and if anyone could be an interlocutor on this subject, I believed it would be Kong Nay. So, following our trip to Thach Soly's, Kevin, Sophorn and I journeyed south to the small town of Kampong Trach: the capital of the district where Kong Nay was born, and where he still lived.

Climbing out of our minivan, we found ourselves in a turbulent sea of frenzied hawkers, each one offering us a ride on the back of their motorbike. It took a while to retrieve our bags – Kevin had overpacked, and loading the great bulk of his bag onto his shoulders took some careful handling in order to avoid him scuttling around on his back like an upturned beetle. In all the chaos, Sophorn had discovered that Nay's place was much further than predicted and we'd have to hurry if we were going to make the visit *and* the last bus out of town. There was no time to lose. Wrestling with bags, we frantically clambered onto two motorbikes – Kevin on one, Sophorn and I on the other – and shot off in a cloud of red dust onto the tarmac highway that cut through the farmlands of Kampong Trach. I was sporting a double-turtle-shell look, with backpacks strapped to my chest and back – the placement of my front backpack meant that I teetered precariously on the back edge of the seat. The beauty of the landscape aside, the journey couldn't end quickly enough.

Finally, we peeled off the tarmac onto a potholed dirt road, luggage leaping and jolting us forward, upwards, backwards. I was almost ready to dismount and walk the rest of the way, but I'm glad I didn't. A moment later I looked down and spotted a cobra on the road. It was dead, its head flattened with a blunt instrument, the morning sun yet to suck the blood out of its fresh body.

As our wheels propelled us deeper into farmland, I thought about the man I was about to meet. A certifiable troubadour, I'd read that he'd busked his way around much of Cambodia and Vietnam and performed at some of the world's most renowned music festivals and prestigious universities. The *chapei dang veng* is the instrument of the quintessential bard, by Cambodian standards; the archetypal raconteur. Together, the roots of both instrument and player can be traced as far back as the walls of the Angkorian temples. As a poor boy, Nay found a calling. As a blind man, he'd survived the killing fields. His stories were legendary, and Kong Nay is considered a living treasure by Cambodians, young and old. When, at last, we turned into his driveway, I was overwrought from both the journey and the imminent prospect of finally meeting the man Cambodians call 'the master of *chapei*'.

We pulled up opposite one of two buildings on the property, a traditional stilted Khmer house where Nay's large family were gathered and lounging around their patriarch on an open-air platform beneath the main house. Our bike engines spluttered to a halt, calling an abrupt end to the siesta and, one by one, the family stirred and rose to their feet, Kong Nay's wife Tat Chen leading Nay by the arm and ushering us all into the second property. Inside the austere cement bungalow there were a few sleeping mats scattered on the floor, an electric floor fan, and Kong Nay's famous *chapei* resting against chipped blue window shutters. He positioned himself near it on a raised area, tucking his legs beneath him in the most anatomy-defying way. A contorted *baba* in lotus position, his posture was the result of all the hours, days, months and years of his life spent playing *chapei*.

Born into a rural farming family (the fifth of eleven children), Nay contracted smallpox at the age of four – his hidden, sunken eyes and pockmarked face bearing the scars of his affliction. The young boy was oblivious to his disability until he was around seven years old, when he asked his mother why his siblings always led him around. But his blindness heightened other senses, particularly auditory. And it was around this age that Kong Nay heard a *chapei* for the first time – an event that would alter the course of his life.

Nay's musical journey began as a young child in the rice fields, where he'd sing for small change from neighbouring farmers. Early on, Nay's mother instilled in her son a sense of independence and a need to one day support himself. While his music didn't require sight to play, with so many mouths to feed, his father was reluctant to part with the money for a *chapei*, though he eventually relented when his son turned thirteen and he could no longer stand Nay's pleading. Nay's uncle, Kong Tith, was a *chapei* player and became his teacher. Tith wasn't sure at first how he would teach a blind boy music, but Nay explained to me how he persuaded him: 'My uncle asked me how I would be able to study the *chapei* if I could not see the musical notes. I answered him, "Yes, it's true that I can't see the notes of the music, so you play and I'll listen." He played the first song for me, called *'Phat Cheay'* ['The Wind'].'

Nay told me in coarse Khmer that every *chapei* player had to master this song before moving on to anything else. Nay's uncle would play the melody, Nay would then hum it to commit it to memory, and then he would move his fingers around the *chapei* neck to feel for the pitch and find the right notes. Once he'd conquered 'The Wind' Nay's next challenge was to learn the art of rhyme. To do this, his uncle told him, 'If you want to find the rhyme, you have to study poems.' And so Nay turned once more to his father, pleading with him to buy him a book of Cambodian folktales. The teenager asked family members, friends, even local monks, to read him the stories, which included tales like, 'The Girl Who Flowed Like the Wind' and 'Sovannavong' (the name of a mythical Cambodian king).

Mastering the art of *chapei* rhyming is no mean feat. Not only do players need to be adept at playing the instrument itself – with steadfast rhythms and lightning-fast hands – it's also tradition to improvise, and they have only a matter of seconds during an extended intro in which to put together a story in their head. And not only that, but a story that rhymes. *Chapei* song lyrics are commonly considered the folk protest songs of Cambodian music: they have to be entertaining, in places comical, and often scathing. From satire to fantasy to folktales, I've heard lyrics ranging from a description of a nose being so large that if a tank fell into one of its nostrils it would take half a day to get across, to serious social commentary and educational themes. Ancient tales and Buddhist mythology have often been made all the more accessible by *chapei* songs. In the early days of the Covid-19 pandemic, Nay performed a song about

Covid-19 safety tips, extolling the virtues of washing the nooks and crannies of one's hands for twenty seconds and the merits of social distancing. To see this display of quick-witted talent in the flesh is quite something – a true art form. Nay's wry sense of humour, coupled with his storytelling skills and confidence, leant him an air of whimsy, and an almost supernatural quality. Spellbound, I hung onto his every word, mannerism and joke in our short time together.

On her deathbed, Nay's mother had warned her son that if his father were to take another wife, Nay should leave and seek refuge in the temple; for she was convinced that another woman would not tolerate a dead woman's son, much less a disabled and dependent one. However, Nay's father never did remarry, and Kong Nay was cradled by his father and uncle throughout this painful period, devoting all his time to refining his art in the hope of one day honouring what his mother had taught him. And he did. While still a teenager, Nay entered into the most independent of professions: the life of a troubadour, travelling with his *chapei* around Takéo and Kampot provinces in southern Cambodia, and even as far as Kampuchea Krom in Vietnam.

It was around the age of eighteen, on a visit back home, that a girl from Nay's home town stole his heart. He can still recall the exact date it happened: 'On the eighth day of the waxing moon in the third month of the lunar calendar, 1963,' he told me without missing a beat, as if its memory were as fresh as yesterday. Her name was Tat Chen and she instantly took an interest in the young Nay, often stopping to talk to him on her way to visit her sister's house. She'd first laid eyes on him when they were much younger, long before 1963, when he was just a little boy holding onto his mother's skirt. 'He was hopping up and down like a frog,' she called to me across the room, cackling. Years later Chen fell in love with Nay, watching him play his *chapei* and sharing laughter in handfuls of precious, stolen conversations. And even though

Nay couldn't see Chen with his eyes, he could feel her beauty – it was in the kind questions she asked him, her sweet voice and gentle, caring nature.

Thirteen days after that fateful first encounter, Kong Nay summoned the courage to confess his love to Tat Chen, and she reciprocated immediately. But the path of true love never did run smooth. Chen fell out of favour with her parents, who were concerned for the tough life they believed she might live married to a blind man. Love prevailed in the end, and her parents eventually agreed to Nay's proposal. Shortly after they were wed, the money Nay earned from performing paid for a small piece of land to farm, a tile-roof house and, in time, a family.

While Chen tended their farm and raised the children, Nay made whatever money he could playing *chapei*. And though his performances were traditional, Nay wasn't a purest. He took inspiration from music all around him. From the *mahori* orchestras at weddings to Ros Sereysothea, Sinn Sisamouth and the pop music he heard on the radio, which never failed to lift his spirits. 'The foreign countries have their own culture and Cambodia has its own culture,' Nay explained, 'so when some of the singers merged the music it was a cultural exchange, they influenced each other. I went to New York recently and I played *chapei* with a jazz player from New York. I played my *chapei* Khmer-style and he played music from his culture, and when it merged I felt happy hearing the music we were making. We were trading off each other, me with my voice and *chapei*, and he with his voice and his trumpet.'

Cambodian pop stars blending influences from all over the world with their own roots music to produce that special sound has a long, deep history: from Sisamouth and Cuba to the *yé-yé* bands and the British invasion. I would have expected this attitude and pastiche to sweep across other more classical forms of Cambodian music, and yet, classical music has always struck me as too rigid and untouchable a format to allow such adaptation. It's the ceremony and tradition of it all. But hearing Nay speak of jazz and *chapei* it made perfect sense: there is something incredibly bluesy about the *chapei* sound and jazz and blues come from the same place after all. Nay has the imagination and the feel to blend musical forms – be it the lyrical themes of songs by Sinn Sisamouth, or the string equivalent of a jazz trumpet's buzz – and yet, still retain the integrity of the instrument.

During the Lon Nol era Nay was further refining his craft and raising children, all the time moving on to avoid a civil war tearing apart southern Cambodia. Kampong Trach, where the Kong family lived, had seen a lull in fighting between the colonialists and their rebel enemies, the anti-colonialist Khmer Issarak movement. This lull took place between the mid-1950s and late 1960s but, by 1968, the surrounding area fell again into rebel hands. The Khmer Issarak were gone by then; replaced by the Khmer Rouge, who renamed the territory 'the Southwestern Zone'. The zone was run by the infamous Khmer Rouge commander Ta Mok, known later as 'Brother Number Four' to his friends in the Khmer Rouge, or 'the Butcher' to his foes. A veteran fighter of the Khmer Issarak movement, Mok was renowned for his guerrilla roots and ruthless cruelty.

Apart from occasional ceasefires, Kampot province suffered much fighting between Lon Nol's Khmer Republic army, the Forces Armées Nationales Khmères (FANK), the Khmer Rouge and South Vietnam's Army of the Republic of Vietnam (ARVN). The fighting started in the early 1970s, right up to April 1975, when, following a two-month-long battle that saw both FANK and the Khmer Rouge suffer heavy casualties, the province's prized capital, Kampot city and its port, was won by the communists. Throughout the years of fighting, those loyal to the exiled Prince Norodom Sihanouk, those fleeing the US Airforce's MK-82 bombs, those who had lost their livelihoods and their loved ones, were either captured by the Khmer Rouge along with their land, or enticed to join the guerrillas in the forest – often under false pretences. Some were drawn to the cause by the promise of cheaper taxes and more rice. Many more obediently heeded Sihanouk's call to join the cause in a radio broadcast he made in exile in 1970. They believed that supporting the Khmer Rouge would put an end to the war and bring Sihanouk back to power – not quite, of course, what the Khmer Rouge had in mind. The Paris Set – high-ranking Khmer Rouge including Pol Pot, Khieu Samphan and Ieng Sary – were anti-monarchy and despised Sihanouk. They used him like a puppet, a propaganda tool to sway Cambodian peasants to their side. Pol Pot, who the *New Yorker* journalist Philip Gourevitch argued 'was Sihanouk's way back to power after being ousted by Lon Nol', found himself in a marriage of convenience with the former head of state. He saw Sihanouk as his 'perfect cover story', and Sihanouk's name provided the regime with its most effective recruitment tool for the Cambodian peasants-turned cadres adored their king. Caught up in the fighting, Nay moved his family first to nearby Prek Samnang village, before they were captured by the new regime and moved to a village called Damnak Kantuot. Here, he was ordered to play *chapei* for Angkar. 'They did not allow me to sing traditional folk stories,' he told me, batting away a fly. 'They asked me to sing only about their politics. First, the Khmer Rouge would tell me a story, and then they would ask me to play the *chapei* to explain the story to the people. Songs like "The Bourgeoisie Taking Advantage of the Poor".'

Under the regime, musicians were summoned to 'entertain' the workers while they took a rare break. It was another opportunity for the Khmer Rouge to brainwash their slaves with extreme communist ideology; the singers singing prescribed lyrics extolling 'glorious Angkar' through loud speakers set on tall poles around the camps. I was relieved but not surprised that the resourceful Nay had found a way to work and survive in what was such a perilous and unforgiving situation for a blind man. But, sadly, it was not to last. In 1977, they moved him on to another detail. He was to make bamboo baskets for collecting soil. Nay pleaded with the collective leader that without his eyes he couldn't make the baskets, so his collective leader proposed he produce string cow reins instead, but, again, Nay protested. 'Well, if you can't make baskets or string,' the collective leader concluded, 'then you can strip palm leaves for making brooms.' Nay's quota was to strip forty fronds a day, but the food he received in exchange was a sick person's ration: just one large spoon of rice a day. Starving and frail, Nay's determination prevailed and he managed to survive on these meagre rations for well over a year. Although the Khmer Rouge did not persecute the disabled in an organized fashion (like they did the Vietnamese, the Chams and other minorities), they neglected or killed anyone who was not 'useful' in their new agrarian society. As a result, many disabled, elderly and infirm died of starvation.

By the mid-1970s it was no secret that the Khmer Rouge had designs on Kampuchea Krom – the southern part of Vietnam that was once part of the Angkorian empire – and Phú Quốc island, known to the Khmers, who had until 1939 laid claim to the island, by its Khmer name Koh Tral. The Khmer Rouge led sorties and raids into Vietnam from the mid-1970s, some successful, some utter failures. In 1975 they exercised their claim to Phú Quốc, capturing Thổ Chu island, 120 kilometres to the south. They took around 500 inhabitants back to Cambodia and killed them all. On 20 April 1978, cadres from the Southwestern Zone crossed the border into Vietnam's An Giang province and butchered more than 3,000 Vietnamese civilians during twelve days of bloodshed. For the Vietnamese government this event marked an end to their agreed ceasefire with the Khmer Rouge, and they began to mobilize their military to quash Pol Pot once and for all. With the backing of Soviet aid, on Christmas Day 1978 Vietnam invaded Cambodia. Kampot was attacked, first by airstrikes, scattering the Southwestern Zone's leadership and driving the Khmer Rouge army deeper west. Following a successful naval landing, further Vietnamese troops advanced into Kampot province, liberating villages as they went. For Nay that fateful day came on 7 January 1979, and, by all accounts, not a moment too soon. He told me, 'The leader of the collective asked me to change my location. He told me to move to "phoumi thmei" ("new village") [which was code for "death"].'

There was no love lost between the Khmer Rouge and anyone unable to fulfil their work quota. As early as 1976 the astute Nay was aware of the phrase 'phoumi thmei' when a friend tipped him off to the truth behind the Khmer Rouge's promises of limitless food and freedom to 'grow your own' in the 'new village'. This cruel deception became apparent when Tat Chen and subsequently, Nay, discovered the clothes of the families taken to the new village were later returned and redistributed among the remaining villagers. So when they heard the words 'phoumi thmei' slip from the collective leader's lips, Nay and Chen knew what was coming. Nay, his family and all other villagers deemed unfit to work (the disabled, women who had just delivered babies, and the elderly) were to be evacuated and executed. On 7 January 1979, just as they were being herded towards an ox cart bound for 'phoumi thmei', gunshots could be heard in the distance. Within moments, chaos ensued.

Remarkably, with possibly moments to spare, the KUFNS (the Kampuchean United Front for National Salvation) – an army made up of Eastern Cambodian troops, revolutionaries and defectors from the Khmer Rouge's purges – attacked, and the Khmer Rouge collective leader and his troops fell back, never to be seen again. At the eleventh hour, Nay and his family were saved.

In the years to follow, Kong Nay reclaimed his life as a troubadour, playing for handfuls of rice and small change, travelling as far as Kampuchea Krom in Vietnam in order to feed his family. But the mid-1980s brought about a shift in Nay's fortunes. Word of his talents spread into the upper echelons of war-torn Cambodia's newly reorganized society, with ministers inviting him to play at their ceremonial events. His fame spread internationally and in 1997 he received his first invitation to play in Paris. Since then Nay has performed in thirteen countries across the globe, including festivals like WOMAD in the UK and a number of prestigious conservatoires and universities.

When Nay spoke of the merging of cultures and musical styles – of a trumpet and a *chapei* – it was a natural celebration, not an anomaly. And, after all, where would music be without collaboration, without exploration? There would surely be no emergence of musical genres, no blues, no rock 'n' roll, no jazz, no music of any complexity whatsoever, beyond perhaps a tribal drum circle.

Kong Nay impressed on me that while it is important to explore and learn from other cultures, it is equally important not to lose sight of your own. These words hold a particular and pressing relevance for Cambodia, where dance and music were only taught orally until the twentieth century, and some of the rarer ancient art forms were lost when the musicians that held that knowledge died in the Khmer Rouge genocide, leaving no written or recorded trace behind. As a survivor himself, Nay knows first hand the role that the masters have played in preserving centuries of tradition. He knows the years of dedication and practice it takes to achieve this title. He spends much of his time these days teaching students who come from far and wide, and is proud to be part of the Ministry of Culture Fine Arts programme 'Heritage of Survivors'. He has never forgotten his own struggle, and despite living a modest life, still devotes much of his time to worthy arts and disability causes.

The genocide claimed the lives of many of Cambodia's traditional folk musicians, the great *chapei* players included. Only a small handful survived and the preservation of *chapei* music weighed heavily on just a couple of masters: Kong Nay and Prach Chhoun, who, like Nay, was also blind and learned his craft from a monk while living in a pagoda as a boy. Had it not been for them, this art form may have been lost, silenced forever. Nay feels the great weight of this responsibility to share his knowledge and pass it on, to keep the instrument alive. UNESCO recently honoured the *chapei dang veng* with a place on their World Heritage safe-guarding list. Nay himself is considered a national treasure. I looked at him, then I looked at his *chapei* behind him, its smooth, white bone frets and tuning pegs, and its dark, heavily varnished body shining in the light. That's when the collective magnitude hit me: what if Nay hadn't made it? It was as if he could read my mind, because the next thing I knew, Nay asked if he could play a song for us.

His grandson placed the *chapei* into his grandfather's arms like a court servant presenting an offering at the feet of a king. I watched as Nay adjusted himself and took a moment to focus before he began playing. The air was charged with anticipation, all eyes eagerly awaiting his first note. Suddenly, his *chapei* rung out a brutal start-stop rhythm with punctuated stabs, alternating fast strums and pauses, lasting long enough for Nay to work up some lyrics. His gravelly, guttural blues voice rose and bent up to a note that came from somewhere deep inside – and even in the 40 degree heat, I felt a shiver ripple down my spine. As Nay spat out his words, I experienced his mastery in all its glory. Not only the exquisite playing of the instrument, but the talent of his ad-libbing and wordsmith-wizardry.

As he came to the end of the first verse, Nay called out our names. I was taken by surprise but immediately understood why he had spent so much time clarifying the pronunciation of our names when we first arrived. All this time he had been preparing this gift. He sang of the journey of Sophorn, Kevin and Dee, and the two motorbike drivers who, cross-legged behind us, let out hoots of excitement when they heard the word '*moto-dup*'. When Nay was finished and the applause died down, he handed his *chapei* to one of his grandsons. The small child was swamped by the huge instrument, but when he unassumingly took the strings in his tiny hands and played his grandfather's songs with such finesse, I was again rendered speechless. I was watching a master in the making.

Kong Nay.

Around us the generations of his family chattered – Tat Chen and her friend horizontally batting flies and passing around a Khmer delicacy of bamboo leaves and sticky rice called *krolan* for us all to share. Nay sat stoically to attention, sipping a well-earned beer and listening to every note his grandson played above the chatter. Before we knew it, our precious time had gone in a flash. With the last bus to Kampot scheduled within the hour we thanked Kong Nay and his family for the time we had been so fortunate to spend with them, boarded our motorbikes and headed back to the bus stop in town.

Public minivans in Cambodia are an experience not for the faint of heart. They are often driven at breakneck speed, which on unsurfaced roads is like riding a bucking bronco. Scoring a driver who isn't a lunatic hellbent on squeezing in an extra fare from the day is luck of the draw. A knowing, amused smile would spread across my face whenever I saw unfortunate passengers emerge at rest stops rubbing their battered heads or twisting from side to side to loosen neck injuries and stretch out cramps. By then, I knew those aches and injuries all too well. Depending on the price of the ticket, public minivans can range from business class (air conditioning and one person per seat), to economy (bursting with people – sometimes with passengers on the roof, or perched precariously on luggage in the boot with the back door open). Our situation leaving Kampong Trach was entry level economy. That said, the back door shut and there was no one on the roof – and, mercifully on this occasion, our driver was not a lunatic and the journey was only an hour. But as more and more passengers piled on at road stops – including the Cambodian Von Trapp family with a seemingly endless line of children filing in at one point – space was tight to say the least. Eventually, with twenty-six people and their luggage squeezed into an eleven-seater minivan, we reached our personal record for the highest number of passengers. I had to trade my seat to perch on a sack of cockles, but, the smiles, the babes in arms, the food and chatter all made the adventure. Reaching our destination, Kevin, Sophorn and I tumbled out of the van, stretched out our cramps, and walked into the town centre to hire a bike and unwind for a few days beside the still waters of the lazy Kampot River, the smiling faces walking along its banks, seemingly a lifetime away from the not so distant past Nay had talked of.

7

Old Pot Still Cooks Good Rice

*Sereysothea's voice is a gift from God. When she sings,
I fall in love.*

Lay Mealea, singer

Ros Sereysothea.

The north-western city of Battambang is famous for its surrounding rice bowl agriculture, decaying colonial buildings, and for playing home to Cambodia's friendliest people as well as a wealth of famous artists. It remains home to a gumptious tuk tuk driver called Scorpio. Popular on tourist site forums and reputable among the locals, I found him to be resourceful, confident and jocose on all matters but religion, which he took very seriously. Whenever the matter arose, his plump lips would turn down, his round, dancing eyes freeze into a hard stare, and he'd lower his voice to a whisper as if he were unveiling the location of the holy grail. Less driver, and more of an unofficial and underappreciated tour guide in a tuk tuk, he wasted no time strong-arming Kevin and me into committing to his services for the duration of our three-day city break. Scorpio struck me as a big fish in a small pond and, within moments of meeting him, my imagination sparked: I pictured him, holster slung, striding forth with great big spurred steps into the local saloons and homesteads of his town. But in spite of his often roguish nature, his motives for the most part were sincere, and if it weren't for him, we would not have got beyond the temple gates.

Wat Damrey Sor (The Temple of the White Elephant) can be found on the outskirts of Battambang city in north-west Cambodia. Organized into a series of colourful platforms, the large complex of dilapidated outbuildings is interlinked by dirt paths surrounding a central edifice, the paint of its ornate frescoes, peeling. Hues of faded teal, red, orange and yellow paint cover large exterior walls and intricately portray ancient Buddhist stories within the various temple structures. Chirruping sparrows – peacebreakers – dart between flowering tamarind trees scattered throughout the compound, shading monks and temple workers as they sew and wash robes away from the merciless midday sun.

It was shortly after we'd arrived in Cambodia for the second time and Kevin was yet to start his teaching job at the School of English under the iron rod of headteacher, Wendy, who didn't suffer fools. Kevin had a knack for charming formidable older women, mainly because he was honest and came across as self assured but respectful, never seeming to care a toss about their concerns and power plays. He batted these displays away with charm and humour and could crack a smile from the hardest set frown. He was also a wonderful travel partner and, given that he had the time, joined me in venturing north for a few days. It was April, the hottest month of the year, when temperatures reach a feel factor of 45 degrees Celsius and the breeze is absent. Kevin was sweating buckets from the undersized white shirt we'd stopped off to buy en route to the funeral we were to attend, his 6 foot, 160 lb American frame squeezed into a shirt made for a 5 foot 5 inch, 100 lb Cambodian. It was paired with some ivory harem pants he'd bought for a Muslim wedding the previous year, and lined up next to Scorpio's pristine white shirt and my rumpled, cobbled-together outfit, we formed a somewhat wayward trinity before the chief monk.

Earlier, Scorpio had helped me inscribe a piece of paper with the Khmer characters of the departed's name, and handed it to the monk who chanted as we bowed, hands clasped and raised between closed eyes, before eventually lighting the paper on fire to set her spirit free with our blessings. We watched as tiny pieces of burned paper broke off and fluttered into the air like butterflies. Offerings of sugar, fruit, rice and tea were handed to the venerable father, and Scorpio later informed me that the monks would consume the offerings, and, in doing so, pass these on to the dead, feeding the departed spirit as they journeyed into the afterlife.

By this stage I had spent two years reading, listening and watching anything I could find on the most famous female singer of Cambodia's modern golden age, Ros Sereysothea. Her siblings,

Ros Saboeuth and Ros Saboeun, had kept their sister's legacy alive all these years and both had remained active in reconnecting the surviving musical society of Sereysothea's world following the ravages of the genocide. I'd made travel plans to speak to Saboeuth, but in early March 2014, just one month before my departure, she'd suffered complications after a fall and tragically died, aged seventy-two.

In some strange way, I felt like I'd got to know her somewhat in the previous two years; trawling through footage of interviews of Saboeuth talking about her sister. I felt warmed by her coy giggle and rough provincial accent – there was an absolute honesty that endeared me to her on screen. She'd devoted her life to preserving her sister's legacy, and despite having never met, I felt it only appropriate to travel the ten-hour bus ride to Battambang to honour her spirit as soon as I arrived in Cambodia for the second time. In a way, her death marked the birth of my book.

Buddhist funerals in Cambodia are a process that can last up to a hundred days; a year if you are king. At first the body is cremated and a service is held. This is attended by everyone who knew the individual then is followed by a dinner in a street-side yellow marquee after the ceremony, with traditional *mahori* and *smot* music blasted at ear-shattering volume for days. Anyone can hold their own ceremony for the dead at the temple during the mourning period by offering food, money and well wishes for the afterlife (as we did). A campaign by the Cambodian Vintage Music Archive helped raise money for Saboeuth's struggling family and was backed by many industry figures, from record labels to documentarians. In the end $1,500 was raised to help the family pay for the funeral expenses.

Over the years, my translator and friend Oro had built up a friendship with Ros Sereysothea's remaining sister, Saboeun – along with other members from the Sinn and Ros families – in an effort to enable them to access the rights to their loved ones' music. When Oro told me, a month after Saboeuth's Battambang funeral, that Saboeun was visiting her niece in Phnom Penh, I jumped at the opportunity to interview her. It was to mark the start of an instant and long-lasting friendship between Ros Saboeun and me.

When Oro and I arrived at the house, an elderly, petite lady with jet-black hair emerged from behind the gate. Wearing a long black skirt, a uniform-blue button-down shirt and wedges, she teetered down the bumpy dirt track to our tuk tuk and squealed with delight, embracing Oro and taking me into her warm arms for the first time. I was mesmerized. She had this ebullient sparkle and a maternal manner; gathering us up, holding us back from passing cars. Had her energy been immortalized in a soundtrack it would be French bubble pop or Gilberto Gil; Saboeun flouncing freely down a promenade with grace and style. It was in the way she carried herself – her walk, her freewheeling attitude to life, the bounce in her step; an energy which kept her eternally youthful. It cast her into a stratosphere of her own and I knew instantly that she was special.

As we journeyed to the restaurant in our tuk tuk, Saboeun lifted a brown envelope out of her bag and began to pass around the contents. First was a print of Ros Sereysothea wearing a cosmic-patterned A-line dress and a bouffant bob. Saboeun duly gifted the photo to me, and it still hangs proud above my dresser to this day. We passed around photographs of Saboeun taken in Vietnam in the early 1980s, channelling Bianca Jagger in a white trouser suit and fedora, and a stunning headshot of her aged twenty, to which she remarked wistfully: 'I used to be a beauty queen but I am not beautiful any more.' Indeed, she was by then seventy years old and was missing a few teeth, but the years hadn't taken away Saboeun's elfin charm. Where her skin had loosened, her cheekbones were accentuated; her eyes were larger and deeper, fuller with life, its joys and its sorrows.

It was noon, and when we pulled up to Doors nightclub the bar was stirring, the DJ for the evening was testing his gear and playing 1970s Khmer rock. It felt wild and strange to be talking with Saboeun about Sereysothea to her sister's backing track, Ros Sereysothea's hit song 'Chnam Oun Dop-Pram Muy' ('I'm Sixteen'). The title track of a feature film released in 1971, 'I'm Sixteen' is a storming psychedelic garage rocker expressing the quixotic buoyancy of youth. I was a convert from the first time I heard the first dirty guitar note on a friend's rooftop balcony in Phnom Penh in 2012, and when Sereysothea's clear and perfect soprano launched in, I was floored. By the time she sang her last note I wanted to know all there was to know about the mystery singer. She transported me, pitch perfect, with a vibrato that seemed to radiate every cell in my body. I'd never heard a voice quite like hers before, and doubt I will again. The British rock journalist Nik Cohn wrote in the *Guardian*, 'Her voice was the perfect teen-dream confection, equal parts heartbreak, flirtation, and true romance. Even though I couldn't understand a word, she affected me more strongly than any female pop singer since Ronnie Spector of the Ronettes.'

She is to this day undoubtedly the most famous female singer in Cambodian popular culture, her fame only surpassed by Sinn Sisamouth, her close friend and duet partner. Beyond her remarkable and unrivalled vocal chords is a diverse and gargantuan back catalogue containing hundreds of songs that are equally extraordinary. From recording 'Bompae', a classic Cambodian lullaby her mother taught her, to popular heartache ballads like 'Roses You Draw', downtrodden rock dirges 'Wicked Husband' and 'Broken-hearted Woman' and psychedelic satire like 'Old Pot Still Cooks Good Rice', her songs reflect every aspect of 1960s and 1970s Cambodian life, as refracted through the lens of a woman like Sothea. Her lyrics traversed all the Greek loves, from the strength of familial ties to the mania of obsessive love, and there remains a timeless quality to her music sixty years on.

As the DJ played on we tucked into some burgers, and began talking about what it was like growing up in the Ros family, specifically, what growing up with Sereysothea was like. Saboeun began naturally at the beginning, listing the names, ages, offspring and professions of her parents and siblings between burger bites as I furiously scribed their details one by one. The first in line was Saboeun, born in 1942. She had four children, who all tragically passed away. Next came her sister, Ros Saboeuth in 1944. She played the *roneat*, a traditional wooden xylophone, and is survived by one daughter, who lives in Phnom Penh at the house where we collected Saboeun earlier that morning. The only brother, Sokunthea, was born in 1946, and was a paratrooper for the Lon Nol regime. He died in 1978, during the genocide. Fourth in line was Ros Sereysothea, born in 1948. Saboeun believes she passed away the same year as her brother. Sereysothea gave birth to four children but none of them survived the genocide either. The next two girls died young of illness: Ros Sareth, born in 1952, died aged three years old, and Ros Saroeun, born in 1954, also died the following year, 1955. The final Ros girl was Sophean, born in 1958. She died when she was twenty years old, and, like her brother, Sokunthea, she too was a paratrooper for the Lon Nol regime.

'My father was a military man in the colonial time,' Saboeun continued. 'When Cambodia was liberated from the French colony, he was appointed to a position in the Ministry of Defence called the "black troop" [perhaps named after the black socks they wore]. After that he got a job painting on walls – like Buddha stories – and also worked as a traditional healer.'

There are widespread rumours and stories, originating from a Cambodian author called Seng Dara, of Sereysothea's humble beginnings – a clichéd rags-to-riches tale. Saboeun was keen to set the record straight: 'My mother had a rice field and she also ran a small business from the house, selling things. We [children] worked on the rice, and we all went to school until we received our high school diplomas. I made it to year ten and Sereysothea – or "Sothea" as we called her in our family – made it to year eight. There was enough money to support the children to do this. My father never let us succumb to selling snails for money, or anything like that.'

A natural sponge for music, Sothea soaked up anything she listened to. Saboeun remembered her sister – as far back as a three-year-old – imitating the songs she'd heard at weddings, from the radio blasting from lamp post speakers in town, and the Lakhon Bassac (Khmer opera) songs their mother sang to lull her children to sleep. Many years later, Sothea would record one of her mother's lullabies with the renowned producer Voy Ho called 'Bom Pae', which simply means 'Lullaby' in Khmer.

Sothea joined a singing club in 1960 when she was twelve years old and spent the next few years honing her vocal skills both at school and at home, as well as playing an active role in the school's running club. Quiet and distant, she wasn't one for words; her natural personality was at odds with the confident stage performer she would grow up to be. These inner tensions extended to other areas of her nature: Saboeun talked of a picky and sometimes mean sister, but, in equal measures, a gentle and kind child.

For the Ros siblings it was a relatively peaceful time to grow up in Battambang city. By 1953 it belonged to Cambodia once more, following a long period of occupation by, first, the Thais, then the French, followed by the Japanese during the Second World War. The former trading post and second most populous Cambodian city received a good deal of infrastructure and support from the government, with Sihanouk ploughing money into education, sport and industry across Cambodia, and championing the arts, both ancient and modern. In the late 1950s, when they were all teens and pre-teens, the Ros children created a four-piece folk band. Like the jug bands of early twentieth century America and the skiffle bands of 1950s Britain, Saboeun fashioned instruments from household items. She constructed her own washboard bass out of a washing line, some wood and corrugated iron to resonate the Ros family's gutbucket folk sound. They merged modern instruments such as Saboeun's handmade guitar with traditional Cambodian instruments like Saboeuth's *roneat thung*, a low-pitched wooden xylophone. Sothea sang, and even at a young age and with no formal training, her natural talent entranced her audience, earning her the moniker 'Mey Rey' (Khmer for 'Cicada') from the village elders. While the Quarrymen were plucking their tea-chest bass thousands of miles to the west, Ros Sokunthea kept time on his makeshift bass for the Ros family jug band. The highlight of the Ros band's short career was seemingly a gig at a Battambang county clerk's housewarming party. Saboeun smiled with great pride recounting this brief but happy time, before finalizing this chapter of her life with a sigh: 'I liked artistic work and I liked being artistic, but I didn't turn out to be an artist.'

When she was twelve years old, Saboeun's father, Ros Sabun, divorced her mother, Nath Samean, and, shortly after, remarried. It was a traumatic turn of events for the entire Ros family, Sabun included. Saboeun kept the diaries of her mother and the whole tragic story filled its pages – who the other woman was, what she did for a living, the surreal drama of how she came to seduce Saboeun's father: 'She pretended that she was sick in her stomach and she called my father to look after her. She said to *her* father that if my father didn't marry her, she would die. When he heard this, her father was so scared that he begged my father to marry his daughter – just to promise her he would until she recovered, and after that he said my father could break his promise – but they married and, after that, my father discovered that her illness wasn't real, she'd faked it. She was just using him, but by then it was too late.'

Despite the heartache, the family did what Cambodians often do so well – they picked up the broken pieces and carried on as best they could. Samean eventually remarried and went on to have another child, her last, four years later.

While Sabun didn't let his children go hungry, money for child support was tight. In 1966, in an effort to support her family, Sereysothea, then eighteen years old, entered a singing contest in Battambang and pipped fifty other contestants to first prize. She caught the eye of army commander, Colonel Chay Lay, who was in charge of a musical troupe called Lomhea Yothea. Sothea was recruited into the band and was soon leaving her classroom studies and beloved running club behind in favour of nights performing at the popular Battambang restaurant Stung Khieu. Here she sang the sentimental string-laden swing songs by writers like Peou Sipho, and elsewhere she picked up wedding-singer gigs, singing *mahori* wedding songs backed by traditional gong chimes and wooden xylophones. Session musicians – like the future Drakkar band drummer Ouk Sam Ath – and troubadours came through town on the club circuits, and stories of her talent reached as far as Phnom Penh. It wasn't long before she caught the eyes of some very big cats indeed.

Numerous reports exist of Sinn Sisamouth and another famous singer, a crooner called Im Song Seum, keeping tabs on the blossoming singer and biding their time to bring her to Phnom Penh. By then, it had been a year since she'd joined Lomhea Yothea and, all around her, Sothea was being encouraged to go to the capital to seek her fame and fortune – not only by her own more seasoned band members but also other Phnom Penh-based industry figures passing through Stung Khieu. Empowered by the growing support from family, peers and friends, when the stars did finally align it was 1967; the year that Sereysothea relocated to the capital, and where, shortly after, she burst onto the music scene with her first hit song, 'Stung Khieu' ('Blue River').

Upon arriving in Phnom Penh, her cousin and fellow Battambang native, Im Song Seum, took Sothea to a place called Sala
Pov Om, a private school-cum-boarding house with cheap rented
rooms for artists. A pit stop on her rise to fame, she lived there
with her mother, another up and coming singer from Battambang,
the aforementioned singer and radio presenter Huoy Meas, and
Meas's drummer husband, Yel Om Sophanarak. Huoy Meas,
go-go singer Pen Ran and Sothea had all attended the singing
club of Battambang's Wat Kam Pheng primary school during their
childhood and, reunited in Phnom Penh, the friendships within
this alumnus grew stronger. Pretty soon, Sothea started recording
duets with Im Song Seum and was invited to sing alongside Pen
Ran in Chariya's distillery band, SKD. At Sihanouk's biannual
state congress celebration, Sothea was discovered by thousands
of Cambodians – it marked a turning point on her road to fame.

Later that year Sothea released her first soundtrack, for the
movie *Preah Leak Sinavong Neang Pream Kesor* – a love story
about a prince called Leak Sinavong and a woman called Pream
Kesor. Following a six-month stint in SKD, Sothea adopted the
punishing schedule of a 1960s performer, her manager, known
only as 'Mr Sok', often cramming her schedule with at least two
gigs a night. Sothea was a regular on the bill at the Lotus D'Or, the
floating supper club boat on the Mekong, as well as the Magetat
nightclub, and another nearby restaurant Saboeun called 'Baler'.
As for her days, she filled them recording starry-eyed duets with
Sisamouth and starring in the RNK radio band, performing live
on air to a vast audience. And it was at RNK radio that Sothea
met her future husband, the classical singer and palace favourite,
Sos Mat.

They married in 1968 for six short months, before divorcing.
Numerous reports highlighted their connection as a passionate
and tempestuous one. However, Saboeun was afraid to talk to me
about the reported affairs and domestic abuse Sothea allegedly

suffered at the hands of her husband, for fear of reprisal from Sos Mat's son and family. But speak to anyone and they will all say the same thing of Sothea: her love life was, for the most part, full of heartache and violence. 'I feel bad for my sister, who encountered so much bad love and all this mess,' Saboeun told me, lowering her gaze. 'Sothea had money but she had bad love and bad husbands.'

The dark-skinned beauty was never short of admirers; from producers to nightclub owners, to singing partners and military men. Her numerous relationships were riddled with drama, thwarted by disagreements, jealousy and rage. Following a public altercation with Sos Mat in a Phnom Penh nightclub, and their subsequent separation, Sereysothea reportedly returned to Battambang, turning her back on music. A couple of months passed before her friend, champion and duet partner, Sisamouth, was said to have wooed her back to the city with a promise of protection against her ex-husband, his friend, Sos Mat. When Sereysothea returned to the capital, Sisamouth kept his promise, and she came back to a rising career and a new relationship. He was Huoy Siphan, son of the successful film and music producer Van Chann, who mysteriously disappeared in 1969, though his businesses continued to be run prosperously by his wife until 1975. Sereysothea and Siphan married and within a short time she became pregnant with her first child, a boy they named Sopanara. Her relationship with Siphan wasn't perfect but it was relatively peaceful in comparison to some of the other unions she made in her short life.

The longest-standing relationship Sereysothea seemed to have with a man was the working relationship she had with the singer Sinn Sisamouth. Their romantic duets – spanning every genre from sentimental *romvong* to sassy garage rock – garnered widespread speculation that their relationship was more than platonic. But this was never the case: the relationship was based on an ethos of hard work, discipline, respect and friendship, and it spanned almost the entirety of Sereysothea's career as well as a large portion of Sisamouth's. Sereysothea was Sisamouth's queen, he her king. He affectionately called her his '*ah tea*' ('little sister') and she called him '*bong*' ('friend'). Together, they were the nation's sweethearts. In their duet, 'We Sing Together' the pair proclaimed:

> *We sing our lives, we sing our love*
> *We sing our destiny, forgetting our suffering and pain*
> *We sing to understand each other, [singing is] our*
>   *language of communication*
> *We sing with joy in our heart of each other's company*

There is a magic that happens when their two voices collide. In their romantic ballad 'Snaeh Yerng' ('Love Us') Sereysothea enters in the second verse – the first time I heard her voice burst through I felt like I'd been punched in the side, tears welled in my eyes, such was her power. At times she could dominate a song, at other times her partner came out on top. But mostly they complemented each other completely. Their music spanned every genre: from traditional folk ballads to bouncing bossa nova to psychedelic foot stompers and everything in between. From the achingly poetic 'Thavary My Love', featured on the *Don't Think I've Forgotten* soundtrack – a song that may not be out of place on Miles Davis's *Sketches of Spain* – to the rockier end of their spectrum (tracks like 'The Mango Branch'), the potpourri of their collaborative prowess knew no bounds. While they both had other singing partners, their work together was prolific. Their talents won them accolades from Prince Sihanouk, who christened Sisamouth 'the Master' and 'the King of Cambodian Music' while describing Sereysothea 'the Golden Voice of the Capital'.

The pair would often practise duets at Sothea's house before recording in the studio. As Sothea couldn't read music, Sisamouth often took this time to teach her the music by singing the notes first. He was both her partner and her teacher in many ways, often correcting her approach to a song, and directing her on where she should bend or cut notes.

A rare stage photograph of Sinn Sisamouth and Ros Sereysothea.

'Sothea never took care of her voice,' Saboeun told me in all seriousness. 'But she followed the advice of a famous *ayai* [a form of repartee performance] theatre actor who advised her to eat *prahok* [a paste made from fermented fish and chillies, used as a dipping sauce or sauce base], which warmed up her vocal chords and made her voice sound great. She also liked to eat *toek kroeung* [a fish paste with vegetables, fried garlic and eggplant] before she performed. On the other hand, even when Sinn Sisamouth laughed or cleared his throat he was mindful of his voice. No smoking, no drinking . . . ah-heh-heh,' Saboeun half whispered, impersonating Sisamouth's feeble, muffled cough. However, despite Sothea's carefree approach to her craft, so at odds with

168

Sisamouth's, the singers bonded over their shared reserve and the value they placed on kindness – both in themselves and others.

More often than not, Sereysothea recorded at RNK radio studio, the Mekong studio and Van Chann, with its thick soundproofing, hot studio and cold bright lights. There was no vocal booth, instead the singers stood around a microphone in the centre, surrounded by musicians. When the engineer signalled the tape was rolling, Saboeun would sit dutifully silent in the corner until each take was finished, and when Sothea sang on Cambodian film soundtracks, her eldest sister would catch a glimpse of upcoming releases, watching Sothea sync her vocals to a rolling film-screen in the studio.

Ros Sereysothea record sleeve.

During her industrious seven-year career, Sereysothea also had a sojourn in front of the camera, acting in at least two movies, and occasionally performing theme tunes or title tracks at cinemas on opening night. Music fan and makeup artist Ok Silyauth remembered her voice being just as beautiful live as it was on record, when he saw her perform 'Tnae na bong Veul Vin' ('When You Come Back') for the opening of the film *Jomreang Eth Preang Thok* (*The Song Extemporaneous*, directed, written and produced by Sinn Sisamouth), at the popular Hemakcheat Cinema in Phnom Penh.

As Sereysothea's fame grew with the increase in film work in the late 1960s, Saboeun would fly alone back and forth – from her own family commitments in Battambang, to her sister in Phnom Penh – occasionally taking family road trips when the roads were passable. When she was absent, Saboeun and her other proud Battambang-based sisters would gather around the radio whenever they heard Sothea's voice. But Saboeun's happiest memories of her sister centred on her biannual visits back home to Battambang for Ancestor's Day and Khmer New Year. She described these times as sacred.

I knew the time I had with Saboeun was also sacred, and fast coming to an end. As we packed up to leave I asked if I too could make the trip to Battambang to visit her, which she warmly accepted. Before parting, we hit the road again for a tour of her sister's old homes and Phnom Penh haunts, including the two-storey grey cinderblock home en route to the airport, where Sisamouth and Sothea often practised. Saboeun, Oro and I strolled around to the end of the block where all the artists used to gather at what was once a corner café. The present-day restaurant was fairly unremarkable, but back in its heyday, the music would have blasted, as crockery clinked and the young, beautiful and talented passed the time between performances with laughter and excitement for each new day of their golden age.

We returned afterwards to Oro's flat by the riverside to listen to some of the Cambodian Vintage Music Archive's original

Ros Sereysothea 45s, Saboeun's face beeming at the sight of her sister's record sleeves. I'd listened to records in that same Phnom Penh townhouse on other occasions, chasing monkeys off the balcony as Oro excavated the rarest records from his safe and delicately laid them down on the turntable with all the diligence of an archaeologist on site at a dig. It was always an event when one of those records saw daylight.

I'd watched him digitize records there too: a painstaking process that could take up to an hour to expertly clean a record before transferring the vinyl then scanning the sleeve. The operation from first meeting a collector to digitizing their records is often a long road, Oro had once told me, and could end in heartache, with collectors changing their minds at the last minute and slamming the door on a carefully cultivated relationship with the archive. Collectors are often reluctant to have their collections played or even looked at, such is the bond they have with their treasures. 'They don't want people to harm their records,' Oro explained reverently. 'They genuinely take care of them like they're family; they love them, they sleep with them . . .'

Other times, Oro would stumble on the rarest of records – breakthrough titles like Sereysothea's 'Stung Khieu' and Yol Aularong's 'Navanny' – only to find the vinyl and sleeves had succumbed to the ravages of time and the merciless Cambodian heat and rain. But every now and then, new discoveries and successes make it all worthwhile. I was privy to this on occasion. In those moments, and moments like this one, listening to Ros Sereysothea records with Saboeun, the complexities of Oro's character purified, his rancour melted away, only to be replaced by a joy so unadulterated and so true to be contagious. Oro could at times be disagreeable and even unkind – whether rebuking Sophorn for mistranslations or making his disgust known to me over a sentimental effigy of Shiva (the Hindu god of protection) that was not the cash gift he was hoping for. His passion and energy for the music and the archive comes from both the saint and sinner residing within. And it's relentless; a true calling.

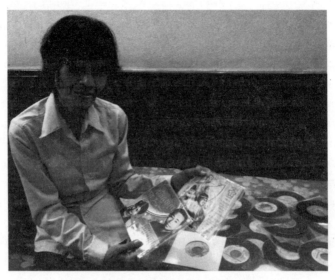

Saboeun looking through the CVMA archive.

After settling our stomachs with Saboeun's favourite bitter melon soup and Oro's prized saltfish we returned Saboeun to her niece's house in the north of the city. By then it was dark, and the alley unlit. We hugged goodbye and walked Saboeun to the gate of her niece's house before one final wave. As Oro and I approached the tuk tuk we could see our driver flailing his arms vigorously. Slowly, one by one, fat, flying bugs emerged from the dark and batted into our torsos, arms, faces and legs. In all the confusion we began to scream. Clambering as fast as we could into the tuk tuk Oro and I held onto each other as all around us a swarm of thousands of cockroaches took to the air in all directions. When we finally reached the end of the alley and left the swarm behind, we separated from one other and composed ourselves momentarily before turning to each other and bursting into hysterical laughter. It was a moment that felt so pure, a moment in which we bonded; one that would be followed by many more memories on the course of this journey.

A few months passed before I managed to make that trip to Cambodia's rice bowl, Battambang. In the end Oro and Sophorn were too busy to join me, so I was put in touch with a young translator and film student from Battambang city named Pry Nehru. Nehru spoke perfect English, had a firm grasp on both Eastern and Western culture, and a kind, modest and genuine character. A wide smile cracked across his handsome face when I arrived at Battambang's popular Jaan Bai café and, after exchanging *sampeahs*, we quickly got down to business, laying out our plans for reading over the Phnom Penh interview transcript with Saboeun and asking a few more questions about Sereysothea's later life. As we paused to drink our coffee, I had the opportunity to learn a little more about Nehru and his own backstory.

He grew up in war-torn Battambang, where fighting between Khmer Rouge forces and the Vietnam-backed Kampuchean People's Revolutionary Armed Forces carried on until 1996. One of Nehru's earliest memories was of seeing a fighter with an AK-47 walking across a bridge.

As he scattered dates like seeds into the conversation it dawned on me that we were around the same age. While I was living the life of a care-free British teenager dodging homework and sneaking off to gigs, Nehru was jumping into trenches with other civilians to escape open fire. He was smart as a whip and, in spite of the turmoil that afflicted his childhood, this professional, creative and talented guy had managed to flourish, both educationally and in his work in the film industry.

The following afternoon I met Nehru in town, hopped on the back of his moped and headed for Saboeun's neighbourhood. We left the colonial mansions behind and welcomed the transition from smaller houses to sparse communes on the city outskirts.

When we arrived at Saboeun's commune it was clear the monsoon had made its mark on the dirt roads all around, leaving dinosaur-sized puddles in its wake. We skipped over missing timbers on a raised walkway connecting the shacks, and eventually came to the Ros residence at the end of a quiet cul-de-sac. From the porch, Saboeun's eldest grandson rose to greet us and welcomed us inside with a gentle smile and an apology that the devout Saboeun was held up at the temple but would be with us shortly. Walking inside her small dark home was like a journey into the past. A wall spanning almost the entire length of Saboeun's single-room house was covered in framed photos of Sereysothea: a shrine to a dead sister, a homage to her life. Some photos looked original, some bought; some were superimposed onto real or drawn backgrounds. There were photos and frames of all sizes; pictures of Saboeun in religious settings like Angkor Wat, and some of her other siblings and children, a *mélange* of black and white and colour, both recent and old.

Along the bed sat four quiet grandchildren. The eldest boy

Saboeun's wall of photos.

motioned us to sit on a couple of plastic chairs, upon which Saboeun had set out packets of raisins, bananas and bottles of water. I placed the welcome package she'd left for us on my lap and looked around at the little she had in her home and felt my heart melt and break simultaneously. So often in Cambodia I was floored with kindness from people who had little in the way of money and possessions – whether it was the poncho off their back in a rainstorm or a pile of raisins set out like an offering. I learned a lot more about what it truly means to give from my short time in Cambodia than I ever learned in a lifetime in the West.

To pass the time Nehru and I tried to initiate small talk with the timid teenagers, but our numerous attempts were met only with polite and awkward smiles until, bursting in with her usual hive of activity and an energy and movement that defied her years, Saboeun broke the silence and relieved us all. It was wonderful to see her again. She talked a million words a minute in Khmer and reorganized our piles of offerings between hugs, excitedly adding more raisins to the mounds and hurriedly motioning us to sit again, introducing us to her grandchildren. When that was all done, from behind me I pulled out the gift I'd decided some time ago that I would give to her if I was to leave Cambodia.

It was acquired months back, when Kevin was perusing the guitars in a music shop near Phnom Penh's Central Market. He'd come across an acoustic guitar with an action that was 'so incredible' he told me, by a maker called 'Hanks'. My curiosity piqued, I Googled Hanks and found that it was likely to be handmade, from a small shop on Denmark Street, London. 'How had a rare guitar from a small independent shop in my home town ended up six thousand miles away?' I wondered, with delight. 'Well, it's a sign; you *have* to get it,' I told Kevin.

The procurement was an endurance test, an initiation that went on for four very long days. On day one Kevin asked how much the owner wanted, and the shopkeeper stopped fixing a soundboard long enough to peer over his reading glasses, take the guitar in his hands and reply with an ironclad, '$75.'

'How about $60?' Kevin counter-offered.

'No.'

'No negotiation on $75?'

'No,' the shopkeeper repeated, firm and final, and, lowering his eyes, returned to fixing his soundboard.

Dejected, Kevin left the shop, replayed the scenario in his head and started scheming new tactics. But all his schemes amounted to nothing. He played out the same unsuccessful scene the next day and the following day, until, finally, on day four, when obsession reached breaking point, Kevin once again returned to the shop.

'You again?' the owner questioned, over his reading glasses.

With a sigh Kevin conceded, 'OK, $75.'

The shopkeeper stopped what he was doing and put down his tools. With a supercilious smile he wagged his index finger and declared, 'I knew you'd be back. It's hard to put a price on this guitar because it's magic; the best in my shop. That will be $75.' And he threw a couple of picks in for good measure.

Kevin later told me that he'd danced home down the middle of the street like a wandering, strumming minstrel, leaving laughter, open mouths and near crashes in his wake. His victory dance climaxed when one hysterical man proclaimed Kevin to be the second coming of 'Elvis', to which my husband swung around in the centre of the busy intersection, raised the guitar neck up to the heavens and looked the young Cambodian square in the eye. With a show of bravado, he stomped his foot, flicked back his hair and played a grand staccato rhythm, screaming from his lungs, *'You ain't nothing but a hound dog!'* before twisting on his heels and strumming his way home. I loved him for many reasons, but none more so than his frequent moments of total abandon.

We'd both had the pleasure of playing that guitar in our apartment and whenever we hit the road on our travels across the country. With our reserves dwindling and no job prospects on my horizon, when it came time for us to concede to leaving Cambodia we knew we had to either track down a guitar case or leave the guitar behind. When we couldn't find a case that cost less than the guitar itself, and our remaining time in Phnom Penh began to accelerate at breakneck speed, Kevin and I turned our attention to who we should give the guitar to, and I recalled a story that Saboeun had told me the first time we met.

After the genocide, she went to Vietnam to work for the Department of Women's Affairs. She bought a guitar to rekindle some semblance of her jug-band youth, and it accompanied her as she rebuilt her life. She chuckled dismissively when she told me that this was until a male friend visited her one day and told her that 'women should not play guitar' – then, without protest from Saboeun, claimed the guitar for himself. As much as she laughed it off, I felt the injustice of that act and I knew it hurt her inside. I could think of nobody worthier of 'Hank' than Saboeun. Kevin agreed.

So, the gift I pulled from behind me as I recited this memory was Hank. I told her to use it as she wished, hoping that either she would play it or pass it on to her grandchildren to play for her – but also accepting the possibility that if she was hard up and needed to sell it, then the guitar would still serve a worthy purpose. (I was delighted to see, months later – while promoting the crowdfunding campaign for the documentary film about lost Cambodian rock music *Don't Think I've Forgotten: Cambodia's Lost Rock and Roll* – that the filmmakers had shot Saboeun playing Hank.)

We started where we left off last time – with the year 1970. This was a time of transition for Sereysothea's music, both in genre and style. Radio stations such as Voice of America and

American Forces Vietnam Network began broadcasting from military bases to American troops in 1965, and, gradually, because of their extensive broadcast range, their top 40 hits were picked up by Cambodians, supplementing their own national stations, in effect Americanizing Cambodia's music. By the early 1970s the English and French 45s that had occupied the travelling bags of the 1960s Phnom Penh elite were replaced by American top 40 radio hits and, gradually, cheaper cassettes, making music more accessible to all.

Music making as a whole changed in 1970 with the *coup d'état* that overthrew Prince Norodom Sihanouk, replacing the Sangkum era's propaganda machine with that of the new regime. During the Sangkum period, between 1955 and 1970, there were loose regulations set by the songwriters' association concerning the lyrical content of music. So long as the words of upcoming releases did not criticize the Sangkum government and weren't explicit in sexual content, most songs passed the grade. When the American-backed Lon Nol regime took control of the country, their administration had heard Sangkum-endorsed anti-Vietnamese songs of protest and seen the subsequent anti-Vietnam student protests that had occurred throughout the country and knew that music was a powerful tool for instilling ideas, particularly among the youth. They encouraged the sounds of the early 1970s that lent themselves so well to the fighting spirit of protest songs – from hard rock to psychedelia to bohemian folk – and started out by pressuring artists to perform in military garb, tightening their grasp on the lyrical content of new releases. Popular themes included songs that criticized the previous administration and other neighbouring enemies of the state, and songs that might inspire young men to enlist and take up arms against the encroaching Khmer Rouge guerrilla army. Songs like Sisamouth's 'Tomorrow I'll Join the Army' – the lyrics of which were borrowed from a student's poem – and rockers

Savoy and Yol Aularong's garage screamer, 'Dying Under a Woman's Sword', condemning *'cowards hiding behind women's skirts'*. Having experienced the geopoliticization of lyrics under the Sangkum, and given the record-buying student population had assorted views on Sihanouk as a leader, the transition from the Sangkum to Lon Nol was less a paradigm shift for the average listener – more a shift in enemy focus (namely to Sihanouk and the Khmer Rouge) and a passive compliance to this change, or, at most, acquiescence.

Though she would eventually return to ballads through a female lens and the misty-eyed love songs she was renowned for, throughout the early to mid-1970s Sereysothea embraced new vibes, from garage rock classics like 'Cham 10 Khe Teat' ('Wait 10 More Months') to go-go to flower pop. She wasn't afraid to inject a little humour to her repertoire every now and then with songs like 'Chhnang Jas Bai Chgn-ainj' ('Old Pot Still Cooks Good Rice'), and experiment with covers of American classics like Creedence Clearwater Revival's 'Proud Mary', the Carpenters' 'Yesterday Once More' and a heartbreaking version of their track 'Superstar'. Occasionally she even sang in English, like on her 1973 flower pop track 'Chmreing Somrapp Bong' ('A Song for You'), made famous by the likes of Andy Williams, Donny Hathaway and the Carpenters.

Shortly after the coup, Sereysothea met an army general named Srey Ya, but sadly it was to be another doomed affair in her litany of disastrous relationships. Their union was tumultuous, violent and fraught with heartache and difficulty. During Saboeun's tuk tuk tour of Sothea's Phnom Penh hotspots, I remember my shock at her coolly casual comments as we passed the intersection close to Sothea's home en route to the airport: 'And that is where Srey Ya raped Sothea,' she divulged in a detached tone, a bony finger pointing to an unkept grass verge at a nearby intersection. 'Sothea was kidnapped by Srey Ya's troops. He already had a wife but he kidnapped Sothea and forced her to have sex, and the wife accepted it, because his wife had had three children and could no longer get pregnant.'

How this act progressed into a relationship remains unclear, but, if true, this was certainly the most violent and cruel start to a coupling. Of course, the military held a lot of sway and power at the time, so there was every chance that the marriage was also forced. As for Sereysothea's partner at the time, according to Saboeun, Siphan was intimidated by his lover's new suitor and fled to France, leaving their son, Sopanara, with Sothea. Srey Ya and Sothea went on to have three children together during the early to mid-1970s. The demands of managing a successful career and four young children were high pressure, but, with the help of her entourage, she juggled both roles adeptly, and her fame continued to grow throughout this time.

As well as promoting the new government through her music – Sereysothea was forced to sing songs like 'The Traitor' about the deposed Sihanouk – she also starred in a promotional film for the army in which she donned military garb and exclaimed with pride, 'I look just like a man to the enemy soldiers,' before parachuting out of an aeroplane. Shot in black and white, the smiling, natural beauty joined a swarm of jellyfish-like parachutes exploding across the sky, landing in the monsoon-drenched rice fields, before being scooped up by hordes of excited children. She wasn't forced into it, rather, she was inspired by the parachuting careers of her brother Sokunthea and her sister Sophean. Sereysothea undertook the training to qualify as a paratrooper at the military training ground where her husband worked, mainly so that she could don the badge and experience what they did, according to her sister. It was a six-week course which included several jumps – and a chance for Sothea to relive one of her first passions, cross-country running. She managed to slot her recording dates into the rigorous training schedule, declaring in the September 1971 edition of the *Khmer Republic* magazine: 'But fighting the war is more important than any of that.'

Having two sibling paratroopers already, Saboeun was no stranger to the dangers of the job. She'd accompany Sothea to the military air base where Srey Ya and the paratroopers' regiment were based in Kombol, Kampong Speu Province, south-west of Phnom Penh. Saboeun remembered the rope they'd attach to new recruits in training, the large nets they would jump into, the weeks of running and crawling exercises undertaken, the helicopter rides and the six successful jumps recruits had to complete to get their badge. Sothea enjoyed it so much she jumped seven times, much to the anguish and protestations of Saboeun who accompanied her to the training ground each day. Saboeun acknowledged the impact of her sister's actions at a time when the war affected everyone, young and old, and the government was pushing for songs, poems and media stunts to support the war effort: 'She was already very famous, but in supporting the Lon Nol regime, and that being broadcast on TV, her fame grew even more.' Those caught in the countryside crossfire simply wanted an end to the civil war, and were willing to follow Lon Nol to make that happen.

Throughout the early 1970s Phnom Penh swelled with refugees from the provinces, fleeing if not American bombs in the east then the fighting between Lon Nol's troops and the Khmer Rouge elsewhere across the regions. Along with her compatriots in the music business, Sereysothea had to navigate an increasingly precarious industry, thanks to the air strikes and temporary nightclub and cinema closures. In his book *River of Time* the writer Jon Swain remembered this period, and the shift from the beautiful sensual city in which he came of age. Phnom Penh, he wrote, 'suddenly became a city of refugees, barbed wire, and the nightclubs began to close or they started having wired screens on their windows because grenades might be thrown in. Everyone knew that Lon Nol had lost the war: the unscrupulous generals in their Mercedes; the cyclo-drivers carrying the wounded to hospital; the blind soldier-minstrels wandering the streets; the legless cripples; the fortune-tellers; the women grappling with unaffordable food prices; the shopkeepers; the soldiers; the bar girls . . . At the O-Russey open air market in the central area, women in long coloured sarongs slowly went about, doing their shopping amid the flying splinters of the falling rockets.'

While many musicians left to find work in Thailand or Pailin province, Sereysothea stayed and made the best of an increasingly spacious market, her star rising in the space vacated by some of her peers, and a public's need for hope and distraction in such a desolate and foreboding time. Travel, too, became more hazardous. Sothea flew only when the roads were bad or blocked – such flights became more and more frequent as the Khmer Rouge's territory expanded. Her close-knit family – having enjoyed years of free travel at the behest of their famous relative – found their lives increasingly separate; their travel plans evermore fraught with peril, and often abandoned en route or at the last minute.

In January 1975 the Khmer Rouge began their offensive to capture Phnom Penh. They blocked off all overland routes into the capital and rained gunfire and artillery down upon the river and the air convoys flying aid into the starving city, now bulging at the seams with an escalating refugee crisis. The Lon Nol army were outnumbered and out-manoeuvred, so, in February 1975, John Gunther Dean – an American diplomat gifted with the unenviable task of serving as the United States ambassador to the Khmer Republic – began to evacuate his staff and their dependants. It marked the beginning of an eight-week evacuation, culminating in the infamous Operation Eagle Pull on 12 April – a last-ditch attempt to get as many Cambodians,

Americans and other foreigners out of the country by helicopter and aeroplane before the inevitable fall of the capital. Gunther Dean recalled the operation in detail during the weeks leading up to the fall. In late February 1975 Gunther Dean's team announced that they were willing to evacuate anyone who wanted to go – anyone whose life might be in danger at the hands of the Khmer Rouge. But the bourgeoisie had an optimistic outlook on the future and therein lay their downfall. As Gunther Dean reflected in these interviews, 'There were quite a number of people – both Cambodians and foreigners – who believed one could deal with the Khmer Rouge.' Many of Cambodia's left-leaning intelligentsia were executed for their educated status, or ended up dying in the rice fields later. Among the foreign contingency, Scottish radical and Marxist writer and lecturer Malcolm Caldwell was murdered shortly after meeting Pol Pot, several East German diplomats offered up their support only to be cuffed and led away as prisoners, and, of course, Prince Norodom Sihanouk remained in exile after the Khmer Rouge came to power, only to be wheeled out on occasion and forced to make a show of support for his communist brothers. In the end, Operation Eagle Pull had more helicopters than people to board them. Of the 289 people evacuated, only 159 were Cambodians.

Lon Nol had resigned as premier on 1 April and fled the country in secrecy, eventually settling in California where he died in 1985. For those cabinet members who stayed behind, I'm inclined to believe it was an act of honour. Along with Prime Minister Long Boret, Chariya's father, Deputy Prime Minister Lieutenant General Prince Sisowath Sirik Matak, was one. As Gunther Dean awaited the call to be moved to the evacuation site on 12 April, he spent the final moments in his office, opening a letter received from Matak forty-five minutes earlier. It read:

Phnom Penh, 12 April 1975

Dear Excellency and Friend,

I thank you very sincerely for your letter and for your offer to transport me towards freedom. I cannot, alas, leave in such a cowardly fashion. As for you, and in particular for your great country, I never believed for a moment that you would have this sentiment of abandoning a people which has chosen liberty. You have refused us your protection, and we can do nothing about it. You leave, and my wish is that you and your country will find happiness under this sky. But, mark it well, that if I shall die here on the spot and in my country that I love, it is too bad, because we all are born and must die (one day). I have only committed this mistake of believing in you the Americans. Please accept, Excellency and dear friend, my faithful and friendly sentiments.

(signed) Sirik Matak

Gunther Dean went on to reveal that the tears rolled down his face as he pulled the American flags from their flag-poles, draped them over his shoulders and walked out to the last awaiting helicopter. As for Sirik Matak, Long Boret and the other senior leaders in the Lon Nol cabinet, there are a number of unsubstantiated accounts of where, when and how they were executed, ranging from sports grounds to schools, from beheadings to firing squads. What is a matter of public record is American journalist Sydney Schanberg's account of the last time he saw a puffy-eyed and broken Long Boret, Lon Non (the younger brother of Lon Nol), Brigadier General Chim Chhuon and the fifty or so generals and officials who'd been rounded up at the Ministry of Information, awaiting their fate. Sirik Matak had sought refuge on the soil of the French embassy, perhaps having made the mistake of thinking that the Khmer Rouge would honour international laws surrounding immunity. After hiding in a cupboard for three days, he handed himself over to save the others in the compound. He was led away by Khmer Rouge forces and executed.

To get a sense of the final days before the takeover, I looked through French photographer Roland Neveu's photobook *The Fall of Phnom Penh* for stories and images of sandbagged shopfronts, overcrowded hospitals, rush hour on Monivong Boulevard for the last time in decades . . . Cambodians looking on and lining the fences of the Operation Eagle Pull evacuation site, bodies returned from the last battlegrounds. After the evacuation there was a temporary respite from the fighting. But over the coming days, one by one, the battlegrounds around the suburbs of Phnom Penh were claimed by the Khmer Rouge forces, before their final victory at Pochentong Airport. Small efforts to barricade and protect foreign institutions in the city held through for a few days, while more and more displaced families and deserting Khmer Republic soldiers flooded into the city centre, fleeing its burning outskirts.

On the morning of the fall, shortly after daybreak, Neveu saw a government soldier running with an old M1 rifle in one hand and a guitar in the other, before the streets emptied out and a few cautious, heavily armed Khmer Rouge guerrillas surveyed the intersection outside the French Embassy. Nobody, including Neveu, made a move, until a few brave children stepped out with white flags above their heads and broke the ice. War weary and hopeful inhabitants lined Monivong Boulevard and cheered as truckloads of Khmer Rouge soldiers entered the city. Smiles were exchanged, cigarettes were offered to the newcomers, group photos of cadres and civilians were shot by journalists, and peace was won at long last.

But it was to be short lived. The first wave of Khmer Rouge

to enter north Phnom Penh had been young cadres, awaiting new orders – standing at just a few thousand they were vastly outnumbered by the city's two million inhabitants. It was in their interest to enter the city peacefully and await instruction – as well as the ten thousand or so hardened frontline guerrillas who would bring up the ranks later that day. The second wave wore *krama* scarves, green caps, black shirts and trousers and 'Ho Chi Minh sandals' made from car tyres. By and large they were pedestrian and hostile, in stark contrast to the young cadres of earlier Khmer Rouge battalions. By early afternoon civilians were being turfed out of their homes by soldiers brandishing weapons to a backdrop of bullhorns and loudspeaker announcements ordering a three-day deadline for people to leave the city for a temporary evacuation. Citizens were told to carry only small items of luggage, and to take designated roads into the countryside. They were informed this was to flush out hidden enemies, and that this was an order from Angkar, the ruling body of the Khmer Rouge: everyone needed to follow the principles set by the party. But the explanation that everyone remembers hearing – and which replaced the morning's euphoria with panic – was that, 'The Americans are coming to bomb the city.' We now know, of course, that this was a cruel deception, made believable by America's relentless and illegal bombing of Cambodia during the Vietnam War.

By dusk the Khmer Rouge's mobile units were in place, and the pre-planned mass exodus of Phnom Penh had developed into a heavy flow of people exiting the city – systematic but totally chaotic. Thousands of hospital patients were forced onto the roads, on their crutches, crawling on their elbows and knees, carried on relatives' backs, or carried in their beds. Lost and separated children and parents screamed out for one another, and the bourgeoisie pushed their cars alongside the slum dwellers as, side by side and wave by wave, the penguin columns comprising some two to three million people marched solemnly from the capital. And somewhere in that vast sea of civilians was Ros Sereysothea.

In the days leading up to the fall, Saboeun was desperate to get to her two children who'd been living with their aunt while being schooled in Phnom Penh. There were a number of failed travel attempts – from a military helicopter organized by Sereysothea's husband Srey Ya to another organized by a Battambang embassy worker to accompany the film director Pech Saloeun and his wife, an actress called Vichara Dany – but Saboeun was stranded in Pailin province and missed the departure each time.

As far as Saboeun knows, Sothea was with their mother, Sothea's four children and two of Saboeun's children when the call to evacuate the city came. Saboeun has it on authority from a distant relative who met Sothea on the road, that Srey Ya had disappeared and they were evacuated forty miles west of Phnom Penh to Tro Pieng Tlong village, Dambouk Rung commune, Phnom Sruoch district in Kampong Speu province. It was the hottest month of the year and their relative, Mr Song Hong, told Saboeun that between them they'd juggled carrying Sothea's starving and dehydrated children but, tragically, the heat and the distance was too much for the youngest three children – one just a baby – and they didn't make it. He buried their bodies as they fell, covering the shallow graves with sand and *khlong* leaves. The road took many prisoners – estimates range between 20,000 and 400,000 – mostly the vulnerable: the elderly, the infirm and the young. Many babies and young children starved to death on the road, were separated from their families in the chaos of the evacuation, or died from gastrointestinal afflictions or dehydration.

By the time I came to reflect on it and write this I too had become a mother. I couldn't begin to imagine how Sothea survived this. To lose one child – the pain would be incomprehensible

– but to lose three of her four children, under such cruel and desperate circumstances, and in such a short space of time . . . I can't fathom how anyone recovers from that. Saboeun, of course, suffered that same pain and worse: the unbearable agony of not truly knowing what happened to her children. She has never had a grave site to visit or a chance to put them to rest. Since first learning of the deaths of her children, sister, their mother and her nieces and nephews on her return from Vietnam in 1980, Saboeun has heard many different stories about what happened to them. Sadly, I doubt she'll ever have any conclusive evidence, or anything beyond witness accounts; some more trustworthy than others. She's had time to ponder these sources and tales, and surmise the most reliable accounts of her sister's end, which she went on to disclose to me: 'I believe that Sothea was killed in Kampong Speu in 1978. After they got to Kampong Speu, a few days later, the new arrivals were given the option to carry on to where they were born, and Song Hong told me he went to Battambang. Sothea wanted to go back to Battambang but they [the Khmer Rouge] said, "You have to stay here and sing to the group." Another witness called "Mao" Tiv Heng . . . she has now passed away . . . told me that one day, at four o'clock in the afternoon when she came back to her house, they carried Sothea and her family on an ox cart and they were killed at the nearby pagoda called Choam Sangkae pagoda, Phnom Sruoch district in Kampong Speu province.'

The Khmer Rouge carved the country up into administrative zones, and Phnom Sruoch district bordered both the 'Western' and 'Southwestern' zones on Cambodia's new map. The Western Zone stretched from Kampong Chhnang province just north of Phnom Penh to Koh Kong, the western province that borders Thailand. The Southwestern Zone – where Sereysothea ended up – covered Kampot and Takéo provinces, both bordering Vietnam in the south and Phnom Penh's neighbouring Kandal and Kampong Speu provinces in the middle. Both the Western and Southwestern zones were subject to extensive purges in 1978, the final year of the Khmer Rouge's rule. Fighting with Vietnam in the east (a result of Khmer Rouge excursions into South Vietnam and subsequent attacks like the Ba Chúc massacre), unit rebellions and Cham Muslim uprisings spurred on the search for 'enemies from within', as the Khmer Rouge called them.

Of the ten mass graves found in the Phnom Sruoch district, none of them were located in Choam Sangkae. I could not locate a village in Choam Sangkae's neighbouring commune, Dambouk Rung, called Tro Pieng Tlong, which is not to say that it – or some alternative spelling – did not exist, but nothing remotely related exists there now.

There are a number of stories of Sothea being forced into an arranged – and once again violent – marriage with the son (called 'Trok') of the region's head honcho towards the end. Rumour has it that the marriage did not follow the rules of Angkar and their arguments drew the wrong kind of attention and sealed their fate. Some say she died at the beginning of the genocide, some say at the end; some report she died in hospital from dengue fever, some believe she died in a prison, and some – like Saboeun – believe Mao's simple account.

Of the several thousand biographical records of prisoners captured by the Khmer Rouge, Sothea is not one of them. The bodies in the mass graves remain unidentified. What is known is that there were any number of reasons the Khmer Rouge would want Sothea dead, and there are numerous witness accounts to say that she perished in the genocide, along with her children, Saboeun's children and her mother.

Back in Battambang province, Saboeun had the two youngest of her four children with her but was suffering from the separation of her two older children and had other battles to face as the known sister of the country's most famous singer under a regime that persecuted popular musicians: 'The Khmer Rouge approached me and asked, "Do you sing like your sister?" I replied that I couldn't sing. I said to them, "In Khmer wisdom, we have a saying: some coconuts have water inside, and some don't."'

Among the other Battambang natives that Sothea spent her early career with, little is known of the demise of Pen Ran. Ran's skull is reputed to reside in a memorial stupa in the Wat Troap Kor pagoda in Takéo province, where she was allegedly killed along with her four children during the genocide. Of the artists who disappeared without a trace in 1975 I have so many questions still, but most of all concerning Pen Ran. Some of her music survived but I wanted to know more. And it was the unknown details of her life – who she was; what she liked to do when she wasn't recording; who her friends were; her family; her children; how she behaved as a person – that both fascinated and escaped me. Her sassy, tomboy stage persona seemed at odds with her very private personal life; it was as if no one could get close to really knowing her, not even her fellow musicians. No matter how many people I talked to and how many questions I asked, her story eluded me, and I was unable to gather anything concrete enough to commit to paper. Ran left behind no direct descendants and her sister, Pen Ram – probably the closest person to her – survived the genocide but died in Long Beach in 2005, along with their secrets. There were others too who survived the genocide, but died before my quest began. Others still, wanted to leave the past in the past. We will never know the whole story.

Battambang-born singer Im Song Seum purportedly died of cancer at the age of twenty-nine in 1972. And from tales passed down by Nehru's grandmother – who lived and worked in the same village as Huoy Meas – Nehru was able to corroborate Thach Soly's story, his grandmother claiming that Huoy Meas went under the false name of 'Lom' and lived near a pagoda in front of her house in Ream Kun village, Moung Russey district, Battambang, and that they worked together constructing a dam. She recounted stories of trading snails and freshwater crabs with the singer for a song while a trusted friend kept a look out for villainous cadres.

Saboeun's father, Sabun, died in 1995. In the end, Saboeun outlived all four of her children. Of the two children who stayed with Saboeun during the genocide, one died after the liberation of 1979 having stepped on a landmine, and her last child died in 2003. Saboeun was left bringing up her orphaned grandchildren in her one-room house with very little money. As she recounted each loss, I began to wonder if the Ros family was cursed, and I bartered just how much grief one person could take and yet still embrace life like Saboeun seemed to. In that respect, she was the greatest warrior I'd ever met, and I've had the honour of meeting many extraordinarily resilient fighters in my lifetime.

Over the years Saboeun has been collecting evidence of her sister's songwriting credits in the hope that she might make a claim for the unprotected intellectual property rights. We talked at length with Oro about this in Phnom Penh. It felt utterly unjust that Saboeun's youngest granddaughter, Monica, was selling bangles at local temples when she could have been at school – meanwhile bootleggers were lining their pockets in a country where copyright law simply hasn't been enforced. After several hours of talking, Saboeun's energy levels were waning, the space between her words growing further, her face increasingly less animated. Before we parted, Saboeun invited us all to join her at her temple the next day for a very special ceremony, and we accepted without so much as a second thought. By now the puddles outside had been shrunk by the sun. The slum dwellers turned out to watch us leave, and wedged between Nehru and Kevin I waved goodbye as Saboeun grew smaller in our motorbike's rearview mirror.

*

It was coming up to four o'clock in the morning and the sun was yet to rise when a bleary-eyed Nehru met Kevin and me at the temple gates for the Buddhist ceremony of the dead, Pchum Ben. After all the loss we'd discussed the previous day, Saboeun felt it only fitting we share the festival with her, to honour her sister and all the artists who perished in the genocide. For those who met their end during those years, there was no funeral, no transition between this life and the next; they were all trapped souls. So it felt hugely important and symbolic to again celebrate the dead at Wat Damrey Sor, the place where we had done so for Saboeun's recently departed sister, Saboeuth, some months before. Celebrating Pchum Ben at the same temple, at the end of my time there, felt somewhat cyclical.

As Kevin, Nehru and I approached the main temple hall it was humming with monks chanting *suttas*. Saboeun was outside, handing out plates of offerings for the dead and escorting newcomers into the temple. The early hour could not extinguish her indefatigable energy, and she lit up when we arrived, refusing to take a penny from us for the readymade plates of ceremonial offerings she'd bought and prepared for us. There truly was no end to her energy and kindness.

Inside the temple, we sat cross-legged with match-stick eyes next to Saboeun's granddaughter, Monica, who bore a striking resemblance to her famous great aunt. The chanting was hypnotic, distorting as it travelled through a loud speaker – seemingly never ending – as tired worshippers slowly lurched into the church and plopped down on whatever floor mats were available. By five in the morning the temple was full, and after more than an hour of ceremony the circular chanting ceased with a final bent-note crescendo, signalling the next phase of the ritual.

Peeling ourselves and our paper plates off the floor, we followed the herd, shuffling together in silence towards the old temple building, lighting our small wax candles along the way. The candlelit procession moved like a shoal of moonlit sardines around the central temple's tower – what Khmers call a *prasat* – where everyone gave away their offerings to the ancestors.

I shadowed Monica and quickly realized that the ancestors could take their offerings from just about anywhere within the temple surround. The monks had even provided us with industrial-sized waste 'portals'. Techniques ranged from the elderly gingerly placing cigarettes and incense around the temple walls to teenagers yearning for their beds, blindly lobbing sticky rice balls into the 'portal' bins. All of it was done in electrifying silence, and as I walked around disposing of my own rice balls and cigarettes I reflected on all the artists who'd lost their lives almost forty years ago. But mostly I thought of Sothea. The melody of Sinn Sisamouth's 'Souvenir of Battambang' – the title track of his 1974 album about the love between a woman and a man at Wat Damrey Sor – rang in my head throughout, his Khmer lyrics set to the plagiarized melody of Lee Hazlewood's 'Summer Wine'.

After a few rounds of the *prasat*, the firefly procession slowed to a standstill and silently closed in around a monk in saffron robes who extinguished the ceremony with a final chanting song. The feeling and the moment stayed with me long after. In that last chant, I felt my spirit soar with gratitude for the sensation that comes from new, unforgettable spiritual experiences. As the crowds dissipated and went home to bed, Saboeun, Nehru, Kevin, Monica and I returned to the main temple to say our goodbyes.

Though I've remained in contact with Saboeun long since, and subsequent partings have never been easy, that particular goodbye was perhaps the hardest and I felt a real pull not to leave her. In our handful of meetings up to that point, she'd had a profound and lasting effect on me. Saboeun had taught me humility, love, determination and integrity of spirit. She'd taught me about true loss and what it is to give.

Her sister, Ros Sereysothea, continues to influence and inspire long after her disappearance. My friend Mealea – perhaps the second coming of Sothea – described her idol's voice as 'a gift from God'. She told me simply once, 'When she sings, I fall in love.' And in a 2009 interview with *Cambodia Daily* reporter Clancy McGilligan, film director and fan John Pirozzi talked of Sothea's voice as an instrument: 'It's just so captivating when you hear it, even if you don't understand.'

The elderly and the young of Cambodia celebrate her to this day. There will never be another Ros Sereysothea. She is the nation's sweetheart, revered like a royal, cherished like a deceased relative and immortalized by her music, never straying far from the radio. She remains for many, forever sixteen.

8

Golden Voice Emperor

The people are gone but the pictures remain. Today, it's as if Sinn Sisamouth were still alive. His voice hasn't changed, his pictures haven't changed. So, let's pretend he's alive.

Dy Saveth, actress, filmmaker and singer.
Quoted in the film *Golden Slumbers* directed by
Davy Chou

Sinn Sisamouth and his beloved VW Bug.

Phnom Penh Post reporter Will Jackson chronicled what happened when a film crew arrived in Cambodia to shoot a short biographical piece about the singer Sinn Sisamouth. While filming in a remote rice field in early 2004, the crew took a break and turned the camera on an eight-year-old bystander. They asked him if he knew who Sinn Sisamouth was, and the child responded by singing one of Sisamouth's songs, word for word. Filmmaker Chris Pankhurst stood aghast, and later said, 'I don't know anywhere in the States where you can just walk up to an eight-year-old kid and ask them, "Hey, do you know who Elvis Presley is? Can you sing us a song?"'

Beyond the royal family and the monkhood, Sinn Sisamouth is possibly the closest thing to a deity Cambodia has. 'The Master', 'Elvis of Cambodia', 'the Golden Voice Emperor', 'the King of Khmer Music' – the long list of names synonymous with Samouth (his nickname, pronounced 'Sa-moot') serves only to labour the point. And while Ros Sereysothea may have been 'the Golden Voice of the Capital', Sisamouth held the same title over the entire country. He is immortalized by his legacy, and if it weren't for my own run-in with his voice on that mountain top in Bokor, I may have never written this book.

When my translator, Oro, and I arrived at the Sinn Sisamouth Association in Phnom Penh early one August morning we had just enough time to take in the outside of the locked suburban townhouse before its owner showed up. A makeshift display board of peeling photographs featuring various artists hung proud in the porch way, like a school project that had been left out in the rain. It was a little after eight-thirty in the morning when Sisamouth's son, Chanchhaya, pulled up in a red saloon car with his smiling, diminutive wife. He barely looked up to greet us as he hurriedly jangled keys to rush inside and hastily empty his metallic desk drawers of paperwork pertaining to the Sisamouth Association.

There was no mistaking his heritage – he had the same round face and brow of his father – but while the resemblance was irrefutable, there was a hardness to Chanchhaya's face that I never saw in photos of his father. I was used to seeing Sisamouth in a Kentucky derby tie and tux, his eyes soft and smiling, but the windows to Chanchhaya's soul seemed haunted – and from what I'd heard about the 'Golden Voice Emperor', their manners were nothing alike.

After we all sat down, Chanchhaya started handing me papers on the Sisamouth Association, and it was quickly and gruffly made clear that Chanchhaya's memory wasn't strong enough to answer any questions about his father, and that we should address our questions towards the affairs of the association only. We were not to ask him about his father. We were also curtly informed that our pre-agreed interview hour had in fact been cut down by half. As annoyed as I was, there was no time to dwell on whether or not we'd caught him on a bad day.

Set up in 2003, the main goal of the association was to look for lost documents and music of all singers and composers from Sisamouth's time, with a secondary aspiration to also take back ownership of Sisamouth's childhood house in Stung Treng and turn it into a museum. Sisamouth's remaining son took over the reins as the association's chairman in 2007, and spoke almost tenderly about the eighty-year-old longan tree that his father planted outside his childhood home. Chanchhaya told me of his concerns about the current owner – a distant relative – and how he wanted to mitigate the risk of alterations by purchasing the house. That summer of 2014, when I met Chanchhaya, the family had submitted 181 songs from their own collection (all songs written by Sinn Sisamouth), to the Ministry of Culture and Fine Arts, for protection under intellectual property rights. The move broke new ground for a country so neck deep in corruption and so lawless in its protection of copyright. After nearly a lifetime of struggling to get by – while others profited from his father's music – Chanchhaya was holding out for a victory: 'The initiative came from my mother because she remembered my father telling her, "Even if the country is destroyed, my music and my name can never be destroyed."' It was Sisamouth's hope, Chanchhaya told me, that his children would have a better life. 'That is why the copyright is so important to us,' he intoned solemnly over his reading glasses.

In Cambodia today, the Ministry of Culture and Fine Arts retains the rights to music in the absence of the author or copyright documentation. In the case of the thousands of songs written and produced before the reign of the Khmer Rouge, this accounts for all but 281 songs at the time of writing. For a minimal $7 fee the right to cover a song and reproduce it can be purchased today without any vetting. In February 2020 the Cambodia News English website reported that the current Director of Copyright and Related Rights Division, the ironically named Sim Samuth (no relation) took a public stand against copyright abuse following the unlawful release of a cover of a Sisamouth song. He vowed to educate the performers today on copyright law, but with piracy so high in Asia, and copyright acquisition fees as small as they are, it's hard to see how the ministry will be motivated to enforce the law.

The Sisamouth Association started undertaking this initiative long before Sim Samuth's announcement. For years they have been training a new generation of performers on how to play and write Cambodian music with integrity, much in the way the eponym of the foundation once did. Chanchhaya has scrupulously kept records of – and from – every artist, singer and composer from the past, much like Oro's Cambodian Vintage Music Archive has in cataloguing and digitizing old records, and both organizations have to date played a crucial role in providing evidence to the ministry to challenge copyright abuses. A grave resolve washed over Chanchhaya as he leaned over his desk to labour his final point: 'While these musicians are still alive it is important to talk to them before the information dies with them.' We may have got off to a bad start, but Chanchhaya was indeed a kindred spirit, on the matter of preservation at least.

As we were talking about the importance of the association's work, students started drifting into the townhouse. A steady stream of notes began to fill the air around us, amplifying as more and more new arrivals set up keyboards and noodled on their guitars. Chanchhaya passed us an old Sisamouth songbook, which Oro and I examined with the zeal of a pair of archaeologists uncovering an ancient artefact. The yellowing pages were plastered with notes and illustrations of Sisamouth, and encased in a bright blue and yellow cover, splashed with 1960s Khmer fonts and design.

Vintage Sisamouth songbook.

Perhaps the sight of Sisamouth's face shifted something in Chanchhaya, because, as we thumbed through the pages, for the briefest moment in time, he opened up about his father: 'Early on in his career, my father was invited by the Queen [Kossamak] to perform at the Royal Palace's Chanchhaya pavilion alongside [singer] Sos Mat and [composer] Peou Sipho. He was so proud of this that I was named after that temple. Only the best people were invited to play there.'

'When did you become aware your father was famous?' I asked.

'I was around ten years old, I think,' Chanchhaya continued, eyes downcast, his balding head catching the harsh fluorescent light as he shifted around in his chair. 'He never sang in front of me, but I heard my relatives talking about his fame. We also had rhyming class at school and the teacher would talk about my father's lyrics.'

Sisamouth vehemently disapproved of his children following his path; instead, Chanchhaya told me he wanted his son to pursue a more stable career, like nursing. But growing up surrounded by musicians, and with music in his very genes, Chanchhaya could not deny the desire awoken by the discovery of his father's fame, and so started teaching himself to play music, much to Sisamouth's disapproval.

Chanchhaya was the first to admit that his talent did not rival his father's. However, by then a respected singer in his own right, I got the sense that rather than live in his father's shadow, Chanchhaya's life's work through the association and his own music had all been to honour his father, and nothing more.

Through the course of time and reflection, I grew to learn that Chanchhaya may have been, at times, unreasonable, dour, and even disagreeable, but he was also measured, fair and upfront about himself, his father and his family. And loyal – fiercely loyal to his father's memory, despite their differences. When

I eventually met his mother and listened to her story, I better understood her son's inherent sense of honour.

My short interview with Chanchhaya was over before it had even begun. In the months that followed, my translator, Sophorn, tried – and failed – on a number of occasions to read through our interview and secure Chanchhaya's permission to use it in the book. On every occasion, Chanchhaya would cut more and more words and change more and more text, sending the relentless Sophorn packing each time with a promise that he would approve the revised transcript when he next returned. But Sophorn had an unrivalled threshold for patience, and he possessed the stamina for Chanchhaya's game of cat and mouse, returning time after time for a signature on a dotted line which, sadly, never came.

On 17 December 2014 the Sisamouth family received the approval and empowerment from Prime Minister Hun Sen to exercise management rights over seventy-three of the songs they'd submitted. It was an unprecedented victory, not just for the Sisamouth family and the association, but offered hope for many other surviving families living in abject poverty, without rights to their deceased family member's music. I was elated when I heard the news, but just a month later, on 20 January 2015, I received word that Chanchhaya had died. Sophorn had turned up to an appointment with Chanchhaya in the hope of finalizing the transcript – but was shocked to discover Chanchhaya's corpse laid out on the association's floor; his body still warm. Earlier that morning he'd fallen, hit his head on the bathroom floor and died on impact. Chanchhaya was just fifty-eight years old.

Messages of respect poured in from around the globe for his life's work preserving his father's musical legacy. Articles were written and the funeral was rammed. I was shocked and sad to learn of his passing, particularly in light of the family having only recently received their long-awaited victory. I hoped that in spite of his early demise, December's win had been great enough that Chanchhaya could die happy. I thought of his mother, and how losing her only remaining son would affect her. I knew after first meeting Chanchhaya that the only person who could give me the full story on Sisamouth would be her. So, a month after my interview with her son, I met Sisamouth's widow in the wilds of Stung Treng. She was an entirely different kettle of fish altogether.

By the time plans had been made and bags packed for the border, I'd amassed a small entourage of skilled friends and Sisamouth fans. I brought with me not one but two translators: Sophorn and Oro, as well as a French photographer called Martin Jay who had a calm, conscientious disposition and a pencil-thin moustache that lent him a look of the Great Gatsby. Together we made the bumpy ten-hour journey north along the partially flooded National Highway 7, arriving at the Cambodia–Laos border town of Stung Treng the day before our scheduled interview. While Sophorn and I settled into our basic, deserted guesthouse, the intrepid Oro was champing at the bit to meet the wife of his hero. As soon as the bags had been dropped off he took Martin wandering around the neighbourhood and spent the late afternoon chatting to Sisamouth's widow, Keo Thorng Gnut, outside her house. He came back beaming dreamily; from what he told me, she had been only too happy to oblige a man in his element.

The following morning we rose early to walk the quiet streets across town, retracing Oro and Martin's steps. Stung Treng's centre was rubbish-strewn, unkept and desolate, filling me with the same groundless uneasy feeling that found me in every border town in Cambodia – my first being Koh Kong in 2012 – where a seedy undercurrent polluted the air.

Stung Treng lies at the confluence of the San, Kong and Mekong rivers, its placid red waters a transit highway for goods coming in from Laos to the north and Phnom Penh to the south.

The 'River of Reeds', as the city is known to the Khmer, or 'City of Melons', as it is known to the Laotians, Stung Treng has passed hands between Cambodia, France and Laos for centuries. Perhaps it is this transience and the recent civil war that has infected Stung Treng's capital and stymied progress for its largely impoverished residents. For it felt to me like a place of untapped tourist potential, given its geography and the wider province's abundance of natural beauty and resources. Its surrounding countryside is the gateway to adventure tourism – everything from kayaking through flooded forests to mountain biking down the Ho Chi Minh trail. There are waterfalls to hike to, jungles to trek and endangered species to track down. But the city mainly lives off its port trade, fishing and silk-weaving industries. In the city's centre the corrugated iron covering of the central market shelters dark muddy pathways filled with ramshackle stalls selling silks and foods I'd never seen before, the vendors wearing the floral pyjama uniform of the working-class Khmer woman. But away from the bleak city centre, the roads and houses grow more charming and timeless with every step.

Sisamouth's widow, Keo Thorng Gnut, lives in a traditional wooden house on stilts that had been home to her and Sinn Sisamouth in the early days of their marriage. From atop the balcony, she rose to greet us, and welcomed us in with a brief tour of her home.

As I scanned the usual stock photos of Cambodian royals that adorn the doorways of her generation, a photograph of Gnut bowing to Prime Minister Hun Sen caught my eye. It held pride of place over the door, and I was instantly transported back to my late grandmother's bathroom where a similar photo of her holding a plastic British flag and greeting Prince Charles, probably giving him an earful by the look on her face, hung. The tightly cropped hair and dumpy stature my grandmother shared with Gnut worked only to familiarize her to me. She shared her son

Chanchhaya's serious nature but in rare moments she revealed a smile that had the effect of being both automatic on her lips yet dazzlingly warm from behind her thin-rimmed eye glasses.

In the sparse main room of her timber house there was a bed surrounded by a medical dressing screen, and old family photographs collecting dust on a wooden dresser. Off to the side, her tiny kitchen was sooty from the smoke of endless days spent cooking on a coal-powered oven. There was great charm to its timeless simplicity. Some aged utensils and scorched pots hung on charred walls above the counter top, and a perfect white- and purple-splattered aubergine lay on the counter. Illuminated against the blackened surround, it almost sparkled, as if the artist Jackson Pollock had flicked a brightly soaked paint brush at it. Above, a glass-less window opened out onto a small plot of land that was being cleared of bamboo by a man Gnut would later cook lunch for in return for his labours. Following my gaze she remarked in a reserved, Khmer voice that the land had recently flooded, bringing all the snakes out of hiding, each clinging to life on the tall bamboo.

'She is clearing the land to make way for flowers that her daughter can sell at the market,' Oro interjected softly. If I hadn't completely realized we were out of Phnom Penh, I did now.

We set up our gear on a wooden table on the balcony and Gnut sat neatly on a camp bed and began to answer the tumbling myriad questions I had for her. It was a beautiful spot, full of birdsong and absent of vehicles and the noises of modern life (save for the occasional click of Martin's camera and my furious keyboard-tapping). I wondered if the place had changed much since Gnut was born there some seventy-five years earlier to her Khmer mother, Doung Kham (translation: Golden Kham) and her part-Laotian father, Keo Sut (translation: Pure White). With Laos less than five kilometres away, Gnut's mixed heritage was typical of the residents of Stung Treng. Its influence could be seen in the woven Laotian skirts called *sinhs* – a tighter version of the traditional Cambodian *sampot* – that dotted the cityscapes and market vistas of the town. They were a welcome splash of elegance in a sea of floral pyjamas.

L–r: Sophorn, Oro, Dee, Gnut.

Gnut's Laotian grandmother had woven these skirts since Stung Treng came under the administration of the French protectorate. She was a traditionalist, Gnut told me, who held great sway over the family and didn't see the sense in sending Gnut to school. Instead, she wanted her granddaughter to walk in her footsteps and follow the path of a silk weaver – a noble profession in a province revered for its silk production. So Gnut finished her studies at the age of thirteen and acquired a skill which, unbeknownst at the time, would save her life (and her children's lives) some twenty years later.

Sisamouth too was of mixed Laotian and Khmer heritage on his mother's side; his father, Sinn Leang, was Chinese. A high-ranking soldier in the 'Tea Hean Chean Krohom' (the 'Red Foot Army') – named after the red trousers they wore and not to be confused with the Khmer Rouge. When Sinn Leang's army career ended with Cambodia's declaration of independence in 1953, he went to work for a prison in Battambang where his brother was the governor. Gnut began to share her knowledge of Sisamouth's formulative years – and as she spoke, I gazed out to see the Stung Treng of their childhood, brought back to life: 'Sisamouth was the youngest of four children. He was born in *cheah*, the seventh month of the Khmer calendar; it's between mid-July and mid-August, 1935,' she told me. (Traditionally the Khmer calendar is a variant of the Chinese lunar calendar that differs from the more globally popular Gregorian calendar. It's not common to celebrate birthdays in Cambodia, so the date of a person's birth can easily be forgotten.) 'From what I know,' Gnut continued, 'Sisamouth was a good son, a quiet son; he did housework and helped his parents with home improvements. He built trays of bamboo for planting vegetables and fermenting fish to make *prahok* [the Cambodian cooking paste made from fermented fish]. At night, he would take his step sisters to catch fish by the bridge.'

Sisamouth's father, Sinn Leang, died young, and, when his mother remarried, Sisamouth – an avid learner – didn't want to make waves with his new stepfather, so he fished at night and would go to market the next day to sell the fish in exchange for the money to buy school books. Sisamouth's uncle shared his nephew's passion for traditional music, and alongside Sisamouth's school studies (he later passed his certificate at Stung Treng Secondary), opened up the world of music to a ten-year-old Sisamouth. He taught him how to play the *tro* and the mandolin – an instrument that remained by Sisamouth's side, upon which he wrote many, many songs, throughout his life. A keen scholar from a struggling family, Sisamouth followed the route of many Cambodian boys in his predicament, turning to the monkhood to become what Cambodians call a 'pagoda boy'. To this day, many Cambodian families send their teenage boys to the temple to train. It's a rite of passage for almost all boys aged between sixteen and twenty years old, and brings great merit to their parents. In exchange for food and free education, the boys will take care of the monks and learn the ways of Buddha. Some will continue with a career in the monastic order making the step from *sāmaṇera* (novice) to *bhikkhu* (ordained monk), but most will return to their families within a year.

Life at the pagoda had a great impact on Sisamouth, and alongside the values his parents instilled, temple life enhanced his already calm nature and good intentions. Everywhere I went in search of Sisamouth, I was met with these same sentiments. Universally kind, resolutely polite and well mannered, Sinn Sisamouth gravitated towards like-minded, serene souls. He believed in karma; he respected people, no matter who they were, no matter their background or position. In all my travels, in all my conversations, no one ever had a bad word to say about him.

The temple gave Sisamouth not only a code for living, but his Buddhist language lessons armed him with the knowledge he would come to use later in his career. When struggling to find the perfect word to express how he felt in Khmer, French, Chinese or Thai, he would turn to the ancient Buddhist language, Pāli. Writing the occasional lyric in Pāli only served to elevate his songwriting kudos to an incontestable status among his fans.

It was in the temple that he learned to sing. But, in the end, though he prospered greatly from his time there, Sisamouth didn't ordain in the monkhood. Instead, he went to Phnom Penh to study medicine in the early 1950s, and spent his nights moonlighting as a party singer, actively pursuing his love of music and secretly searching for his big break – much to the disapproval of his parents when they unexpectedly heard his name read aloud on the radio one day.

Sisamouth and Gnut were wed in an arranged marriage in 1955, when he was twenty years old and she was seventeen. Though

Gnut had been informed of the marriage plans by her parents seven years prior, her wedding day was the first time she actually met Sisamouth. 'At that time, you could not refuse a proposal,' she told me sternly, her eyes narrowing.

Not long after the marriage, Sisamouth accepted a new nursing post at the Preah Ket Mealea hospital in Phnom Penh and the couple made the move to the big city. A shy, country girl, Gnut didn't warm to city life, but in Phnom Penh Sisamouth had found his place in the world. Following his return to the capital in 1955, this time with Gnut, the couple brought their first child into the world, a daughter called Yuttana, and Sisamouth caught his first real music break.

In the city he would come to call home, Sinn Sisamouth spent his days working at the hospital and from time to time he spent his nights performing at the Kbal Thnal nightclub, dazzling the patrons with his gifted voice. Word of his agile range and silvery, rich voice travelled and, eventually, through the connections he made at the club and a lot of graft, talent and determination, Sisamouth won an invitation to join the Radiodiffusion Nationale Khmère (RNK) band, then in its infancy and led by the famous composer Peou Sipho. Sisamouth would sing love duets, or *'les belles chansons d'amour'* as they were billed on the programme, with an up and coming fourteen-year-old Sieng Dy, backed by the RNK radio band. He became a featured singer, regularly performing on the radio from the mid-1950s onwards.

With this appointment, his popularity grew and attracted the attention of the Royal Palace where, soon after, he was invited to join the palace musical troupe. By now Sisamouth was mastering not only the sweeping, orchestral love ballads popular on RNK radio in the late 1950s and early 1960s, but also the more traditional Khmer music favoured in palace ceremonies and performances by Queen Kossamak's crowning achievement, the Royal Ballet.

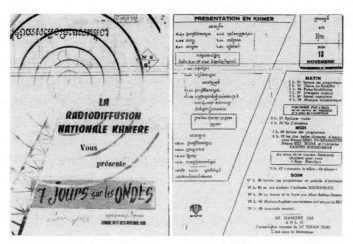

Cover (left) and page (right) from 1950s RNK Radio programmes.

Sihanouk's mother Queen Kossamak was a person of the people, universally loved by the Khmer, and remembered fondly as a moral compass and example to all. When Sihanouk abdicated the throne in 1955, his mother was tasked with 'symbolizing the monarchy' or, as Sihanouk biographer Milton Osborne put it: 'Sihanouk continued to be king in all but name, and his formidable mother, Queen Kossamak, living in the Royal Palace, reinforced all that was traditional, special, even quasi-divine about the concept of monarchy in Cambodia.' Coined the 'Supreme Guardian' by the people, she reinvigorated Cambodia's Royal Ballet, creating new dance forms like apsara in the 1940s. Inspired by the ancient celestial beings of the same name that adorn Cambodia's ancient temples, the dance has become a cultural icon of Khmer art, and the heart of Cambodia's Royal Ballet.

Outside the arts, Queen Kossamak took a keen interest in the health and wellbeing of all people, in particular monks and medics, and held sway over the board of the hospital where Sinn Sisamouth worked. When the lyrical content of a song Sisamouth sang at Kbal Thnal nightclub offended an influential patron, Sisamouth found himself thereafter swiftly demoted at the hospital, and sent to work on the leprosy ward. However, when Queen Kossamak heard of the demotion she arranged for his immediate transfer from the Preah Ket Mealea hospital to the Preah Ang Doung hospital where he worked for a short time before leaving nursing for good to focus solely on the thing he loved most: music.

In the late 1950s Sisamouth split his time between RNK radio and the palace music ensemble. When he sang for courtly ceremonies, religious festivals and Royal Ballet performances throughout the kingdom, Gnut was often there to support him. He had terrible stage fright that only worsened through the years. In front of large crowds Sisamouth's anxiety took hold and his mind often went blank, so he installed someone in the wings to mouth his lines to him in emergencies. I looked down to see Oro, Martin and Sophorn scattered like cross-legged disciples on the ground before Gnut, enraptured as she regaled us with stories of Sisamouth performing, also cross-legged, with the palace orchestra. A smile unfurled on Oro's lips as she described Sisamouth dressed in a crisp white jacket with a mandarin collar singing against a backdrop of ancient stone gopuras. I'd seen this scene myself in old photographs. He seemed to invoke the divine as all around, apsara dancers spun slowly in their brocade and finery.

With Queen Kossamak's endorsement, within the bosom of the palace Sisamouth blossomed. The writers Peou Sipho and Mer Bun were close friends from the beginning, as were the singers Mao Sareth, Keo Sokha and Sieng Dy, and his Royal Palace compatriot Sos Mat. As Sisamouth's fame grew and his schedule intensified, he had little time for family and little in the way of a social life outside of his work. Unsurprisingly, it took a toll on family life. Stalwart in his habits, routines and work ethic, every morning when Sisamouth arose, he'd go to the bathroom and start the day lifting weights and performing a vigorous regime of vocal exercises. He had a studio within a room in his house which he used for writing, and was often holed up for hours with Khmer, Sanskrit and Pāli dictionaries for lyrical inspiration. In fact, Gnut told me the only times he emerged from that room were for meals or studio jobs, to receive any relatives or visitors, or at weekends when he would take his children out to eat. Reserved in manner, Sisamouth was known to be economic with his words and conversation. He was careful of what he ate, and he never drank alcohol or smoked. Happily, the sacrifices he made to keep his voice in fine fettle did not alienate his peers – in fact, his rigid regimen had the effect of garnering only more respect from his fellows.

Nineteen sixty-two, the year rock 'n' roll came to Cambodia, was a turning point for Sisamouth. His catapult to stardom – helped by a genre change and generational shift from Johnny Mathis-style crooning to a new mix of Everley Brothers cool and Paul Anka charm – was inspired by one man, the man who made 1962 what it was: the aforementioned godfather of the Cambodian twist, Chum Kem. Sisamouth had an intuitive ability to seek out and exploit popularity. He saw the ground his Kbal Thnal singing partner Kem was opening up with the twist and, seizing this, began shaking off his traditional palace and French-influenced roots and with his sublime gift for vocal agility began branching out into cha-cha-cha rhythms and genres like Latin, rumba, bossa nova and rock 'n' roll.

The following year, Sin Sisamouth took the country by storm with his first big hit. The song that kickstarted his rocket ascent to nationwide fame was a slow tempo cover of Ary Barroso's 1939 samba classic, 'Aquarela do Brasil', covered earlier in 1963 by Cambodia's favourite Canadian crooner Paul Anka. When it was time for Sisamouth to take on the song, he renamed his contrafactum, 'Champa Battambang' ('The Flower of Battambang').

Up until then Sisamouth had been a rising star, popular with imperialists, the monarchy and patrons of the Kbal Thnal night-club. But 'Champa Battambang' was a watershed moment. With its euphonious melody, modern calypso beat and Khmer under-tones – a cowbell and a violin – it was pleasing to a broad ear. However, it was the song's romantic lyrics about love and longing and the 'Flower of Battambang' – a metaphor for the woman at the centre of the song – that really captured the nation. Released on the Wat-Phnom label it has, over time – along with its singer – become deeply embedded within modern Khmer culture. Passed down through the generations, it seems to recreate a certain nostalgia with each new listener, and also inspired the production of the 2018 feature film demonstrating just that, called *In the life of Music* by Cambodian filmmakers Caylee So and Sok Visal.

With the release of 'Champa Battambang' Sisamouth was becoming as renowned for his songwriting as his honey-sweet voice and staggering vocal control, and by the mid-1960s he was such a prolific songwriter that Gnut remembers he'd order noodles at a restaurant, then set to writing the lyrics and notes of a new song. By the time the steaming noodles arrived at the table five minutes later, he would have finished both the notation and the lyrics. Sisamouth drew inspiration from his own life and from his travels in Cambodia, Hong Kong and France accompanying Prince Sihanouk for ceremonial performances. He'd develop the stories his fans told him, and base songs on tales overheard in restaurants or cafés. His songs were frequently deeply sentimental and full of nostalgia for places he'd been, celebrating love's great joys as well as its heartache and longing. He was a multilinguist and his repertoire fast became as diverse as the languages he could sing in. If he wasn't writing his own music at the dinner table, he would be transcribing whatever song was playing on the restaurant's wireless. Songs like his 1964 doo wop cover of American vocal band, the Cascades' 'Rhythm of the Rain'. Music, for Sisamouth, was all consuming, so much so that he had a hard time stepping outside of his work and into the rhythms of everyday life. By the time Gnut had bore him a fourth child and she'd turned thirty years old, the pressure from his work and the admiration from other females was too much for her to bear. 'I was a singer's wife,' she told me dolefully. 'I had to be calm. It was an arranged marriage . . . and not a happy one.'

In 1968 Gnut took her children and what remained of her dignity, left Sisamouth and moved to a Buddhist monastery where she worked for the monks and studied the teachings of Buddha. Cambodian Buddhists have differing views on divorce and remarriage but, for the most part, divorce, particularly on the part of the woman, is a shameful affair. For women who came from traditional religious families like Gnut's, entering the monastic order after a divorce was often a choice for meritorious gain, both for their next life and those of their family members. It's a choice that reinforces aspects of the *chbab srey* law for women and the societal pressures that condemn divorce.

Though Sisamouth had little time outside his busy schedule for affairs of the heart, he had allegedly begun an affair with a Royal Ballet dancer before he and Gnut split. Nevertheless, Sisamouth was sad about the breakdown of his family and poured his heart into the song 'Oudom Dueng Chet' (loosely translated, 'My Love'). He remained a loving – if not entirely present – father to his children.

Despite his fame Sinn Sisamouth was not a rich man. For someone whose talents were so in demand he earned a moderate income. Bootlegging was as rife then as it is now, and documentation of accreditations was never a strong point of the Cambodian music industry, leaving copyright vulnerable, particularly for someone as busy and prolific as Sisamouth. Still, he earned enough for the family to live in a big house Sisamouth named *Soth Prad* ('Every Day is Good'), south of Phnom Penh's busy Tuol Tom Poung Market. Before the split Gnut remembered the house was always full of visiting musicians coming and going, and when Sisamouth tired of the distractions, he'd retreat to his small place in the seaside town of Kep in southern Cambodia to write. While he was not a materialistic man, he did have one vice, and that was his cars, which he loved to load up with instuments and escape to his place by the sea. He eventually traded up his beloved VW Bug for a more sophisticated Mercedes 220D, which was his most prized possession.

From the mid-1960s Sisamouth had begun creating – and featured on more and more – soundtracks for Khmer movies, which helped maintain his fame and retain his monopoly on the industry: films such as *Thavary Meas Bong* (*Thavary My Love*), starring some of the most popular stars of the time – actors Kong Sam Oeun and Vichara Dany – and *Tep Sodachan* with Saksi Sbong in the lead role of a cursed angel forced to live with a human as punishment. Both were filmed in 1968 and received wide acclaim that has endured to this day. And, it was not only Khmer movies, in their multitude, that Sisamouth produced soundtracks for. Later, as the civil war tightened its grip on the movie industry and plenty of film business moved to Thailand, Sisamouth, already talented at jumping on new trends, employed his multilingual skills and moved where the money was, recording songs in Thai, Chinese and Vietnamese. His favourite studio was a studio called Capitol, in Hong Kong. He was a shrewd businessman, and a bright and opportunistic chameleon, and that is how he stayed at the top of his game for so long.

In 1967 he still dominated the Cambodian music scene, having spent a number of years duetting with the likes of female singers Mao Sareth, Huoy Meas on bolero classics like 'Mother-in-Law', and Pen Ran – Ran whooping and hollering comic call and responses on tracks like 'New Car'. But a decade into his career, Sinn Sisamouth began working with the young Battambang

Sinn Sisamouth record sleeve.

phenomenon, Ros Sereysothea. Cambodia's king and queen of Khmer pop were crowned.

By the age of thirty-two he started losing his hair, and in the latter part of the 1960s Sisamouth's stage fright worsened, so he stopped singing in the nightclubs altogether. The versatility and confidence to adapt his stage presence for a set with an ever-increasing collection of musical genres proved impossible for Sisamouth. He would always be a crooner at heart, most at home performing in the manner of Sinatra and those of his ilk; he was far too shy and serious to jig around the stage to the hand jive. His mammoth back catalogue and the speed in which he wrote and recorded also meant that he struggled to remember lyrics. This was the time of the prompt holding a lyric sheet behind the stage curtain to whisper upcoming lines to Sisamouth out front (as recalled by Sereysothea's sister Saboeun). Naturally shy and personable, Sisamouth's rare performances were, by then, confined to the odd special occasion like Sihanouk's Congress Day celebrations. Instead, he put all his energy into recording, and the results are evident in his catalogue of mid- to late-1960s releases; the apex of his career.

As Sisamouth was riding the wave of success, in Cambodia the rumblings of civil unrest were gaining motion, readying for the political maelstrom to come. Convinced that the communists – specifically, the People's Republic of China (PRC) – would one day dominate Asia, Prince Sihanouk severed diplomatic relations with the USA in 1965, thus planting a time bomb on his position of neutrality and, ultimately, his power in Cambodia. A deal was struck with the People's Republic of China to allow the People's Army of Vietnam (PAVN) and Viet Cong troops to deploy and base themselves and their activities in Cambodia's eastern border regions, and, later, to use Sihanoukville's port to transport arms to the PAVN and Viet Cong bases. These moves to formalize an agreement expanded new routes for the Ho Chi Minh trail, developing what became known as the 'Sihanouk trail', bringing Cambodia's neutrality into question. Ultimately, Sihanouk's tactics to keep the Vietnamese war out of Cambodia and keep both the US and Vietnam onside failed. Antagonized, America answered with the escalation of a bombing campaign that would annihilate civilian villages and help drive swathes of the peasantry (the god-king's most loyal subjects) into the hands of the Khmer Rouge and other rebel factions.

At a grassroots level, Sihanouk was increasingly attacked on all fronts by guerrilla forces. In the blue corner were the anti-communist, anti-monarchy Khmer Serei and the US-backed Kansaing Sar 'White Scarves' – both trained by the US military and partly financed by the CIA – and in the red corner, the Maoist, China- and North Vietnam-backed Khmer Rouge, whom

Norodom Sihanouk severely underestimated. The prince played them all – the guerrillas, the North Vietnamese, the Western and Eastern superpowers – like pawns in a game of chess, not realizing until later (when the ground was swept from beneath his feet) that he'd really lost the game with the decision to switch sides in 1965.

Sihanouk had begun losing favour with the bourgeoisie, city intellectuals and big business in Cambodia. The Chinese-Khmer merchants who monopolized the economy wanted a return of American aid to plump up their fortunes. The rice makers and government – already crippled by a rice revenue loss from the Vietnam War – wanted an end to the smuggling and peasant uprisings of the mid to late 1960s. The right dominated the 1966 elections, and Sihanouk's tactic to squash his leftist opponents simply opened up seats to more of his critics. They had little patience for Sihanouk's blind eye strategy when it came to North Vietnam, and a leadership style they deemed autocratic. The city intellectuals disdained their king for his playboy lifestyle, and serious left-leaning students disliked their leader's increasing focus on his own artistic pursuits.

But, for Cambodia's music, the king's support paved the way for a golden decade and, by and large, he was still unquestionably popular with the majority of his deeply monarchist subjects, many of whom lived in the countryside. Yet, even here, within his most loyal fan base, Sihanouk biographer Milton Osborne argued Sihanouk's decadent exploits were losing him favour. Frequent countryside screenings of Sihanouk-directed feature films – depicting high-society life – served as a potent propaganda weapon for those succeeding in convincing the peasantry of the evils of the monarchy and the bourgeoisie.

All Sihanouk critics wanted an end to any form of corruption – of which they weren't personally benefiting from – which the head of state left systematically unchallenged. The shrewd statesman who had masterfully charmed the media and astutely manoeuvred his political pawns in 1953 was now losing a grip on his beloved kingdom. Much of Sihanouk's legacy is based on his political adroitness and mastery of the balancing act – yet, after his early wonder years, he was fast losing his finesse.

All the while, Cambodia's military was in ascendance. Sihanouk's longstanding ally, Marshall Lon Nol, rose in the ranks of the colonial army to governor of Cambodia's north-eastern province Kratie before entering government. His party – the right-wing, monarchist, pro-independence, Khmer Renovation Party – had been instrumental in the formation of Sihanouk's Sangkum party in 1955. Lon later bounced around a number of the highest positions in the cabinet, from defence and military to the premiership, to retirement and back again; his popularity as fragile and wavering as his health. A timid spokesperson and a mediocre career politician, the marshall was not remembered for his intelligence or courage. His closest ally on the other hand, was an altogether more calculating character. Highly ambitious and politically ruthless, Chariya's father, Brigadier General Sirik Matak, could charm both the high society and political worlds he straddled. Along with Lon Nol, he stoked the fires of anti-Vietnamese sentiment that culminated in Cambodia's Vietnamese population sheltering in churches and schools for fear of reprisal. Together, and with Sihanouk's gaze elsewhere, Matak and Nol set in motion a series of plays that would eventually topple a 1,168-year-old Khmer dynasty and replace it with a republic.

Against a backdrop of violence, peasant rebellions, military threats and anti-Vietnamese demonstrations, Matak moved to weaken the absent head of state. He doggedly challenged Sihanouk's economic policies, reactivated a civil service and reintroduced military pressure to the north-eastern provinces where the Viet Cong was most dense – all against Sihanouk's wishes. From the summer of 1969 Lon and Sirik started calling in their chits among Sihanouk's former domestic and international enemies, and by March of the following year they moved to strike, Matak and his henchmen allegedly coercing his weaker but more senior US-backed partner Lon Nol into signing the necessary paperwork, supposedly at gunpoint.

The following day, 18 March 1970, with the army posted around the capital, the assembly gathered to invoke Article 122 of the constitution, ousting Sihanouk from power in a bloodless coup. Upon hearing this in Moscow the now former head of state immediately fled to China to mount a counterattack, which failed to win back his position but would result in recruiting tens of thousands to the side he vengefully placed his support with, the Chinese-backed Khmer Rouge.

The loss of his 'king' – as Sihanouk remained in name to his supporters long after he abdicated the throne – had a profound effect on Sisamouth. He was a staunch royalist, loyal to Sihanouk, so he boycotted the new regime and Lon Nol's plans to propagandize society. But Sisamouth's actions came at a price. His refusal to play ball cost him work and he was temporarily ostracized from making a living. 'They asked him to sing a song to insult the king, but he refused. His children were brought up to never insult the king, so how could he?' Gnut asked rhetorically.

Fortunately for Sisamouth he had nursing to fall back on, so from 1970 to 1971 he returned to his first profession – but his salary was low and there was a large clef-shaped hole in his heart. He longed to play music again, and it soon became intolerable. Eventually Sisamouth caved in and agreed to Lon Nol's demands in exchange for his return to the industry. The loyalists, of course, spurned him; they couldn't understand how he could work with the 'king' and now insult him. Sisamouth responded, 'What else *can* I do?'

I did eventually track down the lyrics contained within the

song Gnut talked of – 'The King Sold the Land to the Viet Cong' – which included ultranationalist digs at Sihanouk, questioning his loyalty to his country and ability to stand up to the likes of Mao Tse-tung and the Viet Cong. Its scathing lyrics accuse the head of state of selling Cambodia out to the Viet Cong and other neighbouring countries.

Caught between a rock and a hard place, the bargain Sisamouth struck with the regime did recover his career – and while Samouth's moral compass no doubt paid a price for his betrayal, he'd held out in defiance longer than most. He returned not to his trademark suit but to military garb and the rank of lieutenant in Lon Nol's Khmer Republic – but also to the studio, creating the music he loved.

During the early to mid-1970s he recorded mostly at the famous Van Chann Studios, playing his mandolin bare-chested, dripping with sweat in the hot live room under the watchful eye of producer Voy Ho who was, at the time, at the forefront of Cambodian sound. Though separated, Gnut was still mother to Sisamouth's children, and he still loved her Laotian cooking that reminded him of his mother's. From time to time she would cook for his musicians outside Van Chann's studio; the men topless in their combats, the women, by then, trading their 1960s beehives for relaxed, 1970s hippy locks, Gnut crouching over hot coals stirring soup for hungry players. As she talked, I felt myself a ghost meandering through the laughing, chattering crowds of Cambodia's own Motown machine.

As Sisamouth belatedly arrived in the new decade, he thrust himself head first into the sounds of 1970s Cambodia – psychedelia, jerk and go-go dance songs like 'A Go-Go', with its squalling, Sonics-like guitar sound. Having established himself as a relinquished national treasure, Sisamouth had to compete with the *yé-yé* groups and international bands for the teenage market. Artists like the Drakkar band, Yol Aularong and Pou Vannary were coming to define the new era, injecting a heavy dose of free-flowing abandon to the rock 'n' roll and flower pop sweeping the country. And, just as Samouth had done with Chum Kem, he brought his silky voice and fan base to the scene the younger 1970s artists were creating, and with a deft hand turned out a prolific amount of music in 1972 and 1973. Songs like 'Don't Be Mean', with its catchy '*Na-na-na-na-na*' lyric so often repeated at random by my Cambodian friends – and 'I Love Petite Women', a caterwaul of overdriven wandering guitars, high-pitched organ and congas. In addition to his own writing, Sisamouth covered everything from Vietnamese to Thai to American to English songs during the period, including his interpretations of songs written by the Beatles ('Hey Jude'), Procol Harum ('A Whiter Shade of Pale') and the Archies ('Sugar, Sugar') which have become staples of his back catalogue. Even the most upbeat of Western songs could be recycled and turned into tragic love stories by Samouth's hand. While some question the integrity of Sisamouth's output in the 1970s, as an artist and a chameleon, his boundless experimentation produced a plethora of different sounds and styles in those few short years, mostly for just two labels: Heng Heng and Chanchhaya.

As the hits rolled in throughout the early to mid-1970s, Sisamouth was rewarded with a promotion in rank from lieutenant to captain. His role was to carry out the occasional administerial or ad hoc military duty, but chiefly his orders were to use his influence to promote Lon Nol's regime and encourage the country to stop fighting, through his lyrics. A pacifist and royalist at heart, Sisamouth still maintained his links with the palace, continuing to work with their ensemble, according to Gnut. In 1973 he was offered a job in Thailand with a car and a villa for his estranged wife and their children – a chance to flee the war and make a name for himself in Thailand – but, loyal to the core, he refused the offer – a decision Gnut bitterly regrets: 'He couldn't live without all of his family and some of the relatives wanted to stay in Cambodia, so he decided not to go. If he *had* gone there, just think: he could have survived the Khmer Rouge.'

Sisamouth stayed in Phnom Penh with his relatives to battle out the insecure industry he still led. While Phnom Penh's live music scene was suffering a near constant shutdown from the encroaching war and ever more frequent airstrikes, the music industry continued to function fine in studios and on the airwaves, evermore shaped by the sound of American military radio from Vietnam. Some of Samouth's ventures into flower pop and rock 'n' roll, and his hit covers of the Animals' 'House of the Rising Sun' and Santana's 'Black Magic Woman', provided the city – its civilians and refugees – with respite from the encroaching war. While he still wrote prolifically for himself, Samouth's partnership with the producer and writer Voy Ho grew ever closer during this time, and together they churned out more songs than Voy Ho did for any of his other musical partners. It was the golden age for Voy Ho and Van Chann Productions, but sadly, it was not to last.

When the Khmer Rouge took over and evacuated Phnom Penh in April 1975 Sisamouth and Gnut were apart. Just before the city fell, when it was no longer possible to follow his military orders to write and record music, Sisamouth took up position to defend the Royal Palace and its inhabitants – including his beloved Queen Kossamak – from the encroaching Khmer Rouge. Gnut and the children were at the *Soth Prad* house, where Sisamouth stored his paperwork, including his identity card. He'd left it there alongside the paperwork he would usually leave at home on any given day ... except 17 April 1975 wasn't any other day, as Gnut would attest, recounting those final hours to me: 'On the last night [16 April 1975], Sinn Sisamouth was guarding the front entrance to the Royal Palace. Sisamouth didn't go with the rest of our family, he went with a royal dancer to Wat Kean Svay [in Kandal province]. My mother-in-law was with them and she told me this later.

'My children, though almost all grown, were with me. We walked by the river and we saw dead bodies. The Khmer Rouge checked my baggage on the way; they saw my silk skirts, in seven colours for the seven days of the week, the same colours that Sinn Sisamouth dressed in to go to the Royal Palace.' Gnut was referring to the Cambodian ritual of wearing traditional Cambodian silk harem pants, *sampots*, a tradition which dates back to the Funan Empire. Each *sampot* has a colour corresponding to the planet that day of the week is said to represent in character – to abide by this ritual brings the wearer good fortune and prosperity. When a Khmer Rouge soldier inspected Gnut's bag and came across the silk *sampots*, he automatically assumed that Gnut was a silk weaver, which Gnut went along with, confident her teenage training would come to the fore should she need to prove it. She knew full well that if that soldier knew her true identity – as the wife of a captain of the Lon Nol regime and a singer of Westernized pop music to boot – she and their children would have been in grave danger.

The first place they lived was Kaoh Thum in Kandal province in the south-east, before the family was granted a transfer north to Battambang. A dull calm swept over Gnut as she looked out into the distance and said, 'In Kaoh Thum I ate only corn for seven months. People said there was much rice in Battambang, but when we got to Battambang I discovered that there was only one can of rice to feed ten people a day, and that is why I lost my son, Vantha. He was just nineteen, and he died of oedema. After Vantha died, I sold my seven silk skirts for food to save my three other children. And that is how we survived.'

After the genocide, Gnut returned to Stung Treng to find that her marital home had been taken over by a Khmer Rouge chief. Gnut managed to appeal to the chief's humanity in a time when currency was obsolete and squatting was commonplace – her only currency was emotion and words. She argued that the house had sentimental value to her. There were plenty of other empty buildings and so, eventually, she won over the chief and he agreed to give her back her home. She has lived a life of poverty there ever since. True to her traditional values, she never remarried.

As for Sisamouth, Gnut doesn't know exactly what happened to him beyond her mother-in-law's account of the evacuation. Gnut never received any news from her husband and never said anything because she was afraid that the Khmer Rouge would kill him if she did. The disappearance and demise of Sinn Sisamouth – like much of his life – remain a mystery. Alleged lovers and love children have come out of the woodwork since his death, with varying degrees of authenticity. Many musicians I spoke to claimed to have a story about Sisamouth or have written a song for the Master . . . again, I suspect not all of them truthful. But who am I to judge people who have been through so much? Perhaps a little white lie to bring some magic and meaning to a life lost is not such a sin when life is torn in two by war and genocide?

Some of Sinn Sisamouth's fans say he wrote a song a day; some say five a day. Some say he wrote 1,000 or 2,000 songs – even as many as 10,000 – in the course of his life. Wikipedia currently lists 1,200 of them. Some say he liked watching French movies, eating Laotian food, Chinese noodles and *bobor* (chicken porridge). Some say he didn't eat certain things; some say he ate everything. Some say he was quiet; some say he loved to tell jokes and make people laugh. As time went on it seemed the more information I uncovered, the less I categorically knew. However, the one thing I am certain of is that Sisamouth was a chameleon who could shapeshift into any number of guises; and it was his adaptability and talent that helped him survive more years in Cambodia's music industry than any other famous musician. Yet no one of his stature could have survived the Khmer Rouge and what was to come.

There are a number of reports from reliable sources that say he disappeared in the days after the evacuation, on National Road 1 by the Champa Pagoda, some fifteen kilometres from Phnom Penh. Some say he was turned back by cadres on the road from Phnom Penh; some say he was killed elsewhere in Kandal province; others mention Battambang, Siem Reap, Preah Vihear, Kampong Cham . . . the list goes on. Some believe he met his end in prison; some that he was tortured; some are convinced he was shot; some say his tongue was cut out before death. Some allege to have been imprisoned with Sisamouth during the genocide; and some say that shortly after the evacuation he was returning to Phnom Penh on the orders of Angkar, was accosted by cadres on the road and performed his dying wish – a song – before being shot at point-blank range. Sadly, as with the lives of so many of his peers, we'll never know the real story. When interviewed for John Pirozzi's film *Don't Think I've Forgotten* Sisamouth's son Chanchhaya put it best when he said, 'I've heard so many different stories about how my father died. I've heard thirty different ways he died, but how can a person die thirty times?'

Amid the unsolved mysteries and disputed facts of his life, Sisamouth, the legend, is very much alive and well in Cambodia today, known by all and loved by many. In a BBC radio special on Cambodian music the *Sunday Times* newspaper correspondent Jon Swain remembered a time some months after the Vietnamese had overthrown the Khmer Rouge, when Sisamouth's songs returned to the radio. He recalled, 'People's faces lit up when they heard his voice.' Even in death, he brought joy and pleasure to his people. In a *Phnom Penh Post* article from 1995 Moeun Chhean Nariddh wrote, 'He has been dead for nearly twenty years, but the songs of Sinn Sisamouth are still the soundtrack of the daily lives of the Khmer people.'

In the decades since Sisamouth's death, much has happened, many new singers have emerged, but Sisamouth remains undoubtedly the king of Khmer pop. Filmmakers are making movies about him, and yet it remains to be seen if we will ever know the definitive story to much of his extraordinary life, and death. But we do know that there was no other like him, nor will there ever be again. Sisamouth's output was phenomenal, his mark on Cambodian popular culture as unique as it is unrivalled.

As for Gnut, she had dedicated her life to her husband, and despite the separations has remained loyal to the end. From the indignity and loneliness of 'being a singer's wife' to her rags-to-riches-to-rags tale, life has not been kind to Gnut. She has, nevertheless, borne these trials and tribulations with poise and pride, and remained fair to Sisamouth in her account of him. An act of grace I was awed by more than once.

There was so much more I wanted to ask her, so much left unanswered, so much left unsaid. But the day was drawing to a close, Gnut was tired and a thunderstorm was gathering fast. Oro helped her down the wooden steps to the family corner shop where they went to wait out the storm with plenty of unabridged Khmer.

As for Sophorn, Martin and me, we crumpled, exhausted, onto a platform under the stilts of the house, our initial perfunctory

Clockwise from left: Dee, Gnut, Oro, Martin and Sophorn.

conversation muted by the deafening deluge. We watched the rain flash-flood the muddy ground, rapidly filling ceramic water butts as violent waterfalls cascaded out of the gutters, fat raindrops splitting on the sides of banisters.

Sisamouth had a knack for transporting the listener to faraway places and bringing nature to life. I knew a Sisamouth song called 'Under the Sound of Rain', and as I sat in a place where Sisamouth may have once sat, watching rain just like this, I felt the words more poignantly than ever before:

> *My love, turn around and look at me*
> *Listen to the thunder harmonizing with the rain*
> *A rhythmic pounding sound sings*
> *Narrating a story of nostalgia*
>
> *The rain continues to fall with the sound of water dripping*
> *They speak to one another while reminiscing*
> *They sing to soothe and comfort you, my love*
> *Falling melancholy as it touches the earth*
>
> *The rain falls hard soaking the ground*
> *I'm here embracing you in my arms*
> *Keeping you wrapped, every minute*
> *I would never want to disappoint you*
>
> *The sound of the rain mesmerizes*
> *Soothing us both*
> *Whispering to us, telling us*
> *That this love is our destiny*

For the best part of an hour the heavens opened violently, before finally the rain lightened enough for us to run down the street to a noodle house for some dinner. Before departing, Gnut offered to watch our bags for us, and handed us all plastic ponchos which she wouldn't take a dime for. It was a simple act of kindness, and one I thanked her for profusely when we returned to collect the bags and say our last goodbyes. Her smile made another rare appearance, but I was coming to learn that it was in action that her warmth burned brightest.

When we reached our guesthouse later that evening, our quiet dwelling from the previous night was long gone. Our empty floor now reeked of the damp escaping from the dozen or so cell-like rooms along the corridor. Each room was now open-doored and filled with men who looked like off-duty soldiers, their dark muscles clad in black vests and green combat trousers. An entire platoon was lounging on beds, five to a room, cheering and clamouring, playing cards and drinking beer. Testosterone laced the atmosphere, and our dank little guesthouse now felt more like a prison than a hotel. Frightened, we scuttled the length of the corridor to our balcony rooms and locked the doors fast.

Across the hall, I could hear Oro passively-aggressively slamming the windows – to no avail – in protest at the cigarette smoke and drunken caterwauls of soldiers on the balcony. However, in the room I shared with Sophorn, smoke and noise weren't the only pests invading our space. Despite our closed windows and blasting aircon, a mosquito had got in, and neither Sophorn or I had brought anti-malarial medicine. I waved and clapped my hands maniacally to no end, and every time I locked onto the mosquito circling within Sophorn's reach I would shout, 'Catch it, catch it, Sophorn!' But Sophorn's efforts were lackadaisical, at best. When he did eventually get lucky, Sophorn opened up his hands to inspect the deceased, and in all earnestness turned to me and said, 'I should not have killed it, it was too young,' before flicking the little creature off his palm and returning to his work. Five minutes later another invader heralded a further fifteen minutes of flailing and impassioned pleading from me, before Sophorn reluctantly caught the second mosquito – despite his worst efforts. Again, he took a moment to reflect before opening his mouth to say, 'I should not have killed this one either . . . it was his wife.' I felt immediate remorse for asking my karmic friend to kill the mosquitos – to contravene the first Buddhist precept – and, in equal measure, an absolute love for the gentle man he was. He literally couldn't hurt a fly.

By this point it had been nine hours since my last cigarette and, given I was a habitual and fairly heavy smoker, I was deep in the throws of nicotine withdrawal. However, Stung Treng and a balcony of hostile drunken soldiers was not the best place for a Western woman to light up, but in the end the cigarette prevailed over common sense and I reasoned that if I played it cool, then everything would be all right. I tried – and failed – to channel some Chrissie Hynde sophistication, and wafted out, barely detected, for a quiet moment on a windswept veranda. The reality was more like Ru Paul taking the stage at a Boston Tea Party rally as my nerves got the better of me and I flounced out, bellowing hello in Khmer, '*Suasaday!*', to gasps from twenty or so men as I lit up for the tensest three minutes of my life. I practically hoovered up the cigarette, and as I started to make my way back to my room one of the soldiers lurched drunkenly over the threshold of the balcony. His eyes were menacing, bloodshot and full of hate. I squeezed past him, back to the wall, and swiftly locked my door with an impending sense of pitchforks at dawn and the vision of my dead body floating down the Mekong. The sense of relief and comfort I felt when Sophorn looked up at me with his innocent eyes and the lock clicked in my hand was palpable.

Despite my worst premonitions, I eventually slept that night and woke up alive and well the following morning. As it came time for us to leave, Gnut surprised us by pulling up on the back of her daughter's motorbike. She had no idea that we'd been staying there, but she'd seen some sacks from the rice harvest piled high on the lobby floor while searching for some ingredients for *krolan* (bamboo shoots stuffed with sticky rice) to give us for the journey and, as luck would have it, found both rice and us at the same time. After a brief exchange with Oro she sped off again and asked us to wait for her to return.

Outside, the hungover troop, now multiplied and in its entirety, lined the benches and curb of the unkept boulevard, smoking and lounging in the morning sun. The eldest of the troop was sitting by us in the lobby, quietly chatting with the guesthouse owner. I was struck by his stoicism; his calm and knowing eyes, so at odds with his younger platoon. While I checked us out with the concierge, I could overhear Oro intervene in the man's conversation, delicately investigating in Khmer. I was desperate to know the outcome of their talks, and wasted no time in badgering Oro as we walked away to meet the others at the bus stop.

'And?' I began eagerly. 'What did you find out?'

Oro shot me a sideways glance and, sensing my avidity, formu-lated his words slow and Svengali-like, stringing out each word for as long as he could: 'Well . . . he said they live in the forest and they come into the town once every few months to get supplies. He was the commander . . . and they are Khmer Rouge.'

'Are you serious?' I asked, my voice rising an octave. 'You believe him?'

'Yes. Why not? That is what he said,' Oro replied nonchalantly.

Dumbfounded, I refused to let go. 'You're telling me that we just spent the night sharing a hotel with the Khmer Rouge?'

'Yes . . . but don't worry, Dee,' he chuckled. 'They don't have power any more.'

I felt like I'd been hit by a truck. In my naivety, I thought the Khmer Rouge had all but gone. But the history *is* recent and I would later hear tales of whole villages still being ruled in fear by gun-slinging ex-murderers, torturers and bullies – hardened and determined in their beliefs. It was therefore not a far stretch to imagine the existence of guerrillas hiding in forests that once hid legions of them – and what had initially struck me as odd about the mountainous supply of rice sacks in the lobby was now beginning to make sense. The wilderness surrounding Stung Treng and its proximity to the border with Laos had made it a hotbed for communist insurgent activity in the past. The factors that once drove recruitment to the communist call still exist in the corrupt and divided Cambodia of today. You only had to look around Stung Treng – the gateway to Cambodian ecotourism and Laos – to see the disparity: border-crossing backpackers languishing in the guesthouse lobbies stood in sharp contrast to many of the hardworking locals living on less than a dollar a day, navigating poor roads strewn with rubbish and without a hope of repair.

We caught up with Martin and Sophorn loitering outside one such guesthouse. Just as Oro and I caught their attention, Gnut reappeared on the back of a motorbike, a large black bag under one arm. As promised, and in a touching, parting gesture, she'd returned with the *krolan*, and we collectively bid our goodbyes one last time.

There was one more important stop we had to make before leaving Stung Treng. As we walked alongside the Mekong to our destination, Gnut called Oro's phone to check we were safely away. Not one for sycophancy, what you saw was what you got with Gnut – her kindness spoke not in words, but action.

After hanging up and relaying her message, Oro passed around the *krolan* and wasted no time launching into a tirade about his long-distance love troubles to a rather despondent Martin. I tried to mind my own business, walking silently beside Sophorn, my mind wandering, until Oro's words and all munching of *krolan* faded into muffled background noise. As we parted with the Mekong and turned into a warren of dirt paths and peaceful, picturesque hamlets, I took some time to reflect on the past couple of days and piece together the woman we'd spent it with. I thought about how different her life had been when her husband was alive. She was unhappy in romantic love but she'd lived for her children, and while their home was broken, they were loved and never needed for anything while Sisamouth was alive.

Like so many others, Gnut made the long journey home from the rice fields in 1979 with no real prospects of ever regaining anything like the material comforts of the life she'd once had. She'd had to survive and grieve with the constant threat of poverty lurking at her door – a full circle from rags to riches to rags, Stung Treng to Phnom Penh and back again, and all that went in between. The questions of her husband's fate left unanswered to this day. I was lost in these thoughts when the boys and I turned a final corner and found ourselves within a clustered hamlet of traditional Khmer homes. Oro looked at a photo of our destination on his phone before looking straight ahead and announcing, 'That's it – Sisamouth's childhood home,' with a smile wider than any I'd seen before forming on his face.

The hamlet was a little piece of paradise with well-kept

Sinn Sisamouth's childhood home.

gardens and bougainvillea decorating almost every household's exterior. There, in the middle of it all, on ten-foot stilts, stood the house and the longan tree Chanchhaya had told us his father planted as a boy. Fortunately for us, the occupiers – a young family – were in and happy to welcome us.

As I stepped over the threshold I felt the magic of the place instantly: from the timber underfoot – worn smooth by almost a century of bare feet – to the rafters. The odd light shard pierced through the roof and windows and brought the poverty of the household into focus; I could have counted their belongings on two hands: the odd farming tool, a couple of buckets for catching leaking water, a scrap of bedding and a spartan collection of cookware.

I felt conflicted for the people on both sides of this land dispute: a tension between the wonder of standing on floors that Sisamouth once trod, in the place he'd spent his childhood, and the desperation of the young family just barely surviving there now. That feeling became an overwhelming all-consuming pressure on my chest and I awkwardly thanked our hosts and made my way back down the wooden steps to join the others by the longan tree. Oro and I took it in turns swinging around its slender trunk, taking in the surrounding bougainvillea, chirruping birds and the experience we'd all been so fortunate to receive. I felt I could breathe again, the heavy sensation on my chest dissipating, replaced by laughter and the light from the sun piercing the clouds, radiating my cells. Oro was skimming the high ground on every turn around the trunk and every near fall made us laugh a laugh so pure, so contagious and collective I don't think any of us wanted to leave that place, that feeling or that moment. It was an enlightenment of sorts; a bonding; a resolution, after all the emotions we'd navigated over the past couple of days. A final parting gift from the Master, before we boarded our van for the long ride home.

9

The Drakkar Band

Music brought social change, it hit the heart of everyone.
I know that the only way to help the country to become
a democracy is freedom of mind . . . Rock 'n' roll music.
Rock 'n' roll makes much more sense than everything else.

Touch Tana, Drakkar

Drakkar 1974 album cover. L–r: Chhattha, Sareth, Sam Ath, Tana.

Drakkar's frontman sauntered in ten minutes late, shoulders dropped, paper under arm, and dressed – from the baseball cap, to the casual suit, to the trainers – like an LA screenwriter. His English was impeccable, his stride formidable, and there was barely a line on his smooth tan face. But I would soon find out that that cool veneer hid a complex, volcanic and fascinating character.

It was the height of summer in Phnom Penh and, amid the buzz and clattering crockery of our riverside café, we were joined by French-born, Bangkok-based ethnomusicologist Edouard Degay Delpeuch. I'd met Edouard earlier that year over email and we'd formed an instant friendship over our shared interest in Cambodian music. The Parisian told me that he was studying 'the larger movement of republishing old media online – as a third voice between world music publications and ethnomusicological publications . . .' My mind trailed off at that sentence. Perhaps the anthropologist was just a little too intellectual for me. But he was warm, with a wry smile and wicked wit, and when he told me he had set up an interview with Touch Tana – the lead singer of psychedelic Cambodia's answer to Pink Floyd, the Drakkar band – and asked if I'd like to join, I was there in a flash.

Within minutes of sitting down to our first interview, Tana launched into a music history lesson stretching all the way to the Dângrêk Mountains on the Thai border, and as far back as the sixth-century Chenla dynasty. But he wasn't showing off; we would come to learn how deeply Cambodia's musical heritage, ancient folklore and even animism had influenced Tana's songwriting process. He delivered all of this in a fast, animated jabber, slowing to a drawl only to labour a point. Neither the arrival of beer, nor a rather acrid-smelling tomato bread, could break Tana's monologue when he was in full flow. Edouard and I buckled up for one motor-mouth of a ride.

*

Touch Tana had been born in Phnom Penh in 1951, at the close of the colonial era. His Chinese grandfather had prospered greatly from the move to Cambodia. Having first built his wealth on a half-ownership of the vast Tonlé Sap lake fishery, he had expanded into transportation, investing in the country's first steam locomotives. By the time Tana's father reached an age to take a role in the family business, the portfolio had expanded even further: Tana's father ended up specializing in sand and distillery transportation, and rubber plantations.

The Touch family was founded on a bedrock of tradition: men were more important than women; their marriages were polygamous (a practice technically illegal in Cambodia, but still widespread); the parenting was strict. Tana painted a picture of his fiercely disciplinarian mother, and how, as a young boy, he had sought refuge in the surrogate embrace of another woman: the loving Vietnamese mother of Mam Molivan, his childhood friend and future bandmate. Recently widowed, Mam's mother treated Tana as if he were her own. So, every day on his way home from primary school, Tana would detour to the Mam household, there enjoying both Madam Molivan's wonderful food and a burgeoning friendship with her son, the young friends 'at one' in those early years of musical exploration and childhood wonder.

Music ran in the Touch family genes. Tana's grandmother had played the *khene* – a free-reed Cambodian mouth organ, resembling a cross between a viola and harmonica in sound, and used to accompany a folk dance of the same name – at the Royal Palace in Phnom Penh. It was hard to believe that the confident man before me had ever been remotely shy or unsure of himself, but he assured me it was in fact his provincial cousin who had encouraged him to play his first note – and to sing with confidence away from the eyes and ears of the city.

Tana was a teenager by the mid-1960s, a time when brass bands and Cambodian folk, early pop and classical music still dominated the radio waves. But an undercurrent was emerging, seeping into the racks of the music shops around the capital, pushing out the old crooners and the 78s and replacing them with rock 'n' roll 45s. The teenager was soon hooked on the sounds of the Rolling Stones and Elvis. His first ever purchase was the Stones' 1964 self-titled debut album, his favourite track 'Walking the Dog' providing the soundtrack to Tana's thirteenth trip around the sun. He loved the Beatles too and often compared his band's dynamic to that of the Merseysiders. He declared he was the John Lennon of the group – the frontman 'who everyone looked at' in spite of the talent of his writing partner and guitarist Touch Chhattha, whom Tana saw as their band's Paul McCartney.

But it wasn't just the Beatles and the Stones who profoundly shaped Tana's musical foundations. For as far back as the early 1960s, when Tana was in his early teens, he and his favourite cousin would sneak a peek through the beaded screen of Cambodia's oldest nightclub, the Kbal Thnal. Perched high on his cousin's shoulders Tana would gape at the wealthy Cambodians and government officers twisting and jiving inside, before the guard inevitably discovered them. The kids would then scurry away only, moments later, to return and for Tana to climb his cousin's shoulders at the same spot – an early sign of his tenacious streak. As he regaled me with his memories, it was easy to picture the crowded, sweating dancefloor, patrons throwing themselves around wildly as Chum Kem took the stage.

Tana had been raised on a RNK radio diet of Sinn Sisamouth, Baksey Cham Krong and Apsara, graduating to the Western sounds of *The Hit Parade* on Saigon's US military radio around 1967. We talked at length about both Western and Eastern music at the time, Tana breathlessly lurching between anecdotes and tales of his own outrageous behaviour, and a deeply intelligent and serious understanding of his country and its music. When I asked him how these Western and Eastern influences merged to create

Cambodia's 1960s sound – specifically, what defined Cambodian music in his eyes – Tana unleashed a poetic diatribe: 'You can play the foreign instruments but the songs come out different. So how is it Cambodian? I'm Cambodian. I was born in Cambodia, my mother was Cambodian, my father was Cambodian – even though he was Chinese-Cambodian hybrid. When you are born in Cambodia and your family is speaking Cambodian and you use Cambodian traditions and culture . . . like when my mother sang to console me as a child to stop me crying. From the first day you hear the Cambodian sound in music, you hear Cambodian melody; later on you grow, you go to the pagoda and you hear the monks praying – it's like a song – this is Cambodian, and everywhere you go you hear the sound of Cambodian music. When you close the page of the Rolling Stones, close the page of the Beatles, you close the page of American songs and you start to write everything your own way. Everything comes from here.'

As Tana pointed to his heart, I began to understand what he meant. What he was trying to tell me was that for the Drakkar band, influence was a process of the mind – of everything he had learned and absorbed. But what he did with that influence was a process of the heart, and of the soul; it's what made the Drakkar sound unique. Yet Tana was just one half of the Drakkar's songwriting partnership, and the truth is the band's origins lie with someone else. I knew that in order to get the full Drakkar story, I would need to track down the other half of this partnership; someone I would find to be completely different to the loquacious and extroverted Touch Tana.

In 1961 – five years before he met Tana, and only eleven years old at the time – Touch Chhattha started the Drakkar band with a revolving door of school friends. Chhattha took the name from a French Viking movie, *Les Drakkars*, and during those early

years they'd experimented with various styles and formations
– traditional folk, R&B and pop – before settling on hard rock
in the late 1960s. I met Chhattha on Phnom Penh's riverside
late that summer of 2014. The contrast between Tana and his
bandmate was remarkable. For where Tana strode in with confidence and bravado, instantly taking charge, Chhattha was more
timid and polite, delicately built with, at times, something of a
deer-in-the-headlights look. John Pirozzi, the film director, had
described him as 'one of the nicest people in the world', and I
quickly saw why.

Chhattha came prepared with photos of himself at different
stages of his life, the earliest from his Drakkar youth, pictured
with long hair and a bandana and wielding what looked like a
Gibson guitar. There was also a photo of him and his TVK TV
band compatriots from the Lon Nol era, dressed head to toe
in military gear, and another shot from the 1990s – Chhattha
decorated in medals from the government and the king for his
years of service at RNK radio.

Touch Chhattha in the late 1960s.

The son of a well-off jeweller, Chhattha had never wanted for anything growing up. He began learning the guitar at the age of nine, taking instinctively to the instrument. Songbooks were responsible for most of Chhattha's musical education, but he also played with the great Cambodian music teachers, Mam Boutnaray and Thach Soly, who taught the rich and (later) famous children of the elite classes. By the time he had crossed paths with the latter, however, Chhattha's skill had surpassed Soly's teachings, and instead the boy helped Thach tutor his other students.

It wasn't until the mid-1960s that a chance meeting with Tana led Chhattha to a practice at mutual friend Mam Molivan's house, with the trio bonding over their mutual love of Voice of America, the Beatles and the Rolling Stones. Within a short time a new incarnation of the Drakkar band was born, and it wasn't long before the outfit were playing shows. Their first was a party at the American Embassy. They didn't have a setlist, they hadn't so much as practised. Backstage, as they watched the other bands perform, their nerves began to fray. Yet, somehow, that fear brought Tana's confident alter ego to the fore, which carried the rest of the band through their impromptu setlist of covers, and their audience followed.

Between 1967 and 1970, in its first formation with Tana on backing vocals rather than lead, the Drakkar played around fifty shows, fast becoming the band of choice for wealthy teenagers' parties. They were teenagers themselves, of course, and parental discipline was more absent for some members than for others. Molivan's father, a high-ranking official, had died years before and, according to Tana, Chhattha's Chinese father was more concerned with his jewellery business than with the whereabouts of his teenage son. Tana's family, however, was different – his mother would berate him for playing music, so he'd have to sneak out of the house in the dead of night to practise. When his parents begrudgingly bought him a guitar as a reward for doing well in an exam, it came with one condition: that he had to promise never to become a professional musician. They felt that path was beneath him.

The Drakkar line-up at the time featured Tana and Chhattha on guitars and backing vocals, Mam Molivan on bass and backing vocals, and a singer by the name of Tan Phanareth on lead vocal. There were no keys, nor a permanent drummer, and it wasn't until the second formation that Tana's gravelly voice took centre stage. As for the band's repertoire, their originals were preceded by Western covers, a popular practice at the time. But despite Phanareth's romantic serenades and the band's nascent pop and folk meanderings, their attitude was explosive from the start, with Tana's onstage bravado and offstage antics earning him a reputation among Cambodia's *yé-yé* groups. Long before he took the vocal mic from Phanareth, Tana was stirring up trouble, both heckling other bands on their bill from within the crowd and borrowing his bandmates' mics onstage to intimidate, provoke and pick fights with the audience. Those wild antics are encapsulated perfectly in the story of Tana's first introduction to the singer and future psychedelic garage rocker, Yol Aularong.

Aularong was the son of the secretary of the French Embassy, and had been educated in France. Hindered throughout his adult life by a hip injury he sustained during a childhood fight, Aularong was a rebel from the outset. Inspired by the Rolling Stones and French folk singer and garage rocker Antoine, Aularong – Lara, as he became known – was described by Ben Sisario of the *New York Times* as 'a charismatic proto-punk who mocked conformist society', and by Nik Cohn in the *Guardian* as 'a certifiable maniac'. His longstanding friendship with Tana had begun inauspiciously at a house party of a government minister's son. As Tana recalled: 'When I first met Aularong, it was at a party and he sang James Brown's "Papa's Got a Brand New Bag". He was wearing big flares and the material was cheap – we called it "Olympic", as in the cloth you buy in Olympic Market [a three-storey Phnom Penh market selling inexpensive clothes and textiles]. At the party many people were talking about Drakkar and Aularong got angry. I also laughed when he was performing because he used to shout and jump up and down like a frog, and he got angry about that. After he performed, another band played, and then the Amara band played. Yol Aularong was close to the Amara band, and the guy in Amara played the Bee Gees song "I've Gotta Get a Message to You", but when he sang, he didn't know much English. In the song it says, "Now for once in your life you're alone . . ." But he sang something like "Number one in your life . . ." and I was laughing, you know, mocking him. And he got really upset like, "Oh, this guy, he looks down on everybody." After that we played – [for] about one hour – [and by this time] many people wanted to fight me. Molivan got worried about how he would return home [safely], and I said, "Don't worry, I will sort it out."'

Tana got down from the stage and grabbed a T-bone knife off a table, shouting at everyone to get out or fight. When Aularong accused Tana of mocking him, he retorted: 'Who said that? Who said that I'm mocking you? Was it you?' Eventually, after a tense pause Aularong, presumably realizing there was no easy way out of this, ceded to Tana and, in a gesture of peace, extended a hand.

But just a few months later Tana and Aularong locked horns again. There was an incident involving Tana's sister and a barage of paper balls hurled by school boys – one of which was Aulorang. Tana ran a surveillance operation near the school gates to stake out the daily paper-ball gauntlet his sister ran, and ended up confronting Aularong's gang and its ringleader – who Tana called 'the Godfather' – with a baseball bat in one hand, an ice saw in the other.

Another time, the pair ran into each other in downtown Phnom Penh. Aularong was cycling home and, spotting his nemesis a hundred metres away, and with no escape route in the crowd, leapt off his bike, dropped to his knees and held out a hand in friendship. From that day on Tana and Aularong continued in their dramas and rivalries – but they also shared coffee-shop companionship, their love of music and Chinese deep-fried doughnut sticks called *yu char kway*. On occasions they worked together. Aularong even 'corrupted [me] with cigarettes', Tana snorted. In fact, according to Tana, Aularong's hit song, a psychedelic garage stomper called 'Café Kmao' ('Black Coffee'), was all about their chain-smoking coffee-shop days.

But there was pity in the relationship, too. Aularong's father had died young and unexpectedly from a neurological problem. The condition's name eluded Tana, but it could have been a stroke, or perhaps a brain tumour. In the following years Tana would sometimes spend the night at Aularong's family home. It was clear that the Yol family were struggling financially, and that Lara's mother was a shell of her former self.

Fortune favours the brave, and 1970 turned out to be Tana's year. Then nineteen years old, he became Artistic Programme Director for RNK radio, organizing much of the music programming each week. He worked there at the same time as his bandmate, Chhattha, who started earlier that same year as a session player and political commentator. Drakkar had for a time taken a break while band members finished university and started jobs. But despite the band's hiatus, and the mounting tremors of the Cambodian civil war, Chhattha remembered this as a time of great passion and happiness. For within the station it felt like a small family business, the staff often working around the clock and sleeping in shifts for the love of the job.

Under the orders of the radio station's director general, a Mr Lee Him Uon, Tana was tasked with bringing together musicians from the Royal Palace, the University of Fine Arts and the *yé-yé* groups to create a diversified sixteen-hour daily broadcast for the now-militarized station. He slipped naturally into his position of power, connecting up these musical factions for the first time ever. Despite short breaks here and there, it was a role that Tana would continue in until late 1973.

When he wasn't at the radio station Tana was a fixture on the Phnom Penh gig circuit, where he made a connection with a young man, Kosal, whose father ran Kbal Thnal, the very same club Tana used to climb onto his cousin's shoulders and peek into as a child. Kosal Jnr introduced Tana to Kosal Snr who, according to Tana, was a flamboyant aesthete who favoured good-looking young men, and was so incorrigibly charming and persuasive that people could not refuse his business proposals. In the same breath that Tana told me of Kosal's adeptness for diplomacy, he mentioned that the nightclub owner had 'employed' a customs officer. And, in the corrupt Cambodian society of the time, I took this to mean that Kosal had the customs officer in his pocket, so to speak. When they first met, Kosal Snr fawned over the nineteen-year-old, wasting no time in offering Tana a job organizing a new house band for a sum that Tana simply could not refuse. Kosal knew Som Sareth, Tana's choice for lead guitar, and agreed with the decision. Tana also recommended Oer Sam Ol on bass, having worked with him previously at a gig at the Magetat nightclub. In addition, Tana put forward a keyboard player, a brass section including a trumpet, trombone and an alto and tenor sax, and proposed, finally, Cambodia's very own Ringo Starr, Ouk Sam Ath, on drums. Ouk Sam Ath had previously been a bass player in Battambang, his Beatle mop earning him the nickname 'Tol' (as in Bea-'tol'), but as a drummer he would go on to become one of the most sought after and accomplished session musicians in Phnom Penh.

Tana, however, bored easily and, with all his requests met, he decided to stir it up a little by adding his wild man friend

Yol Aularong into the mix on lead vocal. Aularong, of course, brought his rock 'n' roll antics to the club, though in more sombre moments Tana would join him on stage to duet Sam & Dave songs. Within a short time the band's brand of brassy R&B and Santana-style rock was attracting more and more fans – Kosal's investment seemed to be paying off. A month in, Tana begged Kosal to take on one more player: his childhood friend and ex-bandmate Mam Molivan. Molivan's handsome face must have won over Kosal, for he soon completed the line-up. These were happy times. Tana had finally found himself, beyond the beaded curtain of his childhood mischief and curiosity.

In the summer of that same year, 1970, as the Khmer Rouge rebel army gained ground in the countryside, Tana received a further proposal, this time from the US Embassy. Once again, it was unrefusable. The embassy was looking for bands to play for the Cambodian, South Vietnamese and American troops serving or training in Vietnam. Tana put his work at the Kbal Thnal nightclub and RNK radio on hiatus, agreeing to take a rock band to entertain allied troops at a US-run military training centre in the Mekong Delta for the month of September 1970.

He quickly scrabbled together a band – Som Sareth on lead guitar, Oer Sam Ol on bass guitar, Ouk Sam Ath on drums and Tana on rhythm guitar and vocals – and the four-piece crossed the border into war-torn Vietnam. The musicians were assigned to entertain the troops alongside American, Thai and Korean bands. At the same time Cambodia's most famous singer Sinn Sisamouth was releasing his cover of the Animals' 'The House of the Rising Sun' in Phnom Penh – a five-minute heavy, overdriven version he renamed 'I'm Still Waiting for You' – the Animals' 1965 hit 'We've Gotta Get Out of This Place' was having a revival in Vietnam, becoming something of an anthem for the American troops – to the point where every visiting band to the recreation tent at the training base at Long Hai finished their set with a rousing version, the beer-fuelled, chain-smoking, card-playing audience erupting into a mass singalong for the chorus. Tana's band duly played shows filled with Rolling Stones covers to as many as 10,000 soldiers on occasion, and they loved every minute of the excitement. So much so, in fact, that when the initial one-month contract was extended to three, the band happily accepted.

There were more than two hundred musicians on private entertainment and touring contracts from Australia alone, and many of the American, Korean, Australian, Kiwi, Filipino, Thai, Vietnamese and Cambodian musicians that entertained the troops died in crossfire while on the job. Fortunately Tana and his band returned to Phnom Penh unscathed in November 1970. But when they did so they found the dancing bars were closed and the Cambodian civil war edging ever closer to the city. So the session players like Ouk Sam Ath, who had no other fall-back, returned from riding their Vietnam wave to a home town of little prospect, until the nightclubs opened up again (albeit temporarily) early the following year.

For Tana, however, his lucky streak showed no sign of ending. He'd now landed a contract to write and record forty songs at the famous Van Chann recording studio, which housed the best equipment in town. Freshly inspired by the new sounds he heard in Vietnam, the now long-haired and hippyish Tana set to churning out Drakkar-style rock and pop songs as fast as he could write them. He rapidly put together bands and session players, and in just one month had come close to meeting the full quota of songs needed. 'When we recorded a song, in my mind I would already be working on another song. Everyone said, "He has a machine head." I could write up to four songs a day – lyrics, melody, all arrangements. And I worked also for the RNK radio, but I spent all my free time in the studio. At night I would get ideas. I was young, and we went out past midnight every day, but just before I'd fall asleep I'd get an idea for the next day, and another one, and another . . . maybe just the introduction, no chorus. The studio would (officially) open at nine o'clock in the morning but I would come at seven o'clock. I would be alone until the band came at eight o'clock, and I would start with the first song. When the band came I'd tell them how to play. Then I'd get out to write another song, and we'd invite the singer – for example, Ros Sereysothea – to come. She'd come to the studio, and I'd train her how to sing it, and then we'd record. After recording we'd relax a little bit then change to another singer, for example Pen Ran, because the second song suited Pen Ran . . . then while Ros Sereysothea was being taken back home and Pen Ran was being collected to come in, during that time I'd train the band for the second song. So then I'd teach Pen Ran how to sing it. Then after the second one, we'd go back to get Ros Sereysothea.'

Fuelled by the stamina of youth and his newfound success, at the end of the day Tana would take the studio musicians out to celebrate the day's work in fashionable Phnom Penh bars, flashing his cash among the big-league producers he was coming to rival – people like the writer and producer Voy Ho. Aularong often tagged along for a free drink, regardless of whether he'd sung for Tana that day or not. But the 'machine head' couldn't keep up with the relentless pace he'd set himself. Within a month Tana had burned out, and he had no choice but to submit his work a few songs short of the quota.

Burned out or not, Tana wrote and recorded some of his self-declared best work around this time – in addition to writing popular classical-influenced songs like Cambodia's rebel soul singer Pen Ran's 'Bang Khoeung Roeung Awey?' ('What Made You Angry?'). This also included Aularong's first hit song 'Navanny' ('Number One'), a witty account of the life of a teacher's pet. Lara's career was still fledging and, like many of his friends', was suffering from the club closures. For him, 'Navanny' couldn't have come at a better time.

Unfortunately, initially, the record company hated the riff-heavy, proto-punk 'Navanny', with its catchy call-and-response vocals. So, without their knowledge, Tana surreptitiously arranged for the song to be played live on TV. Overnight the performance put Aularong on the map. With the help of his uncle, a famous arranger and violinist called Hass Salan, Aularong then went on to have even bigger hits with psychedelic tracks like 'Café Kmao', a duet with singer Va Savoy called 'Sou Slarp Kroam Kombut Srey' ('Dying Under a Woman's Sword'), which was a war cry to all young men avoiding Lon Nol's army, the Van Morrison 'Gloria' contrafactum, 'Yuvajon Kouch Chet' ('Broken Hearted Man'), and 'Cyclo', a witty celebration of bicycle rickshaws and beautiful women.

His work as a contracted songwriter also brought Tana into contact with one of his favourite childhood singers, Mao Sareth. At the time, Sareth was just twenty-six years old and, according to Tana, broken, her successful teenage pop career long behind her. But he was quick to discard more famous and commercial singers in favour of his childhood heroine. Mao Sareth, with her thick beehive and heavy-frame glasses, was a singer's singer. She inspired so many who came after her, including her Battambang native, Ros Sereysothea. After releasing her first hit, 'Samrek Tonaha' ('A Scream Of Desire') in 1959 about the pain of unrequited love, Mao Sareth followed this up with a catalogue of tearjerkers like 'Mek Khmao Ngo Ngith' ('The Dark Sky'), prom floor classics, and duets with Sisamouth like their bubble-pop, pro-Sihanouk-era song, 'Tasona Krong Phnom Penh' ('Phnom Penh is a Good City'). For several years her music dominated Cambodian ballrooms and the radio, before finally falling out of favour with her label, Wat-Phnom, and the public.

Together Tana and Sareth recorded a track named 'Boer Bang

Min Mayta' ('Have You No Mercy?'), debuting the hard-rock howler on live TV. A reinvention and departure from the Chantels-like serenades and Sarah Vaughan-style vibrato Sareth was famous for, 'Boer Bang Min Mayta' starts off with dreamy vocals and hazy guitars tripping off a laid-back staccato drum roll, before moving into blazing solos and balls out rock 'n' roll, until Sareth lulls us back one last time for the finale.

In late 1971 Tana handed the remainder of his contract's song quota over to Aularong and his uncle Hass Salan to finish, leaving himself free to reignite the Drakkar. Much had happened in the year since they last wrote and played together. Chhattha and Tana were now that little bit older, that bit wiser to the world and music – that bit ballsier, too – and ready for a change of direction. So over the next couple of years the pair cultivated a new psychedelic sound, alongside their day jobs, marriage – Tana married a glamorous movie star – and Tana's odd studio job.

Joining them in the final Drakkar line-up was the rest of the Vietnam War band: Ouk Sam Ath on drums, Oer Sam Ol on bass, and Som Sareth on lead guitar. Chhattha sang and played rhythm guitar, with Tana singing and playing keys, borrowing a Farfisa organ when he could – or, when the Farfisa was unavailable, using a Yamaha YC-30 or an Ace Tone.

Their latest incarnation introduced dynamic percussion into the mix, embellishing Ouk Sam Ath's splashy drumming style with congos and timbales, paving new musical ground in Cambodia, and cultivating a harder rock sound wrought from new influences like Santana. They performed live only when a special occasion might lure Chhattha and Tana from their radio desks and the others from their own paid gigs, recordings and nightclub residencies. But the real focus was on recording an album in a series of snatched moments between 1972 and 1973. That album was *Drakkar 74*.

Drakkar had never done anything by the book, and this album was no different. Rather than take the commercial route and risk selling their souls to a 'Chinese producer interested only in profit', they slowly crafted the record in a home studio with one of Cambodia's most enterprising sound men, Mol Kagnol.

Tana had met the Baksey Cham Krong guitarist Mol Kagnol halfway through 1972, just as the Khmer Rouge insurgents, deep in the countryside, were organizing battalion-size units and readying to collectivize parts of the country. The pair – the older master Kagnol and his adoring protégé, Tana – quickly established a mentor–mentee relationship which has endured to this day, even if it's now conducted across oceans. When Tana spoke of Kagnol, his demeanour shifted: he softened, there was a sparkle in his eye and reverence in every word. He told me, 'One day, Oer Sam Ol said to me, "Tana, you know Kagnol wants to build a studio – you want to come and see it?" Kagnol had an eight-track console and he wanted to test the machine's recording quality. So I said, "OK, I'll bring the instruments." Som Sareth was a fast psychedelic player, but Mol Kagnol was the seasoning. He instinctively made the music flavourful. We didn't invite him to play on *Drakkar 74* but he plugged in and played anyway. His guitar was handmade, but modelled on a Hofner, and the sound was indescribable. When he played he was like Jimi Hendrix: he could play this guitar and make it sound like a *takhe* [the traditional Cambodian string instrument, shaped like a cross between a sitar and a lute] – I don't know how he did it. He knew how to create sound, and he knew how to control the sound. When we left the studio each night, Kagnol would be tweaking electrics and working on sounds. That is why I cannot say how much I respect him; he was a great acoustic and technical engineer and musician. He made me feel confident, and I couldn't interfere. He'd tease me: "You want to tell me to change anything?" And I'd say, "No, no . . ."'

Most of the album was recorded at Kagnol's Phnom Penh one-room apartment, which had been transformed into a recording studio through remarkable feats of creativity that involved soundproofing the walls and using burlap sacks to create a makeshift drum cabin; washing lines were strung up and draped with heavy hessian sheets to muffle sound too. What made these feats incredible was not merely the engineering – *that*, I suspect, was largely instinctive – but the sound that the set-up created. It was rough and dirty and full of soul – a sound to rival any unabashedly raucous garage rock demo, bursting with sweat, testosterone and frenzy.

The sound captured the mood and energy of the music, but it was almost too raw and the recording needed a little more clarity. So, they did away with their amplifiers in the end, and recorded the keyboard, bass and electric guitars directly through the channels of the console, which Kagnol controlled from the centre of the room as the band recorded live. With a lightning-fast mandolin strum, the man responsible for bringing surf guitar to Cambodia brought his phenomenal *takhe* impression to the song 'Sarawan Chan Penh Boromei' ('Dancing Saravan Under the Full Moon'), transforming his handmade electric guitar into some mystical, otherworldly instrument.

Drakkar's work resulted in a nine-song album that ran the gamut from prom-style ballads and two-minute pop songs to all out psychedelic rock, distortion riffs and epic Farfisa organ and guitar solos. Hand cymbals lent a distinctly Cambodian feel to the album's rather traditional opener 'Boeur Chhang Ban Onn' ('If You Want to Marry Me'), sung by Pen Ran who, in turn, was followed by guest appearances from Mao Sareth on the banger 'Boer Bang Min Maytha' and the sweet sound of the lesser-known Keo Sokha on 'Sarawan Chan Penh Boromei'.

Avoiding the fat cat producers and their factory lines, Tana took it on himself to copy one thousand cassettes. Tana claimed he borrowed the equivalent of $18,000 USD from his brother (and heir to the Touch family fortune), bought a Hitachi tape-copying machine with a maximum capacity of ten tapes at a time and 1,000 blank cassettes, slotted in the master, and laboriously started production. If done alone, as Tana claimed, the whole process must have taken around seventy-five hours. But, despite being titled *Drakkar 74*, the indefatigable Tana managed to get the record ready for release by the end of 1973.

Yet it seemed Tana's lucky streak had come to an end: the album tanked, selling a mere hundred copies in its first month. To add to the pain, Tana's job at RNK radio had been abruptly terminated. So, unemployed, heartbroken, and deeply indebted to his brother, Tana moved out east to the gem mining province, Pailin, in the hope of earning enough to repay the money he'd squandered on the album.

Pailin's precious gems have been one of Cambodia's great treasures for centuries. Legend has it that hunters at the base of sacred Yat Mountain came across a forest spirit who took the form of an old woman and told them to leave the forest unharmed and head to the river to find their fortune. When they arrived at the river the men saw otters playing with blue and red stones, which turned out to be sapphires and rubies. Formed millions of years ago by volcanic mountains to the west, east and south of Pailin, these valuable rocks travelled downstream and deposited themselves on the beds and banks of past and existing rivers.

Away from the mountains and the rivers, the city itself now resembles just about any other Cambodian city, its roads busy with cars, motorbikes and small motorized tractors pulling carts, and lined with food stalls, print shops and hotels. It's hard to believe that Pailin has survived some of the worst fighting between the Khmer Rouge and Vietnam – by 1996 the bombed-out buidings, tanks and rubble resembled Aleppo in Syria circa 2016. Pailin has also weathered centuries of plundering from Burmese, Thai and Russian gem miners, and the subsequent exhaustion of her mining industry. Many veteran miners now work in the growing casino industry, coffee plantations, tobacco and sugarcane fields; the sizeable poor left as panhandlers, swishing river gravel cyclically in the hope of a fortuitous glint of red, blue or gold. Pailin was a retirement home for senior Khmer Rouge officials – land granted in an unofficial peace settlement – until the tide turned and previously pardoned residents, Brother Number 2 Nuon Chea and Brother Number 3 Khieu Samphan, were captured by the authorities in 2007 to stand trial for war crimes.

But before all this, Pailin in the early 1970s was a boomtown, a wildwest frontier, full of opportunity for individual panhandlers as well as large mining corporations. By the time Tana arrived, early in 1974, there was a good deal of trade with nearby Thailand, and the mines were still protected by a large garrison against the likelihood of an attack by the Khmer Rouge, who by then had taken over all of Cambodia bar its major cities. At the start of 1974 there were around ten nightclubs in Pailin's capital playing host to entertainers who, struggling for work in Phnom Penh, had moved to Thailand or Pailin. However, Tana wasn't interested in short change from the nightclubs, he was there to make it big – and spent much of that year building up his emerging gem business, seeking out investors and land to mine.

Back in the capital, meanwhile, his brother had been keeping an eye on the Drakkar album sales. Having already resigned himself to the fact that *Drakkar 74* would never turn a profit, Tana was shocked to receive a call from his brother late in 1974 informing him that the album had suddenly – and for no apparent reason – taken off, and they'd sold out completely. So the band had a second pressing of 20,000 cassettes professionally produced – and a few months later, in early 1975, these, too, had sold out. The Cambodian music economy in the 1960s and 1970s was primarily driven by the sale of the 7-inch singles and the cassette format. Soundtracks sold, and once in a while a compilation album did too, but albums by a single artist were rare. Best sellers by the likes of Sisamouth or producer Voy Ho might have shifted around 15,000 units to the small record-buying contingent of Cambodia's 7,000,000 population, two thirds of whom were then living hand to mouth. By these calculations, and according to Tana, this officially made *Drakkar 74* Cambodia's highest grossing album.

Meanwhile, in Pailin, Tana had acquired a hectare of rambutan orchard in a dubious fifty–fifty deal with the provincial governor. By March Tana's team had set to bulldozing the land in search of mineral ore – and they found a lot. Word of his newfound wealth quickly spread, and by the time Tana had reached Bangkok on business on 16 April he was being treated like royalty. But rumours of Phnom Penh's imminent fall to the Khmer Rouge had also reached Bangkok. Tana was warned not to return to Pailin. The allure of danger, power and wealth, however, was too much to resist. So, mistakenly believing that working on arable land would mean amnesty, Tana the gem king travelled to a remote location within the Cardamom Mountains, south-east of Pailin, to collect a hydraulic excavator.

He returned to Pailin with the excavator at dawn on 19 April 1975. By mid-morning that day, a company of Khmer Rouge troops had marched through his mine, waving their black flags. With the arrival of the Khmer Rouge soldiers, Tana's skills at political manoeuvring and cunning were being sharpened every day. He appeased the passing army, providing them with food and vehicles, which they used to capture one of Lon Nol's fleeing brothers on the Thai border. On 25 April, Tana heard that there had been an announcement in town: all people, except those who worked the land, were ordered to leave on the road to Battambang. The same announcement was repeated the following day and, that night, in secret, Tana got together with the other wealthy mine owners to plot their escape to Thailand. They scheduled their departure for the following night. Tana diverted the Khmer Rouge soldiers' attention by providing lunch for them the next day. Lunch, inevitably, turned into a rowdy dinner, but eventually the soldiers left and, at ten o' clock that night, Tana and his workers set off for the Thai border, twelve miles away.

With only two cars onsite, many of Tana's workers were forced to walk behind the vehicles. But fear took hold of the workers, and it wasn't long before many ran off into the jungle, never to be seen again. When the rest of the group arrived at the city of Ba Yakha, they decided to take a secret but longer route past the bridge and on to the border. But before they could leave the city, a fight broke out between two men over money, with one threatening to tell the Khmer Rouge. Around fifteen minutes later, the group heard the sound of B40 rocket explosions in the distance and around a hundred motorcyclists. Tana was convinced that this was the end. Luckily the group froze and hid, and the motorcycle army passed by, unaware of the travellers hiding in the suburban brush. Nevertheless, the experience was enough to shake their confidence and the remaining group returned back to Pailin, now entirely deserted but for abandoned, barking dogs.

Around three-thirty that morning, Tana heard the sound of artillery near his house. An hour later a Khmer Rouge officer came to the door asking if he had a bulldozer driver. Tana lied and said he didn't, but his frightened driver, who was staying with Tana in his house, overheard and quickly blurted out that he was there. Hauled before the officer, the driver was swiftly taken away. He returned later that morning, shaken, exhausted and mute. It would be Tana's first inkling of what the Khmer Rouge were capable of.

On 28 April Tana was told by a Khmer Rouge officer that he

was no longer required. He would need to prepare to leave like everyone else. By now all the banks and shops were shut, so the remaining workers spent the final couple of days in the village scrabbling together whatever food and drink they could find to pack for the road – a little saltfish, fermented fish paste, rice and *cacao* in place of coffee.

Tana and his workers left on 30 April. Looking back at the deserted village, now host to an influx of exhausted new workers for the nearby fields, Tana began to smell an unpleasant stench. The smell extinguished the hunger in his stomach. The air was buzzing with countless flies. The bulldozer, Mr Cherk, also refused what little food they had, instead remaining mute. But when Tana offered Cherk a cigarette, he lit it and began to open up: 'Young boss, I buried all my bosses that I've worked for since I came to Pailin. They were shot, but they were still alive; they opened their eyes. The Khmer Rouge came and checked the bodies [for the valuables and gems they were carrying], every Khmer Rouge soldier got one bag of gems, great gem stones. Women, men; they stripped them down to their underwear. There were about a hundred people they shot, lying everywhere. They told me to bulldoze the hole, and then push the bodies into the hole and cover them with soil.'

Tana walked on in shocked silence, realizing that the unpleasant smell and the flies came from rotting corpses. He remembered what had happened just days ago when the Khmer Rouge commander had found out he'd lied about not having a bulldozer driver at his mining site. The commander wasn't happy about being lied to, but had taken a shine to Tana and had given him these parting words of advice: 'Please try to behave to survive. I like you, but I cannot help you.'

Tana being Tana, however, it wasn't long before he started to test the boundaries of this warning. He recalled, 'I'm lucky. They wanted to kill me too many times, but I am brave; they could not scare me. They tricked me, they conspired, and they were well organized.'

Tana was referring to one of the scrapes he found himself in during the Khmer Rouge rule. The musician found some solace in break times at his new village – located somewhere between Pailin and Battambang – when guitar playing was permitted so long as Khmer Rouge revolutionary songs were sung. There were moments of great risk, however, when officers secretly asked him to sing them old songs from the bygone era, or, after a little convincing, to play songs by Sinn Sisamouth, the Apsara band and even American and British songs. On one occasion he picked the light-hearted 'Ob-La-Di, Ob-La-Da' by the Beatles, and the soldiers went wild. But he made enemies among his fellow farmers and fishermen, who resented his bourgeois roots. On discovering that Tana's first wife had been a movie actress and singer, the villagers were enraged, and, as Tana put it, 'They wanted to kill me. No poor guy can be married to a movie star, and they looked at my face and said, "He is a big guy."' So the other villagers hatched a plot against Tana.

One of Tana's jobs was to fish for the village. One day at a nearby lake, a member of his fishing group had cast a net and caught a shoal of big fish. All the group's members, including Tana, had taken a fish each, hiding it in their clothes to take back to their huts and families. Hiding food from the Khmer Rouge was punishable by death but, seeing his fellow comrades hiding their fish, Tana followed suit. Unfortunately for Tana, the move was a ploy to make trouble for the singer. For when everyone returned to the hut to change their clothes, he realized that they had all thrown their fish back in the lake or handed them in to the cooks when he wasn't looking. They had set him up. One of them he'd known since his primary school days.

Hauled in front of the village on trial, Tana knew he was going to be killed. He could hear the young cadres sing, *'Tonight's the*

night we kill the man, cut out his belly and fill it with grass.' But
Tana was a fighter to the last and, from somewhere deep inside,
he summoned that fearless confidence he discovered at his first
Drakkar show, and stepped into the centre of his 1,000-strong
commune with his head held high: 'I said, "OK, I know it was
my fault. I know I will die, but I want to say something. Will you
allow me to say something?" The head of the village said, "No."
So I said, "I am not asking you. I am asking the collective, the
whole mass. Do you agree for me to talk?" They agreed, and I
said thank you. My voice was strong, and I shouted out, "I have
another request: when I talk I don't want anyone to interrupt me.
Are you agreed?" They agreed. I said, "Thank you. Can I ask you
a question? Between rice robbery and fish robbery, which one has
the greater fault?" They said "Rice!" So I said, "And if they are
punished should the rice killer be killed first, and then the fish
killer be killed later?" "Yes!" they shouted. I thanked them, then
I started to talk. "You know I came here, everyone knows I came
from Phnom Penh city. I don't know how to fish or how to cast a
net, because I am from the city. How could I get a fish without
anyone giving it to me? So, you have evidence that there is a fish
in my box. But you should think how this fish came to be in my
box. I don't want to blame anyone, but all of you agreed that the
rice stealer is the greater thief, and you should kill them first.
The village leader and these guys who complained about me –
now, let's go to their houses and check if they have rice in their
homes. All of us, we don't have rice, we just have rice porridge,
and sometimes it's mixed with corn. But all of them, they have
rice, plenty of rice that they keep at home to make wine, to make
noodles. What a different situation, between us and them."

'And they stood up and shouted, and I said, "Don't be a dog. Sit
down until I finish talking. You cannot interrupt me – the whole
collective agreed to let me talk without interruption." I started
to shout stronger and stronger. I talked for more than two hours.'

Having heard the famous motor-mouth first hand, the idea of Tana arguing his case for two hours didn't surprise me. I was now on the edge of my seat, in awe of his audacity.

The village chief summoned an Angkar official and threatened that heads would roll if proceedings were not brought to an abrupt end, but Tana remained defiant: '"Why do you try to stop me? Because I am right. You organized a crime for me. You want to kill one life? How about your family's lives? Your wife? Your children? Why do you want to kill me?" One red guard begged me to stop. He said, "We'll forget about everything, we apologize, please stop!" So, I said, "OK," and I stopped. It was my fate, or destiny or luck that the Khmer Rouge could not kill me, because I was brave. I just talked.'

The majority of Tana's family were not so lucky. In April 1975, when the Khmer Rouge had ordered the evacuation of Phnom Penh, his father had had to leave Tana's Cambodian mother behind in order to help his other Chinese-speaking wife. But in all the commotion he lost his Chinese wife on the road to Kampong Thom province, north of Phnom Penh. Tana's father survived only because he was lucky enough to meet one of his daughters on the road, who happened to be working for the new regime as a nurse. He escaped, going on to live in France, later joining Tana's stepbrother in the USA and living in Monterey Park, LA, until his death in 1987.

The rest of the family perished in the genocide. The details are a litany of disaster. Tana's mother and one of his sisters were killed by a bomb blast at a naval base on the Tonlé Sap River during the evacuation. His sister's husband was a major in the navy who, despite joining the Khmer Rouge the day before the takeover, was taken to Tuol Sleng Prison in February 1976 and executed. His elder brother was killed in the Kampong Cham–Preah Vihear area. His second sister was killed in a rubber plantation in Kampong Cham. His other sister, niece and nephew were all killed. Their remains lie in unmarked graves across Cambodia.

Of the band's five members, only Chhattha, Tana and Ouk Sam Ath survived. Som Sareth and Oer Sam Ol disappeared during the evacuation, never to be heard of again. As for Yol Aularong, Minh Sothivann – the brother of Apsara's bass player, Minh Prahul – was the last person known to have seen Lara alive. He had been sent to work in Krauko village near Battambang, and there Sothivann recognized him. Aularong was shaking his head from side to side, saying repeatedly, 'I don't understand, I don't understand, what are they going to do to us?' There was no place for visible trauma in the labour camps. Sothivann presumed that Lara did not last long.

After the liberation of Cambodia by the People's Army of Vietnam and the Kampuchean United Front for National Salvation in 1979, Tana made his way through the rice fields and forests of rural Cambodia, carefully avoiding the mines, to a refugee camp in Thailand. There, like many others, he was turned back. For in the months since the Vietnamese invasion of Cambodia, the camps along the Thai–Cambodian border had been flooded with refugees. Faced with a threat to their own national security, the Thai government decided to turn away new arrivals.

Never one to surrender, Tana returned to Phnom Penh, found work for a few years playing music for the Fishery ministry band and focused on obtaining a passport in order to travel the world. In 1983, having made some international connections through the fisheries department – having greased enough palms and saved enough money for a passport – Tana set sail on a new adventure aboard a Russian naval ship, assisting with marine research. The crew's food didn't make the grade, however, and in typically charismatic fashion, Tana quickly blagged a seat for himself at the captain's table, dining on shrimp and squid and drinking wine every day.

In the past couple of decades Tana has showed no signs of slowing down. His stint on the Russian ship opened the door to a new career in marine science, as a conservationist, and he has published research on everything from Mekong dolphins to Asian mussels. His work has earned him the title of 'His Excellency' in research circles, and he was, for a time, an advisor to Cambodia's fisheries department – the very industry which his grandfather once controlled.

As for Chhattha, he never spoke of the genocide. It was, understandably, too traumatic to revisit. He returned to Phnom Penh after the fall of the Khmer Rouge and his experience writing propaganda music under the Lon Nol regime stood him in good stead. In 1979, under the People's Republic of Kampuchea, whose Vietnamese-supported regime lasted from 1979 to 1989, he wrote educational songs with titles like 'Children Need to be Safe', 'Life and Development', 'Handicapped by Mines' and 'Mosquitoes', the latter of which warned his countrymen about the dangers of malaria. The new regime – headed up by former Khmer Rouge cadres and officials who had defected to socialist Vietnam before the invasion – was seen as a global pariah by aid-giving superpowers like the US and UK, who had been engaged in the cold war with the USSR and its allies since 1947. In Cambodia feelings were mixed. Initial jubilation at being saved from the Khmer Rouge was muddied by centuries of warring between Cambodia and Vietnam, some looting of villages by Vietnamese troops during the invasion, and feelings of oppression by some Cambodians, particularly the Mandarin-speaking Chinese-Khmers whose language was silenced by Pol Pot and now discouraged by the PRK. With popularity at a low watermark and a war-torn country to rebuild, the PRK relied heavily on propaganda to motivate Cambodians and keep them onside. In a 1999 *Phnom Penh Post* article entitled 'Lyrics Mirror Political Zigzags' Chhattha remarked on words being as strong as weapons, possessing the power to change a regime – all of which was a far stretch from writing lyrics about girls and rock 'n' roll for the Drakkar. The PRK period was nevertheless a happy and honourable chapter in Chhattha's songwriting career, and he was proud to put his songwriting skills to a virtuous use.

He also continued in his career at the RNK radio. When he had started there, in the early 1970s, staffing levels had hovered at around a hundred. When he retired, the staff numbered 400. His roles ranged from programme organizing to political commentary, to senior management, culminating in being appointed Deputy Director General in 2004. In addition, he has also turned his hand to writing novels, journalism and theatre criticism.

Meanwhile, the joy is that the Drakkar band has had something of a revival since I first interviewed Tana and Chhattha. In 2014, anticipating John Pirozzi's film release, a Hong Kong-based record label called Metal Postcard reissued the *Drakkar 74* album on vinyl. In the years since 2011, the band has also given several interviews and performances, taking their music as far as the USA. Knowing Tana's drive and dogged determination, this touring pace is unlikely to slow. He spent a good amount of time convincing my counterpart, the ethnomusicologist Edouard, and me to help him create a music festival, which in the end turned out to be a well-attended Drakkar show at the Mansion, a colonial ruin-cum-music venue in Phnom Penh.

Some of my most prized time was spent with Chhattha and Tana on this journey. Both men had lived fascinating lives – lives of continual invention and reinvention in the face of extraordinary trauma. When I talked with them about how Cambodia's music today compares to the music they made in the 1960s and 1970s, Tana told me: 'Music brought social change, it hit the heart of everyone. The only way to help the country to become a democracy is freedom of mind . . . rock 'n' roll music. The music of rock 'n' roll in Cambodia helped people to change, to be free.'

Chhattha took the point further: 'The writers now write songs from their head, not their hearts. Every writer during the 1960s and 1970s had a lot of experience. So, every song that they wrote has a spirit. For example, me, I never went to Koh Kong [a province in south-west Cambodia] but when I listened to this song by Sinn Sisamouth, I felt like I was in Koh Kong too. This was the Khmer style, and it was different from now. Today's songs don't have this spirit. The writers now write only for business.'

When it came time to say goodbye, Chhattha left me with such sweet parting words that I understood what Tana meant when he had told me that 'Chhattha could hit my heart'. He touched mine too and I was moved by his sweet, gentle words and their typically magnanimous delivery. He told me, 'I don't have the capacity to write a book myself. Therefore, I'm so happy and I feel so lucky to share my ideas, my heart, my story and my experiences. Thank you.'

Chhattha remains alive and well, although I haven't seen him since 2014. In 2015, the following year, I met Tana again – this time in New York, where he was reunited with his mentor, Mol Kagnol, for the first time in forty years.

10

Cambodia's First Guitar Band

Kamach got all the girls, and I got all the boys . . . boys who wanted to play guitar!

Mol Kagnol, Baksey Cham Krong

Baksey Cham Krong. Front, l–r: Kamach, Kagnol, Samley.

The Pennsylvania Hotel, just down from Times Square, New York, was a hive of activity. Everywhere worker ants were busy scurrying to and from the city outside. In its dimly lit lobby, I spotted a friendly face. I'd met Bounrith, the tour manager, in 2014 when he was managing the Amatak music festival in Cambodia, and was pleased he recognized me instantly. It had been over eight months since I last saw him, and six months since Kevin and I had left Cambodia and moved back to London, having depleted our savings.

We'd settled back into the humdrum of London life and reluctantly rejoined the sea of suited zombie commuters marching soullessly towards their drab offices each morning. After all the vibrancy of Cambodian life, the subway tentacles of Old Street roundabout seemed so grey, ordered and lifeless. I felt like I'd stepped into a dystopian novel about a capitalist experiment gone wrong; a reversal of the movie *The Wizard of Oz*. I felt like I'd seen colour TV for the first time then been forced back; the door to Oz slammed in my face, and I longed for Cambodia, in all its colours, with every inch of my being. So, when an opportunity to experience Cambodian 1960s music live collided with a planned trip to visit family in the States, I wasn't going to miss it for the world.

It was April 2015 when Kevin and I arrived in New York, and spring had announced itself on the blossom-arched streets of Manhattan's West Side. On the Lower East Side, a star-rating or two down from the Pennsylvania, stood our hotel, the infamous St Marks. No longer the roach-infested cesspool of its bygone glory days, the once blighted jazz/punk landmark had fallen out of fashion in the 1980s and reformed itself to a grade-listed state of endearment in the eyes of Manhattan's *new* New Yorkers. Its foundations shook whenever a subway train passed underneath, but it was all our meagre budget could afford, and if I craned my neck out of our fourth-floor window, I could just about see the Chrysler Building. I was in the early stages of pregnancy, and it was a sight that made me want to squeal with delight each morning once I'd peeled my nauseous arms from the toilet bowl.

Three days since the release of John Pirozzi's film about Cambodian rock music, *Don't Think I've Forgotten: Cambodia's Lost Rock and Roll*, the talking heads of the film had begun to surface – some old faces, some new – in the lobby of the Pennsylvania, ready to hit the stage together again for the first time in forty years. I spotted Minh Sothivann first, thanks to his unmistakable and ceaseless smile. It was almost a year to the day since I'd interviewed him about his brother, ex-Apsara bassist Minh Prahul, in Cambodia, only to be surprised by his own incredible tale. He was seated next to Tana, who had taken up a position in the middle of the booth. Centre stage and holding court, he looked every inch the rock star.

Without wasting a moment, Tana introduced me to his ex-producer and mentor, Mol Kagnol, the youngest brother of Baksey Cham Krong, Cambodia's first guitar band. Smooth-faced and calm, Kagnol's almost zen-like disposition struck me first, followed shortly by his wickedly wry sense of humour, which he teased out slowly in a tantalising Cambo-American drawl.

In the preceding few months the *Don't Think . . .* film crew had run a successful Kickstarter campaign to reunite, in song, some of the surviving Cambodian musicians (including the Drakkar and Baksey Cham Krong bands) residing in Cambodia, France and other parts of the States. The crew had spent months co-ordinating flights, accommodation, venues, rehearsals and interviews to culminate in a three-date tour of New York, Silver Spring, Maryland, and Lowell, Massachusetts. Drakkar guitarist Touch Chhattha and drummer Ouk Sam Ath were supposed to join their frontman, Tana, but were unable to receive their visas in time so sadly missed the boat. When I heard of this, I felt so very bad for Chhattha; I know the experience would have meant so much to him.

Tana, on the other hand, was ecstatic to be reunited with Kagnol. He proceeded to tell me that, at the start of rehearsals, Kagnol had arrived in a wheelchair, sitting down to play guitar. But part way through rehearsals he'd ditched the wheelchair for a cane and by the end he was walking unaided. Such was the miracle of music, the group concluded, but Kagnol shrugged it off with a modest, dismissive smile. As he regained strength, his brother Kamach's health unfortunately took a turn for the worse, and on the opening day of the tour, had lost his voice and was resting in his room. I felt for him. Back in my singing days, I seemed to always fall sick before a gig or tour, and trying to get so much as a free warm drink out of the venues I was playing was like asking the Empire for the stolen *Death Star* blueprints.

In the past few months I'd managed, by herculean, dogged efforts, to weasel my way into the film's press schedule to interview the Mol brothers. As Kamach rested, Kagnol and I were ushered with military instruction by the film's press co-ordinator into a quiet hotel bar. I was to have half an hour and not a minute more. We settled onto a couple of wooden stools by the deserted mahogany bar and I learned about Kagnol's early life in Phnom Penh as the youngest of seven brothers. He described his parents as Saigonese – from Vietnam's old capital (now called Ho Chi Minh City) – and in spite of their humble beginnings they'd prospered in Vietnam's silver business during the French colonial rule. In neighbouring Cambodia Kagnol's father, Mol Minh, saw the demand for Cambodian silver balloon under the French protectorate – an industry which achieved global reverence for its silver craftsmen as far back as the Angkor Empire. So, he seized the opportunity to move to Phnom Penh and corner the market. He moved to the right place at the right time and soon became the second wealthiest silversmith in Cambodia. Before long he owned a factory that staffed a few hundred workers and produced silver coveted by Cambodian royalty and the upper class of Phnom Penh society.

Their father's success offered the Mol boys opportunities few in Cambodia could access. Kagnol leant in, cocking one arched eyebrow to disclose: 'I went to a girls' school for the royal family – for some reason my parents took me to that school with permission of the royal family and I wore a sarong. Perhaps it was because we didn't have an equivalent of kindergarten for wealthy families,' he mused with a satirical smile. Certainly at the time there were only elementary, secondary and university schools in Cambodia, and the new secular school system was still distrusted by many Cambodians, who had until 1911 educated their boys in Buddhist wats. Vietnam's secular school system however, was more established, so it didn't surprise me that Kagnol's Vietnamese parents were keen for his education to start young, even if this meant disguising their son's gender to do so.

Kagnol was the last Mol boy to join the family band, and the one to influence the switch from their folk roots in the 1950s to surf rock in the early 1960s. The band's name 'Baksey Cham Krong' is rooted in Khmer mysticism, inspired by a temple and a mystical bird of Cambodian folklore. Legend has it that an ancient Khmer king was saved by and named after a huge bird that swooped down and sheltered him under its wings. The ancient folktale of Baksey Cham Krong tells that upon his coronation King Promakel sought out a fortune teller who told him that the next king would not be his kin but the son of a concubine and the former Khmer king whom Promakel had defeated for the crown. Promakel learned that the boy was now seven years old, lived among the people and bore a chakra sign on his palm.

A farmer named Ta Kohei and his wife adopted the boy when he was a baby. One day they left him alone on a dyke while they worked in the field. An eagle swept down to shelter the baby from the sun, and he was named, forevermore, Baksey Cham Krong: 'the one who is sheltered by the bird's wing'.

Upon hearing the fortune teller's prophesy, Promakel ordered his soldiers to search the land for the boy. When Ta Kohei heard this, he carried the boy on his back and went into hiding. They lived in secrecy for twenty years in a cave in what is now Battambang province, and when King Promakel died, court officials searched the country for Baksey Cham Krong and brought him back to fulfil the prophecy and crown the next king.

The legend of Baksey Cham Krong resonated with the Mol brothers, who based their lyrics mostly on the themes of love and family and virtue. They had a Jackson 5 family band dynamic; their music a mix of crooning and surf guitar – Pat Boone meets Link Wray meets the Shadows. So, I was particularly interested to find out how such a talented dynamic had come to be and how it had traversed such diverse musical tastes. With little time on our side, I probed straight to the heart of the matter with Kagnol: the music. When did he start playing music and what was his first instrument and early musical influences?

'My first taste of sound vibration was a rubber band that I wrapped around my ear and would pluck,' Kagnol demonstrated with an imaginary rubber band. 'I enjoyed the sound of the vibration and I could play it for days. Later on, I got a little more creative with a cigar box, and put the cigar box next to my ear, again with a rubber band to pluck the notes,' he grinned impishly.

The sides of my lips began to curve upwards as Kagnol spoke and I was bewitched. I thought of the tales I'd heard from Tana and others about Kagnol: the inventive, engineering guitarist with a talent for electronics. Only a musical mind could do this – it made perfect sense that his first instrument would be homemade. His first 'bought' instrument was a toy xylophone. He mastered the succession of notes in seconds – 'do, re, me, fa, so, la, ti, do' – before his naturally inquisitive mind turned to skipping notes to create dissonant, minor tones. The xylophone was followed by a toy piano his mother bought him, that in its simplicity was missing sharp and flat keys and was a great disappointment to Kagnol.

When the youngest Mol reached the third grade, he got his hands on a little accordion. His school had gardening activities in the afternoon, and Kagnol would sit and entertain the teachers with his accordion while his older brother, Kamach, sang. This was followed by his first foray with a guitar, around the age of eight years old. His much older brother, Saem, owned an electronics shop, which had an acoustic guitar that Kagnol quickly learned to play but bored of within a few years. The 1950s was the era of the electric guitar, with Fender birthing both the Stratocaster and the Telecaster and Chuck Berry donning his Gibson ES-350T to play 'Johnny B Goode'. Across the Pacific, Kagnol turned to the acoustic guitar, took in the electronics surrounding him in his brother's shop and made a discovery that would change his life. Once again, a rubber band was involved: 'My dad gave me a rubber band and I wrapped it around the acoustic guitar,' Kagnol told me, using his hand to demonstrate. 'I stuck a microphone to the guitar with the rubber band and it vibrated, and then I ran it through an amplifier and speaker. I fell in love with that electric guitar sound.'

A handful of times in my life I've met a musician who just seems destined for their time and their craft, as if it's impossible to imagine them doing anything else. Kagnol struck me this way. We talked of his early musical influences: from Pat Boone to Paul Anka to Elvis Presley. We talked of the Ventures and the Shadows and the birth of Baksey Cham Krong's second formation with its youngest member. But just as we were hitting our stride, the film's press co-ordinator called time, and before I could properly say goodbye *The Wall Street Journal* was ushered in as I was ushered out. The whole thing had the feel of planning a wedding. After months of planning, my time with Kagnol was gone in a flash.

Don't Think I've Forgotten was screened again that night at the Film Forum in SoHo. Ten years in the making, the documentary contains some phenomenal footage of the musicians and Phnom Penh in the swinging 1960s, especially the black and white footage of a long-haired Yol Aularong and singers Pen Ram and Sieng Vanthy in mini-dresses wildly unleashing their music on an outdoor stage. At the time of release there were plans for executive director Youk Chhang's agency, The Documentation Center of Cambodia, to add the film to the organization's mobile film library and tour the country, simultaneously preserving and bringing this history alive for thousands of Cambodians in the farthest flung places.

After the screening, we walked a stone's throw to SoHo's City Winery, for the first leg of the film's music tour. The Winery's queue snaked around the building, fifty people long, for the best part of an hour, as small groups trickled through the door before more replaced them outside: people of all ages and colours – from white to black to Khmer – and all backgrounds, from groups of hard-up Bushwick hipsters to affluent, middle-aged Upper West Side couples; from film-crew friends to curious strangers. It made me reflect on how universal this music was – and still is; how it cuts across all slices of society and across all continents.

Inside, between exposed brick walls, the Winery's floor was set up like a supper club, with a dozen or more large round, white-clothed tables. The lighting was moody and the atmosphere was fired up with anticipation, warmth and love for the performers about to take the stage for the first time in forty years. The late, great 'Big Mike' was there. Kevin and I had spent many a debaucherous night at his dive bar, Sharky's, in Phnom Penh. If there was ever an iconic moment in rock history, Mike was there. In *Woodstock*, the movie, Mike can be seen standing backstage, just over Jimi Hendrix's shoulder. True to form, Mike wasn't going to miss this and had flown all the way from Phnom Penh to New York to be there. People flitted around from table to table, Kevin and I took our seats stage right and, as I sat down at our table and ordered a drink, I scanned the room for other familiar faces. LinDa Saphan, the artist and social anthropologist who helped arrange my interview with Kagnol, her husband, John Pirozzi, and various crew members worked the room. Dengue

Fever's lead singer Chhom Nimol made a grand entrance with a glamorous entourage of glittering young Khmer women fanning out beside her. On the other side of the room, Tana hobnobbed with friends and fans.

A few minutes later the lights dimmed further and a pale purple stage light slowly emerged as the shadows of the night's backing band shifted onstage to take their positions behind the drums and keyboard, the bassist plugging into a bass amp. In those long moments awaiting the first act, the silence was so pronounced I could have heard a pin drop. Baksey Cham Krong eventually appeared one by one, with Mol Kagnol on lead guitar, ex-Baksey Cham Krong and Bayon band guitarist Hong Samley on acoustic rhythm guitar, and Minh Sothivann on an electric rhythm guitar. Mol Kagnol, aided by a walking stick, took his place on a high stool to strap on his electric guitar. Naturally, he started the set with a few impromptu jokes and had the audience eating out of his palm before he'd strummed his first note. The trio kicked off with a fast blues progression, Kagnol's surf guitar reverberating around the room. It was hard to believe that this natural and highly accomplished player had supposedly locked his guitars away upon his musical retirement in 1975 and only dusted them down again recently. They played Baksey Cham Krong's big hits, including their early easy listening standards like 'Pleine Lune' ('Full Moon'), the indelible Santo and Johnny-style riffs of 'Adios Maman Chérie' and their spaghetti western slow *norteño* 'Je Te Quitterai' ('I Will Leave You'). Mol Kagnol rounded out the set with a trailblazing performance of their electrifying skiffle-drum, surf-guitar instrumental 'BCK', Kagnol's fast tremolo howling through their two-minute classic before his signature whammy bar bent for a final time, all too soon.

Second up, Sinn Sisamouth's thirty-year-old grandson, Sethakol, shyly stepped up to the mic in his grandfather's trademark dickie bow and tux. As he crooned the first sentence to

Sisamouth's career-defining hit 'Champa Battambang' the crowd went wild. His talent, nerves and clothing paid homage to his grandfather and endeared him to the crowd, and I found myself swept up in the tide of woops, claps and calls from fans and the older musicians willing him on from the side of the stage. When I closed my eyes, I felt I was hearing the great man sing again.

Minh Sothivann followed Sethakol's set, playfully enacting Yol Aularong's hits, including Aularong favourite 'Cyclo', tilting the neck of his cream Fender Stratocaster on the backbeat and lurching to the mic. 'Cyclo?' he glissandoed, raising a hand to his ear to tease a call and response from the audience. 'CYCLO!' the audience erupted in unison. 'Cyclo?' he teased again. 'CYCLO!' we called back, and the first verse tumbled forth, Sothivann pogoing across the stage between lines, clearly enraptured and having the time of his life.

Of the revivalist generation, California resident and Dengue Fever lead singer Chhom Nimol masterfully took charge of some Ros Sereysothea and Pen Ran songs before welcoming Tana onto the stage to end the show with a few Drakkar and Touch Tana numbers. I wasn't surprised when Tana proudly started his set with his beloved 'Boer Bang Min Maytha', bringing Nimol back on to sing Mao Sareth's part, moving a few audience members to their feet to swerve and sway to the music. The set ended with some hilarious banter between Tana and Kagnol, the protégé and his master, before Tana motioned to all the offstage musicians to return, stand together and take a bow. There were tears onstage and off, every member of the seated audience rising for the duration of a lengthy standing ovation. It was profoundly emotional to witness these musicians reunite again to share their music with the wider world after forty years apart. After all they had suffered and all they had lost, they were able to stand together again and play their music, decades after they began as young men.

City Winery show, l–r: Tana, Kagnol (seated), Sothivann.

I said my goodbyes, watched the crowd filter out, and, just like that, left the whirlwind of New York behind. My interview with Kamach would have to wait a few months, until I met him again, this time in Paris.

The first autumn leaves had started to fall when Kevin and I arrived in the French capital that September. My friend and translator, Martin Jay, met us at the Gare du Nord, which was just a stone's throw from the one-bedroom apartment he shared with a friend. I'd met Martin in Cambodia the previous year, and it was Martin, along with Oro and Sophorn, with whom I'd shared the Keo Thorng Gnut–Khmer Rouge–Stung Treng adventure. A talented storyboard editor and photographer by day, and breakdancer by night, Martin had the most genuine of intentions. He was now living back in Paris, and working with his friend Fabrice Géry on a side project: a record label called Akuphone, releasing obscure and virtually unknown vintage music from the farthest flung corners of the world. The cerebral, sophisticated French cousin of more well-known reissue labels like Sublime Frequencies, Light in the Attic and Dust-to-Digital, founder and crate-digger Fabrice was keen for the label's focus to set it apart, with an interest in political and ritualistic music as well as the usual rare pop and folk music releases. Straddling both 20th-century music and the relics of yore, Fabrice's recherché catalogue spans modern-day jazz, dub, electronic and synth, with echoes of Africa and a little French poetry thrown in the mix. Records like avant-garde trumpet player Jac Berrocal's *Exterior Lux* collaboration with composers David Fenech and Vincent Epplay; Japanese jazz and folk singer Chiemi Eri's 1958–1962 releases – no doubt a precursor to popular 1960s and 1970s blues, jazz and folk sensation Maki Asakawa – and the reggae, afrobeat and free-jazz inflected 'Saba-Saba Fighting' by French-Congolese artist Mushapata, a one-time bodyguard to Bob Marley, whose lyrical fighting spirit was fuelled largely by the ideas of Pan-African martyr Patrice Lumumba. And bands like folktronica outfit Ko Shin Moon, whose extra-terrestrial, kaleidoscopic world is what I imagine Lee 'Scratch' Perry, David Bowie, Bootsy Collins and Roland Kirk might sound like had they formed a band, been abducted by aliens then dumped in Algiers with every instrument ever made and a lifetime's supply of acid. Needless to say, the label was right up my street.

I met Fabrice the day after the Akuphone family celebrated their first release, a collection of 1960s Chinese folk songs by the singer Lily Chao. The following week he and Martin were due to travel to Cambodia to trace the story of a collection of Cambodian liberation songs by the composer and violinist Oum Dara, which Fabrice had exhumed from the racks of a record shop in Turkey. Supposedly recorded in the 1980s, the pro-royalist, anti-Vietnamese protest songs were a mystery. How and where had they been recorded, I wondered? Surely not in a desecrated and war-torn Cambodia? Who were the musicians on the record sleeve photo who'd taken such risks to perform an array of Dara's songs from the 1960s and 1970s – including one that he'd written for Sinn Sisamouth? And, how had this collection ended up in a record shop in Turkey of all places? I'd tried to interview Oum Dara myself while in Cambodia in 2014, but his health was fragile and I'd run out of time to travel to his Siem Reap home. I hoped that one year on Dara was doing better and that the boys might find the answers to the questions we shared.

Martin walked Kevin and me along the Rue du Faubourg Saint-Denis' mile-long array of Indian shops, past the smells of incense, durian and fish, through the black market – the stench of urine under the bridge of La Chapelle métro clinging stubbornly to our nostrils – then onto Rue Pajol where our hotel was located. We reconvened a couple of hours later to eat at the restaurant of a Khmer-Vietnamese lady who was taken by surprise when Martin and I opened our mouths to greet her with the Khmer word for an informal 'hello': '*Suasaday.*' She chuckled and her whole face – which had been severely stretched by a scraped-back bun – softened. '*Soksabay?*' ('How are you?') she asked coyly.

'*Soksabay,*' ('Fine,') Martin smiled.

'*Soksabay, Awkun,*' I added, with thanks, as she passed a few seated diners and motioned for us to sit at one of five unoccupied rectangular tables covered in a faded plastic tablecloth with a floral motif. The décor left a lot to be desired – the minimum of funds and effort had been applied to the drab, tiled room – but therein lay its charm and authenticity. It reminded me of any one of the local Phnom Penh restaurants I used to eat in. However, this time my eyes may have been in Cambodia but my ears were in Paris.

Because of France's colonial past in Cambodia, the country opened its borders to as many as 50,000 Cambodian refugees after the war. The estimated number of the Cambodian diaspora is now around 80,000, which swamps numbers in the UK – less than 1,000 according to the last census – or anywhere else in Europe, for that matter. Many refugees settled in the suburbs of major industrial cities like Lyon or Paris, where they could find enough work to provide for their families. A global currency crisis in the late 1960s, the oil crisis of 1973, subsequent inflation and a recession in the 1980s meant that France during this time was in economic turmoil. However, thanks in part to the media coverage of the genocide, and in part to the passive and enterprising manner of most Khmers – many of whom were already accustomed to French culture – most were able to find work quickly. They went to work for Chinese restauranteurs and shopkeepers, or set up shops themselves, like this one. Martin had stumbled on a rare gem here – an authentic Cambodian restaurant, with the nation's traditional dish, *amok* (fish curry), and other familiar selections on the menu. We humoured our host by ordering in Khmer and gorged ourselves on dishes we'd missed. Long-forgotten smells of lemongrass and ginger filled our nostrils and sapid tastes of fragrant spices, coconut milk and fish oil lingered delightfully on our tongues long after we'd finished eating.

Afterwards, we headed along the canal to meet our mutual friend, Edouard. He was visiting from Bangkok, and I hadn't seen him since he'd invited me to share the adventure of the epic Touch Tana interviews the previous year. His cropped black hair was now long, wild and streaked with white. It was a joy to reunite with him at Chez Adel's quirky 1970s wood-panelled bar for a long and lively night in north Paris with Martin and Edouard's friends.

The following morning, while the Marché Saint-Quentin was stirring, Kevin and I bought some croissants and fruit and made our way to Martin's apartment to prepare for our first interview of the day. Arriving on time, a swathe of lightly styled jet-black hair shuffled through the doorway. He wore a black woollen jumper and a small shoulder bag that rested high on his chest, which, coupled with his 5 feet 2 inch frame and unassuming demeanour, had a charming effect. Following the illness that rendered Kamach missing in action in New York, I'd asked Martin to contact him for an interview in Paris. Martin had spent the ensuing months cultivating a relationship of trust with Kamach, who, Martin told me, was guarded and suspicious of most people. But Martin's persistence paid off, and I was excited to interview Baksey Cham Krong's lead singer – this time in his city.

We began by talking a little of his childhood. The sixth of seven brothers, Kamach apprised me of memories of his neighbourhood in Phnom Penh, his home, and the street outside his father's factory lined with cars visiting one of Cambodia's most coveted silversmiths. Prince Sihanouk was a regular customer, buying presents to take on his foreign tours, and was on first-name terms with Kamach's father, Mol Minh, and his wife.

The Mols suffered the loss of four girls who all died young, but the fortune of seven healthy boys in what the couple believed was a curse borne of the idea that the girls could not support the family fortune, so the gods sent boys. Their first boy, Samot, was born in 1928. When he reached adulthood he gained employment at the tax office but, in his spare time, made and played banjos. Samine was born two years later and ended up working for the military department, but while off duty played guitar. Their brother Samel was born in 1931, played violin and was the writer and arranger for Baksey Cham Krong's first incarnation, and worked as a maths teacher at a college in Battambang. Kamach worshipped Samel. 'Even Sinn Sisamouth could not write like him,' he asserted. 'Samel had a very original way of writing.'

Then there was Saem, born in 1935. Unlike his older brothers, Saem was not musically inclined. But he was the most sociable and outgoing of the brothers, and would go on to follow Samot and his father in turning his hand to creating amps and making things that people couldn't find in Cambodia. He would buy the raw elements for building vocal microphones, electric guitars and amps that he saw on TV broadcasts or read about in his uncle's electronics books. Saem was an untrained but natural engineer, just like his father. But that is where their similarities ended. For where Mol Minh, the grafter from humble beginnings, made inventions to serve a purpose, to be manufactured and sold for a profit, his son Saem was less interested in the financial end game and motivated more by the sheer curiosity of invention.

Fifth in line Samkol didn't play an instrument either, but he too was outgoing, and when he wasn't working his job at the tax office would be indulging in his ardour for organizing parties. The best looking of all the boys, he played a valuable role on the managerial side of the family band, brokering recording deals – from their first vinyl recording through to working with the Capitol record label and, later, the lauded producer Van Chann. Kamach entered the world on 20 September 1941, thirteen years after his oldest brother and five years before the youngest Mol boy, Kagnol, in 1946.

By all accounts, Kamach had a loving but turbulent relationship with his devoted but somewhat overbearing father. 'My father was very serious,' he told me, his face pinched with perturbation. 'He liked justice, and when he felt injustice he suffered a lot. He was very pure and very good, and he suffered when people did not treat him with the same respect he gave to them. He taught us good morals and educated us well. My mother did too. But where my father was a pessimist, my mother was more of a realist. He viewed the world and society one way, and when society and the world let him down he became more pessimistic.' Kamach thought that his father's habit of bestowing harsh views on the world was intended as a kindness to his sons, to prepare them for the cruelties of life. But, in effect, the result just made it harder for the boys to integrate into society. One of his father's techniques for toughening and shaping his boys had a psychologically damaging effect on the more sensitive members of the family like Kamach.

'My father was a perfectionist,' Kamach continued. 'So when

we used to gather around the table for a family meal, he'd say, "Let's critique each other to become better people." What was supposed to be something positive had a negative effect. I loved my father, he wanted his kids to aspire and be better, but asking each other to talk about our weaknesses just created tension between us. He had good intentions but he didn't realize the effect.'

Despite these tensions, Kamach and his father were close. I got the sense all Kamach wanted was to please his father, and that Minh saw in his son a kindred spirit; a seeker with a strong moral compass, constantly searching for the truth. Kamach would devour books on psychology from France and, as he grew, became something of an adviser and confidant to his father.

When he wasn't philosophizing, Kamach spent his time listening to music. He would sit by the family's wireless with pen and paper and wait for Sinn Sisamouth to come on, then furiously scribble down the lyrics in real time. If he missed a word, he'd have to wait patiently by the radio until the next time the song came back around. He was surrounded by music from a young age. Western instruments of just about every shape, size and origin – from a shop-bought accordion and violin to a homemade banjo, mandolin and guitars – charged the frequencies of the Mol household. Samot, Samine and Samel first formed the band in the 1940s, primarily to entertain their family; their original folk and French cabaret formation heavily influenced by the likes of Tino Rossi, Édith Piaf and, later, Paul Anka. Samel took the lead in songwriting and continued to play violin. Samine stuck with guitar too, while Samot added accordion and mandolin to his banjo playing. In the beginning, a friend called Tha Luch sang lead vocal.

The same year that Columbia Records unveiled the first 12-inch, 33⅓ rpm record in the US, in Cambodia Mol Minh had set his tinkering fingers to creating a microphone. It was 1948 and, aside from in RNK radio station, microphones were hard to come by. In order to test his invention's sound, he asked his seven-year-old son Kamach to step up onto a soap-box and read into the device from *Les Milles et Une Nuits* (*One Thousand and One Nights*). In effect, it was to be Kamach's first live performance. Half speaking, half singing out of the speakers, Kamach's sweet, young soprano pleased his neighbours and word spread about the boy's gift. Inevitably, within a few years, the vocalist, Tha Luch, was ousted from the band – regrettably – by Kamach who by now, aged ten years old, was learning to play acoustic guitar under the direction of the Cambodian composer renowned for his chart-topping torch songs and penning poetic lyrics for the likes of Sinn Sisamouth and Ros Sereysothea: Peou Sipho. Kamach passed on Peou Sipho's teachings to the youngest Mol boy, who took to the guitar so naturally it wasn't long before Kagnol surpassed his brother's knowledge of the instrument, and their father was helping fasten makeshift amps to his son's classical gut-string axe. Kamach leaned back, looking pensive. He paused for a moment to capture our full attention, before opening his mouth to say, 'He was like a plant just waiting for the rain, and as soon as the rain came the plant grew very fast. That was Kagnol and the guitar.'

The band became official in 1959. That was the year they stepped out of their practice space and into public view, with concerts and radio recordings. Second-in-line, off-military-duty guitarist Samine wrote the band's first hit, 'Adios, Mama and Papa' while en route to study in Paris. Released on a live radio broadcast in 1959, the song was a farewell to his childhood and an expression of gratitude to the parents who raised him. It laid the foundation of Baksey Cham Krong's pop career, and for that, and its wide-eyed sincerity, it's a song still close to Kamach's heart. But dearest of all to Kamach was a song written originally in 1953 by third in line, Samel, called 'Pleine Lune' ('Full Moon').

It became pivotal to the band's success when recorded live on RNK radio in 1959. It was released later that year on a 7-inch single, and later remastered on the French label Akuphone in 2016.

'The original title was "Don't Follow Mother's Advice",' Kamach told me, his face radiating with nostalgia. 'It was the story of a girl who was abandoned by her husband because she slept with another man before her wedding; the guy then left her and it's his story. She didn't follow the advice of her mother and it was very immoral for a girl to cheat on a man in Cambodia at that time. The story goes that the mother tried to raise her daughter well, tried to give her a good education and show her the right way, but the girl didn't listen.' Kamach broke into song, his voice as pitch perfect as the version he recorded with Baksey Cham Krong in 1959.

In the song, the moon becomes a metaphor for the woman, her sexuality and virginity; the moon being connected to a woman's fertility and cycles, it's beauty waxing and waning with its rhythms – or in this case, sexual status. The lyrics, 'Now your beauty is fading, Oh, full moon, you were beautiful . . .' were characteristic of the views placed on women and the *chbab srey* of 1950s Cambodia. Virginity represented beauty and purity; it is still highly prized and, abominably, an entire swathe of the sex industry – funded by wealthy, older Asian men – relies on farming out the virginity of young, poor girls for a high price.

With a last-minute title change the song's use of metaphors was clever enough to pass the strict vetting of the songwriters' association at the Ministry of Information when it was recorded for a live radio broadcast in 1959. It was later resubmitted to the ministry when it was recorded for a 45 rpm single. To manipulate the establishment's strict rigidity on lyrics deemed too sexual for the time, Samel lied, saying that 'Pleine Lune' was copied from an already established popular Chinese song. In essence, what Samel was saying was, if it was OK for Mao, it was OK for

Cambodia's new world order. The plan worked, and it was only after its release, when some more astute listeners wrote in to complain of the song's vulgarity, did Samel reveal he had in fact written it, and the song was indeed riddled with sexual innuendo. Bowing to public pressure, 'Pleine Lune' was subsequently banned. Baksey Cham Krong had earned their rock 'n' roll stripes.

By 1960 the band were entering their second formation and departing more and more from the innocent, crooner ballads that had brought about their fame, to embrace the sounds of a new decade. Kamach was growing in confidence and had, with the release of 'The Rose of Battambang', begun to take the songwriting mantle from his older brother Samel. With its sixteen-note beat and jangle pop guitar accentuated by a dreamy tremolo riff, Kamach's lyrics sang of a holiday romance experienced while the band were on hiatus and living temporarily in Battambang with Samel. Kamach's heart-throb quiff and large brown eyes sent hysteria coursing through the veins of every red-blooded teenage girl that came to their shows – as Kagnol had once told me with a sly smile: 'Kamach got all the girls, and I got all the boys . . . boys who wanted to play guitar!'

In 1961 the Mol brothers went to the cinema to watch the movie *The Young Ones*, starring Cliff Richard, with a soundtrack by his band the Shadows. It was the height of 'Shadowmania', the year the Shadows toured Asia, and listening to that soundtrack was a moment that changed the band forever. They went back again and again to watch the movie, studying each movement and committing the moves to memory. Soon afterwards, the British invasion landed in Cambodia and plastered itself on 7-inch single import sleeves, the co-ordinated Vox Phantom guitars of Peter Jay and the Jaywalkers in particular catching Kagnol's eye. He was by now fifteen years old and an electric guitar zealot, immersed in American and British pop culture. Kagnol took a drawing he'd made of the Vox Phantom's pentagonal shape to a carpenter to build the body, had it painted the same colour red as a hot rod he'd seen in a magazine, and built the electronics of the guitar himself. This guitar would become as famous throughout Cambodia as Kagnol's playing. Playing that instrument made him so popular with aspiring guitarists that it earned him the moniker 'Uncle Solo', even though Kagnol himself was really no older than the teenage boys who christened him thus. He had, by then, taken Kamach's seat next to the family wireless, which had begun picking up shortwave radio broadcasts from Bangkok of Chuck Berry and Kagnol's favourite band, the Ventures.

As the youngest Mol learned to imitate the surf sounds of his heroes, and Chum Kem achieved both uproar and success with Cambodia's first big rock 'n' roll song, Baksey Cham Krong began the transition from their lovelorn crooner ballads to a new, harder surf sound. Prior to Kem, Baksey had been too frightened of reprisal from the establishment and adhered to the RNK radio's nationalist policy and ban on English language songs. However, with the ground Kem laid, they started shaking off their innocence, even venturing into avant-garde surf instrumentals drenched in spring reverb and testosterone. But, just as soon as we were entering this new chapter in the band's evolution there was a knock at Martin's door.

Kamach's one-time bandmate, Baksey's ex rhythm-guitarist, Hong Samley, also lived in Paris and I was keen to talk to him about his time in both Baksey Cham Krong and, later, the Bayon band. We'd scheduled to interview both musicians that day, but Samley arrived an hour early – the exact scenario that Martin had wanted to avoid, and I soon find out why.

Dressed in a cowboy shirt with metal lapels, modern bifocals, a suit jacket and matching trousers, Samley swaggered into Martin's Parisian salon as if it were a wildwest saloon – and a tension immediately replaced the warm and light space we'd cultivated over the past three hours. What I'd originally thought might be merely age-old bandmate rivalry I soon suspected could have been something that ran far deeper. On the course of my journey I'd often heard Cambodians say things like, 'Cambodians hate each other.' Or, 'Why can't our people just get along?' And I'd heard Kamach talk of this, even within the expat community in France. The age-old rivalries – anti-Vietnamese, anti-Chinese, anti-Thai – hatred seemed to have travelled the distance both in time and place. From what I understand, the strong caste system remains in place within the French-Cambodian society, just as it does in Cambodia. Then there's the factor of trauma: trauma from war, trauma from genocide, trauma from relocation. I'd heard French-Cambodians described as people 'living in the shadows', culturally indistinct from any other Asian immigrant to the average French person. Khmer restaurant and shopworkers who own their own businesses often tout them as 'Chinese' or 'Vietnamese', sacrificing their true identity in favour of what's popular and familiar with their French customer base.

After we'd exchanged pleasantries, Samley sat next to Kevin on a futon a few feet from Martin. Kamach and I continued with the interview as Samley tried his best to distract my husband, who was trying to listen intently to Kamach. As Kevin's politeness started to wear thin, the rest of us tried to ignore the disturbance and keep focused on Kamach.

The early to mid-1960s signalled a time in the Baksey Cham Krong story when the band were on top of their game – but the scene was changing, and other artists were starting to come to prominence. Older hands were also adapting. In 1962 Sinn Sisamouth released his hit song, 'Champa Battambang' ('The Flower of Battambang'), then later released 'The Rose of Tokyo', both of which were suspiciously close in title to Kamach's 1960 surf ballad, 'The Rose of Battambang'.

'What was clever about Sisamouth was that he was aware of what was popular and would follow what was popular,' Kamach told me reverently. He went on to tell me Kagnol once overheard Sisamouth heap accolades upon Kamach's songwriting abilities, and there was a time when Sisamouth tried to win Kamach and Kagnol over to his backing band, but the boys were dedicated to each other. 'We said no because we were loyal to our family,' Kamach confided virtuously. 'When you played for Sisamouth, you gave him everything.'

Kamach and I talked about Baksey Cham Krong's studio career, and how they came to work with Van Chann in the 1960s – that was until Van Chann wanted to work with Sisamouth, and, to the boys' dismay, they were swiftly thrown off the studio roster in favour of Sisamouth's rising star. The boys moved into rival producer Heng Heng's studio, and later found out that Sisamouth, in his newfound fame, had agreed to work with Van Chann on the condition that competitors like Baksey Cham Krong no longer recorded there. (Sisamouth later apologized for the snub, chalking his behaviour down to his ambition and the cut-throat business of 'making it' in the music industry, whatever the cost. Thereafter the Mol brothers and Sisamouth remained on good terms and Baksey Cham Krong did eventually work with Van Chann again.)

With the success of 'Champa Battambang', Sisamouth's fame began to eclipse Baksey Cham Krong's. Later that year, the Apsara band burst onto the scene and with more and more *yé-yé* bands and solo artists emerging, the industry was fast approaching its mid-1960s boom. Much like their heroes the Shadows who were now being superseded by bands like the Beatles and the Rolling Stones in the UK, by the mid-1960s in Cambodia Baksey Cham Krong, progenitors of Cambodian rock, were slowly fading into the background. Work, family and education commitments were largely to blame, but the band continued to release the odd record from time to time: songs like their surf classic 'BCK.' in 1964. As was the case with other Cambodian surf bands like Apsara, Baksey's sound was, for the most part, fixed firmly at the softer end of the surf-rock spectrum – a Ronny & the Daytonas ballad vibe – and they released surf weepies by the bucketload. 'BCK' (sometimes credited as 'SKD'), however, was a deviation and more in tune with the Shadows and Minneapolis band the Trashmen's more jarring sound on tracks like 'Malaguena' and 'A-Bone', though Baksey never quite graduated to the band's rockabilly hits like 'Surfin' Bird'. Kagnol's makeshift Phantom screams to life to signal the beginning of the two-minute surf instrumental, the drumbeat galloping to keep up with Kagnol's fast tremolo picking which transports the listener first to Mexico then back to Cambodia in the second verse, Kagnol's signature muted-string technique transforming his guitar momentarily into the Cambodian folk instrument that Touch Tana talked of, the *takhe*. As surf instrumentals go, it's up there with the Chantays' 'Pipeline' and Dick Dale's 'Misirlou'.

By 1965 Baksey Cham Krong's recording career had all but ground to a halt, and a year later the band played their last show, at the Lycée Sisowath high school – the place they'd played their first gig in 1959. By the time the Mol brothers walked out onto a Cambodian stage for the last time, the band had come full circle, the 1960s were in full swing and, despite Baksey's waning popularity, this show was one of their wildest. Girls screamed in adulation and rushed the stage; oestrogen and teenage fervour almost collapsing the rostrum and calling a premature halt to the show. Fans will remember Baksey Cham Krong going out with a bang, however, in reality, there was no real plan, no cataclysmic finish, no finite moment; more an eventual acknowledgement – years later – of their gentle erosion. One by one, its band members followed other pursuits, and before they knew it, it had been months since they'd last played together. Kamach finished his studies and went to work for a bank in Phnom Penh, and it was only when he visited his brother Kagnol in New York decades later that he acknowledged regret for the way Baksey Cham

Krong had ended. 'We were in Kagnol's basement surrounded by instruments,' Kamach remarked forlornly. 'And we looked at each other deeply and Kagnol said to me, "Just look at what we can do in three or four days. We never took music as far as we could."'

Kagnol got out before the fall of Phnom Penh. His parents had long wished all their boys would eventually grow out of the band and settle down into families and 'proper' careers. Following Baksey Cham Krong's split their youngest son followed the path the rest of his brothers had by then set and appeased his parents' career aspirations with a university qualification in structural engineering, before later answering the call of duty to his country, resigning from his job and signing up to become a helicopter pilot in Lon Nol's Khmer Republic army. He was sent by the army to train at Fort Eustis, Virginia, USA, in the spring of 1975 – the timing of which saved Kagnol's life. In Cambodia, Kamach, their older brothers and their parents were not so lucky.

In March 1975, just one month before the Khmer Rouge takeover of Phnom Penh, Kamach married the woman he would go on to spend the rest of his life with. She was a pretty girl from a wealthy and well connected family and, after five years of war, the wedding provided the new couple with a brief moment of happiness in a time of turmoil. The Mol brothers knew by now that the Khmer Rouge were coming to take the capital, and Samine begged Kamach to ask his new father-in-law to lean on his contacts and find a helicopter to escape the city. But Kamach's father-in-law was a socialist and had different ideas about what was to come. He genuinely believed the Khmer Rouge takeover would be peaceful.

Kamach, on the other hand, knew it wouldn't be: 'When the Khmer Rouge arrived I understood that they were not coming to talk, they were coming to win the war. That evening, the communists said, "We've won the war." And I knew then that they were not coming in peace. In the night, we heard lots of trucks and noise, and in the morning they came with guns and told us to leave the city. They told us, "The Americans are coming to bomb the city." We didn't know what to take so we just took one bag, and left a lot of things – jewels, everything. We had a car just to put our luggage in; there was no petrol any more, so we pushed the car.' By this point Kamach's father-in-law had seen the bodies and witnessed first hand the brutality of the cadres. He'd heard the ominous announcements on tannoys, and he too knew that the Khmer Rouge had not come in peace. He had connections in Vietnam, and persuaded his family and Kamach to head towards the border: 'My family crossed the river to go to the province, and me and my wife's family continued towards Vietnam. That was the last time I saw my family. My fifth brother Mol Samel chose to follow his wife's mother because they were Chinese and knew the way out of Cambodia better than most Cambodians . . . he was supposed to come back but he didn't. Kagnol survived, but my five other brothers died during the genocide.'

Just then, from the corner of the room, Samley's ever-increasing sighing, belching and talking in monologues to Kevin escalated. Like a volcano that had been bubbling away for the past twenty minutes, Samley finally erupted, and there was a sudden flurry of French and Khmer crossfire between him and Kamach. We'd all felt the tension mounting – now it burst into open vitriol between the two musicians. The 19th-century Cambodian King Norodom Narottama had once compared Cambodian people to water buffalo – that is, extremely placid until provoked – and, in true Cambodian style, the acceleration of the exchange went from nought to sixty in a matter of seconds. Martin, Kevin and I were rendered helpless bystanders, our heads swivelling from left to right faster than match point at a Wimbledon final. Though his grasp on Khmer was good, Martin pleaded with the pair to speak in French, in part to slow things down, and in part to bring some kinship to Kamach's cause, for while Martin could speak Khmer it was not his native tongue. Samley eventually complied, and it was then that he shed some light on the issue.

'Why are you talking about personal history?' he vociferated rhetorically, fixing his eyes on me. 'This is supposed to be about music. Why aren't you talking about music? You media journalists are always asking about the Khmer Rouge and are not interested in music. You are just interested in making money for your project and don't give us anything!'

Taken aback, I summoned every ounce of my sangfroid and replied coolly, 'We *have* been talking about music for the past three hours. I just asked Kamach, "When did you come to Paris?" And he chose to tell us about his time in Cambodia during the Khmer Rouge. That is his choice and I am here to listen to the story that he wants to tell. I have no interest in profiting from my book; I have spent all my savings on this project. It's never been about making money for me, but about preserving history . . .' I went on.

It took a while to placate Samley. It was obvious that there was more to all this than met the eye. The pair had history, probably stemming, I sensed, from the rancour Samley still seemed to feel about Kamach's family money and class – and maybe other bandmate rivalries or trauma the conversation could have stirred up. But without understanding every word of what was said in French and Khmer, I wasn't sure of what I might have missed. I knew that confronting or rejecting Samley would have only made things worse for Kamach, who was clearly shaken by the altercation. But, all the same, I wanted to howl. I was caving in with regret over my lack of foresight and the hulking weight of responsibility I felt for not asking Samley, on arrival, to return once we'd finished interviewing Kamach. I felt I'd failed Kamach. To assuage the tension between the pair – sensing Kamach's reluctance to continue and heeding Martin's suggestions to halt and swap – I paused Kamack's interview and gave Samley the spotlight. It was an act of conciliation only in that I knew Samley still had a verbal assault weapon poised and pointed squarely at Kamach's head, so if I offered him centre stage he would most likely take his finger off the trigger. Samley and Kamach swapped seats. I offered Kamach some food, lay a hand on his shoulder and, begrudgingly, Martin and I, with our pulses still beating at double speed, began setting up to interview Kamach's former bandmate.

Hong Samley is one of Cambodia's most celebrated rock guitarists, but his start in life turned out to be quite different to that of the Mol brothers. He was born into a large family, one of twenty children fathered by his father and two wives, as was often the custom in those days. But having a sibling count in double figures is where the similarities between Samley and the Mol brothers end. Samley's father was an electrician who headed up a company that sold air-conditioning repair machines in the post-war economic boom. He made a decent living: enough to put food on the table today, but not enough to not worry about putting food on the table tomorrow. Hong Snr had worked hard to get to the top of his organization and had great hopes that his son, Samley, might follow in his footsteps, both in work and in marriage to a woman of his own Chinese-Khmer ethnicity. Samley would disappoint his father on both fronts: 'My father told me, "If you want to be a musician, you will never be happy."' But in spite of his father's foreboding, Samley would prove him wrong, having forged a successful music career and a happy marriage to a French woman for the past thirty-eight years. 'I have a family, we play and love . . .' he waxed lyrical, puffing his chest out and gazing out on Paris for added effect. 'I am happy when I sing and talk about music – and feel like something is missing when I'm not singing.'

As a young boy Samley hated school. Most of the teachers were ex-monks who ruled with an iron rod – or, in their particular case, canes. Samley was brutalized from the age of five and, as a result of his behaviour and his trauma, he took an average of two years to complete each year grade.

Aged fourteen, his mother died. To distract his son from his grief, Hong Snr bought Samley a guitar. Just two short years later the young Shadows fan auditioned for Baksey Cham Krong. It was 1963. The band liked the sixteen-year-old's playing and admired his honest, lionhearted ambition. He quickly found himself swept up in a world of glittering, high-society parties, playing for Cambodian royalty and the city's most influential families. He was recording RNK radio shows and playing concerts in all manner of venues, including the big stage at Prince Sihanouk's biannual Sangkum Party Congress Day celebrations, alongside the likes of Sisamouth and the bebop and marching bands of the time.

Samley admired Prince Sihanouk. He talked of the background divide he felt between himself and his wealthier bandmates, and of the tensions between what he classed 'the professional working musician' such as himself, and wealthier counterparts. Despite the seismic class divide between Samley and Sihanouk, the pair were united in their belief that societal barriers could be broken by music. In her study 'Norodom Sihanouk and the Political Agenda of Cambodian Music, 1955–1970', Dr LinDa Saphan argued, 'Without this royal figure, many artists before the Khmer Rouge era would not have had the support and encouragement to become artists and to attain a place of value in society.' Samley attributed Sihanouk with both his success by association, and of influencing his own moral compass: 'Later in my career I used to bring unknown musicians onstage to promote their talent,' he told me earnestly. 'Though I often played with the older, established musicians like Sinn Sisamouth, I wanted to also help young unknown musicians because they were scared to be musicians because of the social class barriers – many successful musicians were from the high class. I crossed every class of society with music.'

When Baksey Cham Krong began moving away from live performances to spending more time in the studio with the likes of Van Chann and Heng Heng, the young Samley made his own departure from the band. Up until then, unlike his affluent bandmates who owned their own instruments, he'd been getting by borrowing Fenders, Gibsons and Vox guitars for practices and performances. Even if Samley had saved every penny earned in a year, those guitars were still a bourgeois commodity equivalent to the price of a motorbike in today's money, and out of reach for someone from Samley's lower-middle-class background. So, in 1964, following the release of 'BCK', he quit, and set off to make his fame and fortune with his own brothers, Hong Sambath and Hong Samlot. They called themselves the Bayon band and recorded their first song on RNK radio in 1964, called 'I Take What I Want'. A ballsy introduction, this rather high-handed title was somewhat softened by the rest of the song's fairytale lyrics. 'It was about being at the seaside and needing my love,' Samley euphemized dreamily. 'She's talking and lying with me and I feel lucky because the sky is beautiful, and I have my love with me. And it's a dream.'

Between 1965 and 1966 the Bayon band played lots of embassy parties, and cut out a niche for themselves performing on the political event circuit playing a diverse repertoire of originals and covers, including Stones and Beatles covers for ambassadors and Sihanouk. But the pay wasn't moving Samley any closer towards his dream of owning his own Fender, so, in 1966, the guitarist and his brothers traded the parties for better paid, steady gigs at nightclubs, each earning around 7,000 Riel a month – equivalent to around $1,650 in today's money – at supper clubs like the Magetat, as part of their house band: 'My brothers played with me every night. There were four saxophones, two trumpets, one piano, three female singers and one male singer in the Magetat house band. Sometimes Sihanouk came to party with us at Magetat. Sieng Dy, Sieng Vanthy, Pen Ram (my brother Sambath's wife, sister of Pen Ran), Hong Sambath, Hong Samlot . . . we all played together. We were the Magetat band – professional musicians who had to be able to play every type of music – but people also knew us as the Bayon band. The audience was mostly foreigners, ministers, ambassadors, high-class society. People would eat and dance while we played rock, jerk, the twist, cha-cha-cha, the Madison, blues, Latin . . . and our repertoire included covers of foreign songs, the likes of the Bee Gees and, later, Santana, Chicago . . .'

Samley's brother Samlot was the first to leave the band. He joined a cabaret outfit, and the other boys left the Magetat in 1970 when it closed, to work at the Mekong and Olympia nightclubs. Their fate was sealed in 1971 when Samley, having had enough of mediating the fiery marriage of his bandmate Sambath and his wife Pen Ram, kicked his brother out of the band. The following year, when the civil war began to enforce temporary closures on the nightclubs of Phnom Penh, Samley knew their time, and this life, was up: 'In 1970 the soldiers began to arrive at the cabaret clubs with their guns and grenades. When the nightclubs were shut at night, from January '71 to October '72, I was only allowed to play at the Mekong in the day. At night the clubs were closed.'

Samley was aware of the political situation and, being the cautious, savvy character he was, was less optimistic than many of his contemporaries. He was all too aware of the class tensions and the divide between rich and poor, and he knew there were people in the countryside and mountains outside of Phnom Penh who could well come to kill the city people for their capitalist ideals. It was wartime, and work was hard to come by for a nightclub musician. Samley lived frugally and hustled for whatever work he could find. By 1972 he'd saved enough money to either buy his long-awaited Fender, or a ticket out of Cambodia. He chose the ticket. Samley headed straight for Paris, but adapting to his new life was hard: 'I had good clothes and pay in Cambodia. When I arrived in France I was a dishwasher and I had nothing. I didn't earn enough money from washing dishes to survive so I busked in the streets and cafés of Paris for three years. After, I tried to form a band but in the end I gave up and did a one-man show. But no matter my situation, good or bad, whether I've had work or not, music has been the one constant throughout my life. I've never stopped playing.'

As for Samley's family, his sister-in-law Pen Ram managed to make it to a refugee camp in Thailand before living out her days in America. But his brothers died young in Cambodia. Hearing the fate of his family made me wonder whether Samley's lucky escape had anything to do with his outburst earlier. Whether what I was hearing was an expression of jealousy towards the attention heaped on Kamach by Martin and I, or antipathy towards the media, or if it was, in fact, survivor's guilt. Perhaps listening to Kamach talk of the evacuation of Phnom Penh had triggered something in Samley: trauma for those he lost, or possibly guilt for those he left behind. In her chapter 'Refractions of Home' from the book *Expressions of Cambodia: the Politics of Tradition, Identity and Change*, author Khatharya Um describes survivor's guilt among the California diaspora in Long Beach as instituting a 'land of absence', a 'discontinuous state of being that accompanies a forced and unexpected severance from the ancestral homeland'. Orphaned and marginalized in their new countries, many Cambodian refugees have likened their situation to living their lives in exile, trapped between a past that is lost to both themselves and their motherland. But Samley is a survivor in every sense – *'une forte tête'*, as his French companions would say – and has not let the events of 1975 to 1979 define him, or the events since, exile him. Two years after arriving in Paris he began a new family of his own; he built a new life, and has no desire to return to Cambodia.

When we'd finished Samley's interview, to wrap things up, I took Martin, Kevin, Kamach and Samley out for lunch. Kamach had shut down and barely said a word during the meal, while Samley seemed unconscionably ignorant to the hurt he'd caused, and dominated the lunchtime conversation. When it came time to bid them both goodbye I was so very grateful for their time, and so very exhausted from all the peacekeeping.

The next time I saw Kamach was nineteen months later, in the spring of 2017. Paris was blooming, and as my car motored across the city I watched enchanted as pollen floated over the highways like soft rain. Graffiti-covered bridges flashed by where the undocumented sold their wares and Parisians converged perilously upon one another at junctions. I'd been invited to speak at a screening of *Don't Think I've Forgotten*, alongside Kamach, by Martin and his partner Fabrice Géry of the French record label Akuphone.

I was delighted to hear, following my previous interview with Kamach, and since last seeing Martin and Fabrice, that Akuphone had developed their own relationship with Baksey Cham Krong and remastered and released a 7-inch EP of their first two singles, including their 1959 hit 'Pleine Lune'.

The night before the talk I stayed with Fabrice, his girlfriend, Marie, and their beloved cat, Maurice, at their apartment in Bagnolet on the outskirts of Paris. A wall of sound – some five or six thousand records – covered half the living room, and everywhere the walls were covered in books, cassettes, CDs and, of course, vinyl. Culture filled every nook, and light filled every crevice of their home. We were drip-fed with new and old faces throughout the evening and it was wonderful to see my old comrades from Cambodia – Martin and Edouard Degay

Delpeuch – with whom I had long conversations into the night about Edouard's thesis and the differences between Western and Asian psychology in relation to our work (specifically, how these differences created barriers such as missing words between languages, cultural differences and preconceived expectations based on the ignorance of these differences that we, as researchers of one culture, can mistakenly make upon the people we interview from another culture).

Ever the intrepid adventurer, Edouard had just returned from a video shoot by a church in Roussillon, a Provençal town built on red rock, for Ko Shin Moon. Axel, the band's charismatic front-man, regaled us with funny stories of standing beside the church in a Jesus stance, wearing a Fez hat, his face and arms smeared with red rock pigment as bemused provincial parishioners went about their church business.

The *Don't Think I've Forgotten* screening the following day was held in the old operating theatre of a hospital called Écran Voisin, which was no longer in use and squatted by artists and refugees. I'd kept in touch with Kamach via Martin, and it was wonderful to see and interview him again – this time in a more harmonious setting. We talked more about his move to France in 1975, his relationship with his father, and I learned a little more about his brothers. I met his children and his wife. And, I finally got the answer to my question about his life in Paris.

Following Kamach's father-in-law's relationships with some influential Vietnamese that helped them make their way past Vietnamese border authorities in April 1975, the family initially stayed in Saigon, waiting for the right time to return to Cambodia. But it was a return that never came: 'We stayed in Saigon, but when we heard that things were getting worse in Cambodia we decided to move to France. My father-in-law also had contacts who were able to grant us visas. We settled in the southern suburbs of Paris, in the home of my father-in-law's friends.

I started working as a server in an Asian restaurant. After that, I worked at an insurance company owned by a Cambodian in the 13th arrondissement of Paris. Eventually, I opened up a bakery with my wife's family, but the business didn't work, so we decided to retire.' Kamach finished by telling me earnestly, 'I always kept playing music.'

Seeing *Don't Think I've Forgotten* in French was a new experience for me, but the same sentiment remained. When I looked around the audience and saw silent tears rolling down the dignified face of a Cambodian woman in her sixties, I was moved to tears myself.

My talk which followed the film was a disaster. I'd been briefed to speak for fifteen minutes, but after the audience had spent almost two hours sitting in hard dissection-theatre seats, sore bums and bursting bladders prevailed over any thirst they may have had for further discussion. I and my translator, a jocular French-Canadian college professor called Stefan, battled through the steady exodus until Fabrice's girlfriend, Marie, saved us with a signal to wind up. Kamach – one of the stars of the film, and the star of the night – then took to the stage to sing an a cappella version of 'Full Moon'. His voice, unchanged in forty years, received a well-deserved standing ovation.

Afterwards, in an adjoining room, Fabrice DJ'd a storming set of Cambodian psych, and I watched young Cambodian men and women dancing the *saravan* and *romvong* circle dance moves their parents must have taught them, passing the steps on to the young French men and women who followed their movements in harmony. Over in the corner, Kamach was in his element, autographing records, his family looking on with pride.

We finished the night several flights up on the roof of one of the hospital tenements, toasting Cambodia while watching the sun set over Montmartre. The rooftop was filled with artists, hipsters, a dead-ringer for Andy Warhol's factory favourite, transgender muse Candy Darling, and lots of other fabulous creatures. Stefan, the translator, and I put the political world to rights, discussing the recent events of Brexit, France's newly appointed president Emmanuel Macron, and Quebec native, Stefan's prime minister Justin Trudeau, whom he called 'the happy idiot' ('He's just happy . . . being an idiot.') I'm sure I laughed more than I talked and it was a bittersweet end to my last adventure.

On the Eurostar home I reflected on Kamach's words about *Don't Think I've Forgotten*. As the train descended into the tunnel, and my head entered the pressure vice, I thought about where my own journey with Baksey Cham Krong began in New York. I thought about when I'd first heard their music in Cambodia, and the band's revival in recent years, catalysed by John Pirozzi's film. After the Paris screening I asked Kamach what he thought of the film, and he spoke of a deep sense of nostalgia as well as a sense of joy in the recognition the film has brought to his life. He concluded: 'When I first saw *Don't Think I've Forgotten* it made me feel the cruelty of life and the bad destiny of our culture. But it's also very positive, as it shows the reality of Cambodia. I'm grateful to John for making it.'

When I gave that talk in Paris, it had been five years since my quest began in that hollowed out casino on Bokor Mountain. I had never dreamed the book would take me across three continents in search of answers. And here I was nearing the end of the journey, finding out where the story all began, with five brothers and their guitars.

Baksey Cham Krong changed the course of Cambodian music: they fused modern Western and Asian music and paved the way for the *yé-yé* groups to come; bands like Sophoan, Apsara, Bayon, Amara, Drakkar and many more. Half a century on their revival created a miracle in Kagnol's physical health, and brought happiness and a renewed musical vigour to Kamach's life. They were true pioneers; courageous visionaries who managed to keep their feet firmly planted on the ground, even under a stampede of teenage girls. From the accordion phase to the *yé-yé* phase, from ballads like 'Pleine Lune' to surf instrumentals like 'BCK', they ran the gamut and made an important mark on Cambodian history. Some forty years on from the genocide Kagnol was reunited with a vinyl copy of their music, in a chance meeting with a collector. It's unimaginable how that must have felt for the guitarist, but as for the rest of us, we owe that collector a great debt for smuggling this treasure out of the country – and a debt to Akuphone for reissuing the record all these years later.

The Mol brothers lost twenty members of their family to the war and genocide. There are whole bands that were wiped out during the 1970s, and many were buried along with their music, never to resurface again. Kagnol, Kamach and Samley were the survivors, and, again, thanks to the efforts of those who smuggled their music out of the country – and those who've since reissued it – I was able to write these words, not to mention a large swathe of this book's epilogue. Theoretically, it might seem backwards to end my journey in Paris with the progenitors of the Cambodian rock story – Cambodia's first boy band – but, somehow . . . nothing felt more right.

Epilogue

Lon Nol soldier running, guitar in one hand, gun in the other.

On 7 August 2014 I travelled the sixteen kilometres from central Phnom Penh to the Extraordinary Chambers in the Court of Cambodia to witness the verdict for a Khmer Rouge tribunal case. The Documentation Center of Cambodia (DC-Cam) had invited me to watch from the courthouse gallery as the two remaining leaders of Pol Pot's brotherhood, Nuon Chea and Khieu Samphan, finally faced the scales of justice, some thirty-five years after the genocide had ended.

I arrived to find reporters from around the world frantically clambering through the chaotic entry system, and soon discovered why: the courthouse had run out of passes two hours before the verdict was due to be announced. By an act of grace, Penhsamnang Kan, a research fellow from DC-Cam, gave up her gallery pass for me and remained outside watching the proceedings on television screens with the DC-Cam camera crew. The outdoor screens had no translation facilities, so while Penhsamnang could understand the proceedings, I would have missed almost every word had she not so selflessly traded places with me. I remain eternally grateful to her.

When the courthouse doors opened, the crowd filed in: wave upon wave of squirming sardines. Court booklets underarm and translation headphones clattering, Cambodian civilians of all ages, NGO workers and suited diplomats crowded into the 500-seat public gallery, the largest war crimes courthouse in the world. Beyond the bulletproof glass separating the audience from the courthouse, the civil party witnesses took up their positions behind a wood-panelled booth, and among them I spotted Chum Mey and Bou Meng, the lionized survivors of the Khmer Rouge's notorious detention centre S21. In front of Mey and Meng sat the prosecution, and facing the opposition was the defence team seated with their clients, Nuon Chea and Khieu Samphan. Nuon was in a wheelchair, lips downturned, a stoic look behind black sunglasses. Khieu Samphan on the other hand looked more perturbed, peering through his large spectacles, which only seemed to magnify his frightened eyes. It was hard to comprehend the crimes of these architects of genocide when they appeared so puny and frail. I felt uncomfortable, almost guilty gawking at them; there was something so primitive about the theatre of justice that made me want to look away and yet, I couldn't take my eyes off the two men who'd reportedly shown next to no remorse for their crimes.

Eventually all the court clerks and judges filed in, and His Excellency Nil Nonn proceeded to list off the multitude of counts brought against the defendants for the next one and a half hours. The counts were the result of evidence from a trial lasting more than two and a half years: a total of 222 court days in which

92 testimonies were heard. The case had focused primarily on alleged crimes against humanity related to the forced movement of the population from Phnom Penh and later from other regions (known as phases one and two), and the execution of Khmer Republic soldiers at Tuol Po Chrey execution site immediately after the Khmer Rouge takeover in 1975. It was the second Khmer Rouge tribunal case to be tried at the chambers, and the first to see the highest-ranking officials of Angkar face the strong arm of the law.

After what felt like an eternity listening to the overview and the counts, Nil Nonn called out to the defendants to stand for the verdict. Khieu Samphan stood obediently while Nuon Chea refused to budge from his wheelchair. The judge called out again to Nuon to stand for his verdict. After a long pause, the judge was met with a defiant and blood-curdling, '*NO!*' from Nuon Chea. Again, the judge asked the defendant to stand, more forcibly this time. 'NO!' once again echoed through the courtroom.

Judge Nil Nonn then excused the defendant 'on account of his age and disability' and proceeded to call out Nuon Chea's guilty verdict. Khieu Samphan's guilty verdict followed and, with that, what began in November 2011 was at last finished. The pair were found guilty of crimes against humanity and led away from public view, later to be sentenced to life imprisonment.

There were no fireworks inside the courtroom but there was calm. For many of the NGO staff and their clients, it was hard to imagine an end to the trial after so long. But outside the courthouse Nuon Chea's wife was in hysterics and the civil party witnesses wept in front of cameras, swamping them from all angles.

After thanking Penhsamnang, I left the media circus behind and started off down a dirt track hoping to figure out a way back to Phnom Penh. I ended up hitching a ride in a tuk tuk with two Singaporean economics students from Yale University who had travelled from the US to be there for the trial. One of them was particularly arrogant and his uninformed and unfeeling remarks left a bad taste in my mouth all the way back to the city. Within the gaps of his monologues about the incompetence of the courts and the filth of Phnom Penh, I reflected on Linda Banner's more pragmatic words when I interviewed her the previous year. Linda was, at that time, a sessional lecturer in criminology at Birkbeck University in London, with a specialism in genocide. Her thesis, 'Living in Fear', questioned why there had been no retrospective justice after the Cambodian genocide. We talked about the flaws of the tribunal: from its failure to meet international law standards, to the cultural problems surrounding a Western model of justice being implemented in an Eastern country. We discussed domestic policy in Cambodia – Prime Minster Hun Sen's cabinet selling 'peace' in the form of land settlements to former Khmer Rouge officials and assurances against legal retribution, thus putting an end to the war and achieving 'peace' for their victims – and the geopolitics of the cold war hindering justice. The geopolitics at play were that the US and their allies, the UK, were locked into the cold war between 1947 and 1989 and were intent on 'spreading the curb of communism', so they still trained a Khmer Rouge-led coalition of rebels in military camps along the Thai border to fight back against the Vietnamese-backed PRK, long after the horrors of the genocide were known to the world.

Outside of the odd history and culture buff, I found that most of the Cambodian youth today are particularly disengaged with the country's Khmer Rouge past – a past unspoken of by many of their surviving grandparents. They have enough political issues to deal with now as it is, with an autocratic prime minister who has been in power for almost forty years shutting down at least twelve free media outlets in 2017 alone, and who thinks nothing of exiling political opponents, often ones favoured by the youth. And as for the journalists I spoke to who were working in Cambodia during the tribunal, they were often keen to point out the inadequacies and failings of the expensive and lengthy proceedings.

A few days after the verdict, I attended a panel discussion about the case, which included government and court spokespeople, a civil witness, and Nuon Chea's defence lawyer, Victor Koppe. Koppe said that Nuon Chea's refusal to stand for the verdict was, somewhat ironically, a man taking his last 'stand' in a case that the defence and their client felt was fundamentally flawed and unfair. Two years and three months later, the appeal judgement did reverse a number of convictions on political grounds, acquiting Nuon Chea of any involvement in Tuol Po Chrey, where hundreds of Khmer Republic soldiers and officials were executed by the Khmer Rouge. But, ultimately, the life sentences they'd both been handed down in the 2014 verdict were upheld. In addition, Chea and Samphan both went on to be found guilty, in November 2018, of crimes of rape in the context of forced marriage.

A defendant at an earlier trial, Comrade Duch (Kaing Guek Eav, the commander of S21 prison), and Chea and Samphan are the only three senior leaders of the Khmer Rouge to see the inside of a prison. Two further cases accusing lower-ranking officials of the regime remain at a standstill, due to a supposed 'lack of funds' and will never be heard. At the time of writing, the court is being wound down and will soon cease to exist. The truth is that political interference has dogged the tribunal from the start. Put simply, Cambodia and the United Nations have expressed very different views from the beginning about how many people should be tried for crimes against humanity. As one journalist was quick to point out to me early on, Prime Minister Hun Sen himself is ex-Khmer Rouge. I recalled that same journalist in 2012 wagering that it was unlikely the tribunal would convict any others (following Duch in 2010); that it was not designed to succeed and that convicting lower-ranking Khmer Rouge would be getting too close to the bone for the Cambodian government, many of whom are ex-Khmer Rouge themselves.

Linda Banner, at Birkbeck, offered some alternative solutions to the tribunal model: solutions that commonly feature in studies of the effects of post-traumatic stress disorder on Khmer Rouge survivors, and would be more likely to limit political interference. In her thesis she cites the foundation of 'the middle path' – a Buddhist spiritual practice – as the basis for a non-violent and compassionate approach to reconciling the past and dealing with the present. She explains that the Khmer concept of justice is tied to the *dharma* – a religious concept which Buddha used to define his ideas of cosmic law and order, or a code of conduct. It is also linked to *karma* – the Buddhist and Hindu idea of a law of nature which relates to the moral intent of an action, and the consequences that action has on the future lives of a soul. Linda looked at Cambodian religion, as well as the constructs of law in Cambodian society – from the age-old ways a village chief might resolve conflict between warring villagers by listening to, and mediating disputes, to the foundation of the Cambodian legal system and subsequent lack of Cambodian legal professionals resulting from the class persecution of the genocide, to the country's history of autocratic leadership and other corrupt systems. The Buddha's teachings of 'the middle path' or 'middle way' – meaning neither joining the fight nor hiding from it – seem to reinstate a map for living, destroyed by the Khmer Rouge. It's a significant part of Buddhist teachings, and following it can lead to liberation from suffering. As Jack Kornfield, a leading Buddhist monk, meditation teacher and writer illustrates: 'The middle way describes the middle ground between attachment and aversion, between being and non-being, between form and emptiness, between free will and determinism. When we discover the middle path, we neither remove ourselves from the world nor get lost in it. We learn to embrace tension, paradox, change. Instead of seeking resolution, waiting for the chord at the end of the song, we let ourselves open and relax in the middle. In the middle, we discover that the world is workable.'

What this could mean for the musicians I spoke to is a striking of the balance between denying emotions and dwelling in them too deeply; a reconciliation of the past, an acceptance of one's place in it, and hope for the future. Within the repeated action of voicing emotions and traumas and by participating in memorials and community rituals for the dead, lies new philosophical discoveries: the acceptance of one's past, a freeing from trauma, an acknowledgement of the misdeeds of others, an acceptance of self and one's own place within the order of all things, no matter how cruel. The Buddhist path to enlightenment – the freeing of one's soul – is based on such practice: the social and cultural aspects of our lives and how these shape us, and how we in turn use this experience to shape others. Put simply, how we connect with one another. There are many hypotheses on Buddhist-informed trauma therapies swimming around on thesis papers, and more and more studies, curriculums and practices are being rolled out, championing the impact of mindfulness on anxiety and social behaviour. School children across the globe are learning mindfulness techniques at school to transition them from break time back into the classroom; chronic pain is being curtailed by mindful meditation; mindfulness techniques are being successfully integrated into cognitive and psychotherapies; and practices like Mindfulness Based Stress Reduction are becoming an office workplace standard. Essentially the middle path is about love. As Albert Einstein, John Lennon and other famous philosophers have said in a number of different ways: love is the answer, no matter the question.

And it's this idea of the middle path in action that brings me, finally, to a couple of trailblazers I want to recognize – for without them Cambodian music's role in this reconciliation would be missing, and the music and much of the culture of Cambodia would have been buried by the genocide.

There are a number of cash-poor preservation societies working against the odds to bring Cambodian cultural heritage to new audiences. By preserving evidence of the arts they are undoing the Khmer Rouge's past efforts to crush artistry and, indeed, the spirit of the nation. Perhaps the largest of all is the Cambodia Living Arts organization, founded by Arn Chorn-Pond. A human rights activist, community organizer and musician, Arn has received numerous prestigious awards for his lifetime efforts to transform and heal individuals and communities through music.

Having witnessed the full-blown reality of the killing fields, and experienced the full extent of the Khmer Rouge's cruelty, Arn emerged miraculously in a Thai refugee camp, traumatized and on death's door, suffering from severe malnutrition and cerebral malaria. An American reverend, Peter Pond, who met Arn in the camp, later told the *New York Times* that he was immediately struck by the sick child reaching out to touch him: 'That was Arn Chorn from the very first, reaching out and touching.' Arn was fourteen years old, and, soon after, was granted permission to join Peter and the rest of his family for a new life in the US. Life there – for a traumatized refugee thrust into an American high school with only a few English words to hand – was far from the nightmare's end for Arn, but he persevered, faced his demons and eventually began to find his voice.

But there came a day when Arn knew he had to go back to Cambodia and face his past. He returned to his village to look for his family, but instead found his old music master, poor, drunk and lost without purpose. 'Master Mic' had saved eleven-year-old Arn from the deadly conditions of hard labour in the fields, where Arn had been forced to work every day with little or no food, from 5 a.m. until midnight. Master Mic saved Arn by teaching him how to play music. Armed not with a gun or a hoe, but with a flute,

Epilogue

Arn was enlisted into a traditional music troupe and forced to play
Khmer Rouge propaganda music during workers' breaks, either
acoustically or through loud speakers to 'spur on' the workers
toiling in the fields. The music was traditional Cambodian folk
– instrumental *mahori* and *bassak* theatre style – and the socialist
lyrics extolled the virtues of the Khmer Rouge and collective
hard work while condemning all opposing philosophies. Lost in
the music, Arn found a spiritual escape from the daily killings and
other horrors he witnessed under the regime.

Despite the years apart, their bond remained unbroken, and
though happy to see his young mentee, Master Mic told Arn,
'You must find something for me to do, or I will die.' Traumatized
by the Khmer Rouge and subsequently wrecked by alcoholism,
Mic had all but lost hope. Arn knew he had to do something to
help the man who had once saved him. On the same visit Mic
introduced Arn to one of the last surviving Cambodian opera
singers. Arn remembered listening to her music on the radio
before the days of Pol Pot, and the experience of being among
these two masters changed the course of his life. He realized the
fragility of Cambodia's cultural heritage that had been shaped by
centuries of oral teaching, and, in that moment, found his true
purpose: to find work and a purpose for these two musicians, and
others too, and revive the music they'd played. His foundation,
Cambodian Living Arts, was born.

Since its inception in 1998 the foundation has grown. Arn
is often quoted as suggesting that 90 per cent of Cambodian
musicians were killed during the genocide. So, with cultural
resilience and preservation at the heart of their activities, the
organization has given old masters a platform to share their
precious, near-extinct skills with a post-war generation of
young musicians. From scholarships to international cultural
exchange programmes, Cambodian Living Arts has done more
to resuscitate Cambodia's traditional music, acting and dance

heritage than any other body I know of. Arn Chorn-Pond has, rightly so, been formally commended many times over for the impact he and his growing community has left on their recovering homeland, and, with ever bigger plans, they will continue to expand and change lives in the Greater Mekong region and beyond. The activist in Arn has a stunning, powerful way with words: 'We are carpeting Cambodia in music now, not bombs. It's my dream for every young person, every child in my country, and the world, to carry instruments and sing about love, not carry guns and preach about hate.' The middle path in action.

The music that Arn Chorn-Pond and his members create is deeply rooted in tradition and mastery but transcends and evolves

Nate Hun, CVMA co-founder, with his collection.

with the inescapable effect of time. Young people bring their own influences and fuse these with heritage arts in the same way that their ancestors once did. Evolution is what keeps music interesting. Art collectives like New Cambodian Artists and choreographers like Nget Rady are fusing contemporary dance with more traditional dance forms like Khol, Yike, and Bassac. In 2021 multimillion-streaming hip hop artist VannDa collaborated with 'master of *chapei*' Kong Nay on his single 'Time to Rise', and foreigners are getting involved too. French ethnomusicologist Patrick Kersalé is working with craftsmen to rebuild ancient harps and trumpets that have been extinct for centuries. With no aural reference – only their image plucked from 13th-century temple walls – Patrick and his craftsmen are handing these reborn instruments over to Cambodian students and composers to recreate their sound from scratch.

Another who is confronting Cambodia's past not just simply by recovering and preserving it, but by dynamically engaging with it, is Youk Chhang. His journey began at fourteen years of age, when he was separated from his family in Phnom Penh during the evacuation of the city. He suffered terribly from starvation, imprisonment and grief during the Khmer Rouge rule, as did his mother, who had to watch her son being tortured, and brutally lost her pregnant daughter when the Khmer Rouge accused her of stealing rice. In an act reminiscent of medieval witch trails, they slashed open her stomach to prove this, only to find no rice inside.

Youk survived the genocide, eventually emigrating to America as a refugee. But his experience paved the way for a lifelong commitment to promoting memory and justice in Cambodia. He returned to his homeland in the 1990s, at first working for the UN then later heading up the Documentation Center of Cambodia.

With Youk at the helm DC-Cam has identified hundreds of genocide sites, mapped almost 20,000 mass graves, archived around one million documents – from oral histories to propaganda materials – created texts for the Cambodian national curriculum and provided substantial evidence at the Khmer Rouge war tribunal. DC-Cam has also facilitated reconciliations for communities across Cambodia through initiatives like its Anlong Veng Peace Center near the Thai–Cambodian border. Pol Pot's final resting place can be found at the end of a stony, ochre dirt track in the region's forests, and grief tourists, loyal former cadres and even, purportedly, a tycoon or two still visit the site of his final bunker-like house and funeral pyre. Once a longstanding Khmer Rouge stronghold, DC-Cam has turned the remote area into a centre for education that hosts discussions between former Khmer Rouge cadres and survivors, and provides scholarships for the children of former cadres from Anlong Veng to study at schools in Phnom Penh, as well as scholarships for students from major cities and other provinces to study in Anlong Veng. The idea is to document and talk about history objectively, putting straight misconceptions and old, false narratives; above all, to break down social and generational divides caused by what happened in the 1970s. Anlong Veng is a true example of peacekeeping in action. But Youk believes DC-Cam's greatest achievement to date is simply 'touching the hearts of victims by being there to talk to them.'

When you read or listen to Chhang's words, when you meet the man, he lives up to his placings on *TIME Magazine*'s heroes and influencers lists. Chhang has won the Ramon Magsaysay Award – Asia's version of the Nobel peace prize – and deservedly so. To be in his presence is to be inspired. When I had the privilege of meeting Youk in 2014, he told me that Cambodia was like broken glass and that reconciliation and justice were the glue that would bring those pieces back together. When he went on to list what he and DC-Cam were doing in order to be that glue, I thought he was the closest thing to a hero I might ever meet; he's up there with Gandhi, Mandela, Maya Angelou, the Dalai

Lama . . . His charisma, compassion and generosity for anyone he meets along his cultural and humanitarian path are boundless. He and his team helped me in my quest, connecting me with the right people to kickstart my searches – and while I felt like a lowly amateur in the presence of greatness, with Youk there is no hierarchy and no airs and graces.

When I left the centre for the first time after meeting Youk, the heavens opened to welcome in the rainy season. There were hardly any tuk tuks on the road, but I was in a rush to get home for a call so I made a dash for it from under the centre's awning and managed to flag down a driver so unfortunate or desperate he offered me a ride in the downpour. The tuk tuk's roof and open front provided little cover from the deluge, and I cowered over my soaking rucksack, concealing my precious laptop. I remember the connection and smile I shared with a passer-by on a motorbike – an exchange of pure joy and laughter between two drowned rats marvelling at the majesty of nature. Nothing could dampen my mood, not then, nor five minutes down the road when the tuk tuk's motorbike stalled in a flash flood. I dismounted to help the driver heave the hefty carriage out of deep water but the carriage wheels accidently ran over my feet, pain immediately shooting up from my toes. When we reached high ground I hollered and wooped at the driver, before paying the fare and turning back for my apartment. Holding my rucksack high above my head I waded home, waist-high through dirty street water. In that moment I felt unshakable. Such was the spell Youk Chhang cast.

Cambodia's cultural heritage, the role of cultural identity and the healing power of art are things Youk has often talked about over the course of his involvement in many artistic endeavours and historical projects. He was the executive producer of the film *Don't Think I've Forgotten*. Around the time I met him, Youk was interviewed by Al Jazeera America online. When asked about the film, he told the reporter: 'Music is a way of healing and caring for Khmer society. Music is magical, and can bring both heritage and contemporary feelings to all – to heal. Music can also help restore what we have lost.'

At the heart of Youk's aspirations is the idea of reconciliation. But it wasn't always central to his rhetoric. It's something he told me that he came to in the course of his own searching and healing. Initially, Youk believed finding justice for his family was what mattered most – without it, everything else was meaningless. He has often talked in the media about a primary motivation being to avenge his mother for all her suffering. But over time the work has moved beyond simply justice, transforming and transcending his pain into an understanding and need for reconciliation. Seemingly, and without expecting it, the work of DC-Cam has helped his own healing, and this in turn has helped him heal others. For me, this process, this cycle, is the most inspiring accomplishment and the root of everything this relentless and inexhaustible human has achieved in a remarkable life.

Of course, the past may, for some, never fully be reconciled, or in some cases even recovered. Many pre-war Cambodian memories have been tarnished by age and silenced by trauma; lives and records have been lost on a monumental scale. For Cambodia's pre-war music, memory and preservation are integral to honouring its past but, equally important, is the process of cementing its place in the present and future of Cambodia's music scene. Revivalists are growing in number, both in Cambodia and the wider world. Beyond simply preserving Cambodian rock, some revivalists have also evolved their music further, blending their own original songs with covers from the past and weaving in modern influences and other musical genres, just as their 1960s idols had done with their own music. The aforementioned Cambodian Space Project are a great example of this, and so are the American band Dengue Fever.

With ten albums, a number of soundtracks, a couple of documentary films and even a theatrical play under their belts, Dengue Fever's Cambodian frontwoman Chhom Nimol and her American band of brothers have amassed fans across the globe in a career spanning two decades. They are the original Cambodian 1960s revivalists and yet they have never stood still, transmogrifying from simply psychedelic Cambodian rock into new sounds and new music, including hip hop, afro-beat and Latin grooves. They've inspired both revivalists and new Cambodian bands alike with their no-holds-barred approach to mashing musical genres (from Eastern to Middle-Eastern to Western), their appearance – a motley mix of glitter, Hawaiian shirts and guitarist Zac Holtzman's two-foot-long Rasputin-esque beard – and performances: from a village gig in a Cambodian rice field to a tracklisting on Jim Jarmusch's 2005 *Broken Flowers* soundtrack. Like Zac's custom-made *mastodong* – a double-necked guitar consisting of a Fender Jazzmaster welded on top of a Cambodian *chapei dang veng* – the band is impossible to pigeon hole, explain, predict or contain. And in that way, they embody the spirit of Cambodian modern music: inexplicable and free.

Beyond preserving Cambodian arts, the heritage workers, masters, archivists, campaigners and revivalists have also helped pave the way for the future. Collectively, the influence of preservationists has helped promote independence, originality and cultural pride in the next generation of Cambodian artists – no mean feat when you consider the present-day landscape of all-pervasive k-pop and copyright corruption. Since the 1990s the Cambodian music industry has been dominated largely by outside profiteers from China more interested in mass producing karaoke singles than anything else – mainly Thai and US covers – and in the process almost decimating any hope for a strong Cambodian musical identity. Despite the introduction of copyright law to Cambodia in 2003, an insurmountable piracy problem remains.

These were lost years, and, sadly, the country is still recovering. But thanks to the persistence of those mentioned above there is the faintest call of hope for the voices of a new, digital generation in Cambodian music.

Laura Mam is a Cambodian-American revolutionary on a mission to pioneer such change. Since the start, she's been determined to disrupt Asia's karaoke pop covers machine with her trademark electronic pop originals and her growing empire: her label, Baramey, distributes original Cambodian music through Warner music and is home to artists like rapper, VannDa. Laura's brand partnerships alone – from phone companies to Porsche – must be worth a fortune. In 2018 Mam was honoured with the Arts and Culture Prize from the Women of the Future Awards Southeast Asia in recognition of her efforts to reinvigorate original Cambodian music. Laura really does care about the state of the music scene in Cambodia and is an unstoppable force for good.

At the harder end of the modern Cambodian rock spectrum are artists like Vartey Ganiva – Cambodia's first feminist punk – death metal band Doch Chkae, and the original Cambodian punk–metal outfit Sliten6ix. Since their formation in 2011, a burgeoning underground scene has sprung up in Phnom Penh centred around underground hardcore labels like Yab Moung Records. Yab Moung have joined forces with more mainstream artists like Laura Mam and label KlapYaHandz to fight for Cambodian independence from the karaoke houses, the Asian k-pop machine and piracy problems that are crippling the music industry in Southeast Asia. They embody that same spirit, and are paving the way for a new era of original Cambodian music for the first time since the likes of Sinn Sisamouth and Ros Sereysothea graced the radio waves with new music, sixty years ago. Generation Y are writing their own story on Cambodia, one fit for now. As Laura Mam's creative partner, the independent filmmaker Lomorpich Rithy, told an NPR reporter in 2020:

'We want to use the music as the new narrative for the world to remember Cambodia in a different way. We have been judged by our past, like, "Oh, you are the country of war." That was us before, but it's not us now.'

Laura and her generation are taking up the mantle from the likes of Youk, Arn, Oro, Nate, Dengue Fever and the army of activists, academics, survivors, filmmakers and musicians who've dedicated their lives – or at least large parts of their lives – to keeping Khmer history and cultural heritage alive. With every piece of the puzzle uncovered, every story told, every revival song sung, every paper written, every piece of broken glass coalesced, they are rewriting Cambodian history and reinforcing their rich and remarkable artistic heritage.

The last time I made it up to the abandoned Casino in Bokor I went to pay homage to where I first heard Sinn Sisamouth sing 'A Whiter Shade of Pale'. As Kevin and I meandered back down the mountain on our motorbike, I spotted the unmistakable black wings and gold-crested beak of a great hornbill soaring above our lonely road. We pulled off to the side and to our amazement saw another and another, then yet more – until we counted a flock of fifteen. We watched the rare birds in awe as, one by one, they flitted from tree to tree, their giant wings beating like locomotives, flapping and diving all around us in every direction. Silent, but for the birds' wings, it was a private dance the two of us had been permitted to watch. I stumbled recently upon the Japanese word *yūgen*, which means 'an awareness of the universe that triggers emotional responses too deep and powerful for words'. It's perhaps the closest I will get to describing how I felt in that moment. In half an hour, only one or two bikes passed by, oblivious to the magic stirring from the trees.

Enshrined as mythical avian humanoids in ancient Jain, Buddhist and Hindu stories, in Cambodia the birds have been on the decline since the 1960s to the point where today almost all species of hornbills sit on endangered lists – to see one is lucky, but a flock of fifteen is significant. They adorn the temples and palaces of Cambodia, are celebrated annually at the Hornbill Festival of the Nagas of India, and are sometimes depicted as the anthropomorphic Garuda of ancient Hindu and Buddhist mythology – a symbol of courage, justice and power which adorns the state insignia of Cambodia, as well as the coffins of the Batak people of Java as they journey to the afterlife. I couldn't help but think of the parallels between these rare birds and the rare music and musicians, dead and alive, I had journeyed for so long to uncover. In the storytellers of this book I'd witnessed courage of the utmost – of survival against the odds. I'd witnessed the justice system of an international war tribunal convict the remaining Khmer Rouge brotherhood; I'd scratched under the surface of a country grappling with corruption and the fatalistic strokes that marred the lives of those I'd grown to know and love. Above all, I'd seen, first hand, the healing power of music prevail.

Dee Peyok in Bokor Palace's abandoned newly rendered ballroom.

Epilogue

We stood rooted to the jungle roadside watching these guardians of the living and the dead swoop and dance before our eyes. I silently, privately, thanked Cambodia and bid her farewell before, one by one, the birds disappeared into the jungle.

Acknowledgements

The writing of this book proved easier thanks to the support of my family and my extended family. I want to thank my parents for instilling in me a love of music and travel. Jennifer Brogan, Sarah Woollen, Pry Nehru, Linda Davies, Caroline Redmond, Lim Sophorn, Johnny M-R, Oro, Martin Jay, Joe Wrigley and Lay Mealea. I was bolstered by your unwavering interest and belief. And James Royce, my rudder, and critical eye.

I owe a debt of gratitude to my husband, fellow traveller and comrade in arms, Kevin Peyok. Every mirrored footstep, every ounce of love, strength and tolerance you mustered called this book into existence. Also to my agent, John Ash, for clearing the way and helping me signpost this road less travelled. Ka Bradley at Granta for commissioning the book and for writing the road map. Bella Lacey, Jason Arthur and all of the Granta team for their support. My editor, Ian Preece, for rooting me in the music. And Christine Lo, for keeping the train on the tracks.

More than anything, I want to acknowledge the courage and love shown to me by the Cambodian music community; for peeling back the brush and showing me the road in the first place.

Sources

BOOKS

Bolingbroke-Kent, Antonia, *A Short Ride in the Jungle: The Ho Chi Minh Trail by Motorcycle*, Summersdale, 2014.

Boraden, Nhem, *The Khmer Rouge: Ideology, Militarism, and the Revolution that Consumed a Generation*, Praeger, 2013.

Boswell, Steven, *King Norodom's Head: Phnom Penh Sights Beyond the Guidebooks*, NIAS Press, 2016.

Chanda, Nayan, *Brother Enemy: The War After the War*, Collier Books, 1988.

(Eds) Chau-Pech Ollier, Leakthina, and Winter, Tim, *Expressions of Cambodia: The Politics of Tradition, Identity and Change*, Routledge, 2007.

Dy Khamboly, *A History of Democratic Kampuchea, 1975–1979*, Documentation Center of Cambodia, 2007.

Fletcher Haythorpe, Susan, *Lost Generation: The Story Of Cambodian Rock and Roll*, Matador, 2021.

(Eds) Ines, Sothea, and Sākalvidyālăy Bhūmin Bhnaṃ Beñ Department of Media and Communication, *Dontrey: The Music of Cambodia*, Royal University of Phnom Penh, Department of Media and Communication, 2011.

Kiernan, Ben, *The Pol Pot Regime: Race, Power, and Genocide in Cambodia Under the Khmer Rouge, 1975–1979*, Yale University Press, 2008.

Lewis, Norman, *A Dragon Apparent: Travels in Cambodia, Laos and Vietnam*, Eland, 2003.

Ly, Daravuth and Muan, Ingrid, *Cultures of Independence: An Introduction to Cambodian Arts and Culture in the 1950s and 1960s*, Reyum, 2001.

Maguire, Peter, *Facing Death in Cambodia*, Columbia University Press, 2005.

Martin, Marie Alexandrine, *Cambodia: A Shattered Society*, University of California Press, 1994.

Meas, Sambath, *The Immortal Seeds: Life Goes On for a Khmer Family*, Wheatmark, Inc., 2009.

McCullin, Don, *Unreasonable Behaviour: An Autobiography*, Vintage Digital, 2010.

Miller, Terry E., and Williams, Sean, *The Garland Encyclopaedia of World Music: Southeast Asia*, 1st ed., Routledge, 1998.

Neveu, Roland, *The Fall of Phnom Penh*, Asia Horizons, 2015.

Osborne, Milton, *Phnom Penh: A Cultural and Literary History*, Signal, 2008.

Osborne, Milton, *Sihanouk: Prince of Light, Prince of Darkness*, University of Hawaii Press, 1994.

Ponchaud, François, *Cambodia: Year Zero*; translated from the French by Nancy Amphoux, Holt, Rinehart and Winston, 1978.

Purtill, Corinne, *Ghosts in the Forest – a Father, a War and a Story of Survival*, independently published, 2016.

Puy, Kea, *Radio Profile in Cambodia*, Konrad Adenauer Foundation, 2007.

Shawcross, William, *Sideshow: Kissinger, Nixon and the Destruction of Cambodia*, Simon & Schuster, 1979.

(Ed) Simpson, Andrew, *Language and National Identity in Asia*, Oxford University Press, 2007.

Swain, Jon, *River of Time*, Vintage, 1998.

Thompson, Larry Clinton, *Refugee Workers in the Indochina Exodus, 1975–1982*, McFarland & Co, 2010.

Woodier, Jonathan, *The Media and Political Change in Southeast Asia: Karaoke Culture and the Evolution of Personality Politics*, Edward Elgar, 2008.

Sources

FILMS

Chorn-Pond, Arn, *Music Saved My Life*, TEDxWarwick, 2015.
Chou, Davy, *Le Sommeil d'or*, Vycky Films, Bophana Production,
    Araucania Films, 2012.
Pirozzi, John, *Don't Think I've Forgotten: Cambodia's Lost Rock and
    Roll*, Primitive Nerd, Harmony Productions, Pearl City, 2014.

RADIO

Khmer Rock and the Killing Fields, BBC Radio 4, 2009.
The Songwriter, ABC Radio National, 2014.

JOURNALS AND ACADEMIC STUDIES

Banner, Linda, 'What Kind of Justice Long After Genocide?'
    Criminal Justice Matters, vol. 76, no. 1, June 2009, pp.4–5, Taylor
    & Francis Ltd.
Heuveline, Patrick, 'Between One and Three Million: Towards
    the Demographic Reconstruction of a Decade of Cambodian
    History (1970–79)', *Population Studies, vol. 52, no. 1*, pp.49–65,
    Taylor & Francis, Ltd, 1998.
Lincoln, Martha and Bruce, 'Toward a Critical Hauntology: Bare
    Afterlife and the Ghosts of Ba Chúc', *Comparative Studies in
    Society and History, vol. 57, no. 1*, 2015, pp.191–220, Cambridge
    University Press.
May, Sharon, 'In the Shadow of Angkor: A Search for Cambodian
    Literature', *Mānoa: A Pacific Journal of International Writing, vol.
    16*, January, 2004, pp.27–35, University of Hawaii Press.
Owen, Taylor and Kiernan, Ben, *Bombs Over Cambodia, Walrus
    Magazine*, October 2006, pp.62–69.
Pong-Rasy, Pheng, 'List of Burial Sites', February 2008. http://d.
    dccam.org/Projects/Maps/Mapping.htm
Santiago, Luciano P. R., 'The Heart of Norodom: the State Visit of
    the King of Cambodia in 1872', *Philippine Quarterly of Culture
    and Society, vol. 18, no. 3*, 1990, pp.185–200, University of San
    Carlos.

Saphan, LinDa, 'Cambodian Popular Musical Influences from the 1950s to the Present Day', in: Hyunjoon, Shin and Keewoong, Lee (eds), *Sounds from the Periphery: Modernity and Development of Asia Pop 1960–2000*, Seoul: Chaeryun, 2017.

Saphan, LinDa, 'Gendered Modernity in Cambodia: The Rise of Women in the Music Industry', *Khmer Scholar Journal*, September 2016.

Saphan, LinDa, 'Prince Norodom Sihanouk and the Political Agenda of Cambodian Music, 1955–1970', *International Institute for Asian Studies, vol. 64*, June 2013.

Tyner, James A., Henkin, Samuel, Sirik, Savina and Kimsroy, Sokvisal, 'Phnom Penh During the Cambodian Genocide: A Case of Selective Urbicide', *Environment and Planning A: Economy and Space*, 2014.

ARTICLES AND WEBSITES

'A Home for Cambodia's Children', *New York Times*, 23 September, 1984 https://www.nytimes.com/1984/09/23/magazine/a-home-fo r-cambodia-s-children.html.

'Across Languages and Generations, One Family is Reviving Cambodian Original Music', NPR.Org https://www.npr. org/2020/02/29/810155936/across-languages-and-generations-one -family-is-reviving-cambodian-original-music.

'An End to 90 Years of Colonialism "sans Heurts"' by David Chandler, *Phnom Penh Post* https://www.phnompenhpost.com/ national/end-90-years-colonialism-sans-heurts.

'Angkor Wat – 7th Wonder of the World – Angkor Archaeological Park – Angkor Wat Guide – What to See in Cambodia – Cambodia Major Attractions', Tourism Cambodia https://www. tourismcambodia.com/attractions/angkor/angkor-wat.htm.

'Angkor Wat Used far More Stone than All the Egyptian Pyramids Combined', Seasia.Co https://seasia.co/2017/10/02/angkor-wa t-used-far-more-stone-than-all-the-egyptian-pyramids-combi ned.

'A Voice from the Killing Fields' by Nik Cohn, *Guardian*, 19 May 2007 http://www.theguardian.com/music/2007/may/20/ worldmusic.features.

Sources

'Cambodia, Catholicism, and Cauliflower' by Peter Ford, the
	Diplomat https://thediplomat.com/2017/03/cambodia-catholicis
	m-and-cauliflower/.
'Cambodian Genocide Program', Yale University Genocide
	Studies Program https://gsp.yale.edu/case-studies/
	cambodian-genocide-program.
'Cambodia's Lost Rock 'n' Roll' by Ruper Winchester, Al Jazeera
	America http://america.aljazeera.com/articles/2014/4/9/
	cambodia-s-lost-rocknroll.html.
'Cambodia's Own "Elvis" Thriving' by Moeun Chhean Nariddh,
	Phnom Penh Post https://www.phnompenhpost.com/national/
	cambodias-own-elvis-thriving.
'Cambodian Brits? Yes, They Do Exist' by Emily Wight, *Phnom Penh
	Post* https://www.phnompenhpost.com/post-weekend/cambodia
	n-brits-yes-they-do-exist.
'Chapei Dang Veng' from Cambodian Community Day
	https://www.cambodiancommunityday.org/index.
	php?option=com_content&view=article&id=265&Itemid=732.
'Culture Ministry to Stop Illegal Music Re-Recordings' from
	Cambodia News English https://cne.wtf/2020/02/09/cultur
	e-ministry-to-stop-illegal-music-re-recordings/.
'Dengue Fever Revives and Revamps the Sounds of Cambodia' by
	Andrew Gilbert, *Boston Globe* http://archive.boston.com/ae/
	music/articles/2011/06/07/dengue_fever_revives_and_revamps_
	the_sounds_of_cambodia/.
'Discovering Khmer Rock 'n' Roll' by Clancy McGilligan,
	Cambodia Daily https://english.cambodiadaily.com/news/
	discovering-khmer-rock-1393/.
Documentation Center of Cambodia (DC-Cam) Mapping
	of Cambodia, 1973 http://d.dccam.org/Projects/Maps/
	Mapping1973.htm.
Documentation Center of Cambodia (DC-Cam) Mapping Project,
	1995–Present http://d.dccam.org/Projects/Maps/Mapping.htm.
'*Don't Think I've Forgotten*, a Documentary Revives Cambodia's
	Silenced Sounds' by Ben Sisario, *New York Times* https://www.
	nytimes.com/2015/04/12/movies/dont-think-ive-forgotten-a-d
	ocumentary-revives-cambodias-silenced-sounds.html.
'Elvis of the Kingdom Gets New Star Role' by Will Jackson,

Phnom Penh Post https://www.phnompenhpost.com/7days/
elvis-kingdom-gets-new-star-role.

'Fighting for the Sake of Truth and Justice' by Robert Carmichael,
Phnom Penh Post https://www.phnompenhpost.com/national/
fighting-sake-truth-and-justice.

'Finding the Middle Way' by Jack Kornfield https://jackkornfield.
com/finding-the-middle-way/.

'Khieu Ponnary, 1920–2003' by Charlotte McDonald-Gibson,
Phnom Penh Post https://www.phnompenhpost.com/national/
khieu-ponnary-1920-2003.

'Khmer-Krom: Internal Chaos of Indigenous People' from
Unrepresented Nations and Peoples Organization, 25 October
2006 https://unpo.org/article/5690.

'Khmer Rouge Killed Thousands to Build Airstrip' from *Khmer Times*,
28 July 2015 https://www.khmertimeskh.com/58128/khmer-roug
e-killed-thousands-to-build-airstrip/.

'Lyrics Mirror Political Zig-Zags' by Chea Sotheacheath, *Phnom
Penh Post* https://www.phnompenhpost.com/national/
lyrics-mirror-political-zig-zags.

'Operation Eagle Pull Before the Fall of Phnom Penh' by Liz
Dee, Association for Diplomatic Studies & Training
https://adst.org/2013/04/operation-eagle-pull-before-th
e-fall-of-phnom-penh/.

'Phnom Pen Fell First to Obscure Playboy' by Jean-Jacques Cazeaux
and Claude Juvenal, *Washington Post* https://www.yumpu.
com/en/document/view/39647573/phnom-pen-1975-11-first-t
o-obscure-playboy.

'President Richard Nixon's 14 Addresses to the Nation on
Vietnam' from the Richard Nixon Foundation https://www.
nixonfoundation.org/2017/09/president-richard-nixons-1
4-addresses-nation-vietnam/.

'Preserving a Cultural Tradition: Ten Years After the Khmer Rouge'
by Sam-Ang, *Cultural Survival Quarterly Magazine* http://www.
culturalsurvival.org/publications/cultural-survival-quarterly/
preserving-cultural-tradition-ten-years-after-khmer-rouge.

'Queen of Golden Voice: A Biography of Ros Serey Sothea' from
Khmerisation https://khmerisation.wordpress.com/2007/12/29/
queen-of-golden-voice-a-biography-of-ros-serey-sothea/.

Sources

'Remembering "Big Mike"' from the *Khmer Times*, 11 May 2016
https://www.khmertimeskh.com/23768/remembering-big-
mike/.
'Ros Serei Sothea as a paratrooper', *Khmer Republic Magazine*,
September 1971 http://www.chanbokeo.com/index.
php?gcm=1411&grid=139858&gtop=5197.
'Sinn Sisamouth Song Copyrights Awarded to Family' by Nou
Sotheavy, *Khmer Times* https://www.khmertimeskh.com/53250/
sinn-sisamouth-song-copyrights-awarded-to-family/.
'Vanquished in the '70s, Catholic Church Still on the Mend', *Phnom
Penh Post*, 25 March 2005 https://www.phnompenhpost.com/
national/vanquished-70s-catholic-church-still-mend.

RESOURCE CENTRES

Bophana Center https://bophana.org/
British Library https://www.bl.uk/
Documentation Center of Cambodia http://dccam.org/home
Cambodian Living Arts https://www.cambodianlivingarts.org/
Cambodian Vintage Music Archive https://www.facebook.com/
CambodianVintageMusicArchive/

PLAYLIST

N. B. The song titles listed are written in a mix of English and
Khmer and are based on the most recognizable title
spellings.
'Away from Beloved Lover' performed by Sinn Sisamouth
(sometimes credited as 'Apart from Beloved Lover')
'Bom Pet' performed by Kong Nay
'Kampuchea Twist' performed by Chum Kem (sometimes credited
as 'Twist Twist Khnom')
'Champa Battambang' performed by Sinn Sisamouth
'Pleine Lune' performed by Baksey Cham Krong
'Bat Oun' performed by Apsara band (sometimes credited as 'Batt
Aun' – by Sirivuth)
'A Song of Hopelessness' performed by Sieng Dy

'Mini a Go Go' performed by Pen Ran (sometimes credited as
  'Pan Ron')
'SKD' performed by Baksey Cham Krong (sometimes credited as
  'BCK')
'Yellow Bird' performed by Apsara (sometimes credited to 'Panara
  Sereyvuth')
'I'm Unsatisfied' performed by Pen Ran
'Man of Constant Sorrow' performed by Pen Ran
'Rom Sue Sue (Dance Soul Soul)' performed by Liev Tuk
'Sat Stiang Heur Stouy (Stingray)' performed by Sinn Sisamouth
'Stung Khieu' performed by Ros Sereysothea (sometimes credited as
  'Steung Kiev')
'Console Me' performed by Sieng Vanthy
'Hippie Men' performed by Pen Ran
'Missing Tender Hands' performed by Sinn Sisamouth
'Snaeh Yerng (Love Us)' performed by Ros Sereysothea and Sinn
  Sisamouth
'Monkey Dance' performed by Pen Ran
'Dance a Go Go' performed by Sinn Sisamouth
'Woolly Polly' performed by Ros Sereysothea
'Old Pot Still Cooks Good Rice' performed by Ros Sereysothea
'Yuvajon Kouge Jet (Broken Hearted Man)' performed by Yol
  Aularong
'Three Maidens' performed by Huoy Meas, Pen Ran and Ros
  Sereysothea
'Chnam Oun Dop-Pram Muy' performed by Ros Sereysothea
'Do You Remember?' performed by Liev Tuk
'Chmreing Somrapp Bong (A Song for You)' performed by Ros
  Sereysothea
'I'm Still Waiting for You (House of the Rising Sun)' performed by
  Sinn Sisamouth
'Under the Sound of Rain' performed by Sinn Sisamouth
'Cyclo' performed by Yol Aularong
'Have You No Mercy?' performed by Drakkar, feat. Mao Sareth
'I Love Petite Women' performed by Sinn Sisamouth (sometimes
  credited as 'I Love Petite Girl')
'Sarawan Chan Penh Boromei (Dancing Saravan Under the Full
  Moon)' performed by Drakkar

Credits

All possible care has been taken to trace the rights holders and secure permission for the images reproduced and texts quoted in this book. If there are any omissions, credits can be added in future editions following a request in writing to the publisher. Grateful acknowledgement is made to all copyright holders who have granted their permission.

ILLUSTRATION CREDITS

> *The Cambodian Vintage Music Archive and the Documentation Center of Cambodia are abbreviated as 'CVMA' and 'DC-Cam' respectively.*

p. xv	Bokor Palace Hotel © Ilia Torlin/Shutterstock.com.
p. 1	Sieng Vanthy, Yol Aularong and Pen Ram performing © Institut national de l'audiovisuel, Paris.
p. 6	Cambodian classical and folk instruments © Rebecca Grubba.
p. 13	Norodom Sihanouk © DC-Cam.
p. 21	Cambodian 1960s/1970s record sleeves. Images courtesy of the CVMA.
p. 28	The Khmer Rouge brotherhood. © DC-Cam.
p. 31	Cambodians working on an irrigation project. Dam 'January 1st', Chinith River, Kampong Thom Province, 1976 © DC-Cam.

p. 35   Svay Sor surveys his classroom © Dee Peyok.

p. 49   TVK network television, 1970. Image courtesy of Touch
         Chhattha.

p. 66   Apsara dancers, Royal Palace, 1960s © CPA Media Pte Ltd/
         Alamy Stock Photo.

p. 75   Apsara in early 1960s. Image courtesy of CVMA.

p. 91   Lay Mealea and Joe Wrigley perform with their band, Miss
         Sarawan. © Steve Porte.

p. 103   Film still from *Joie de Vivre*, 1969 © the estate of Prince
         Norodom Sihanouk.

p. 103   Exterior of the Magetat © Rama International.

p. 109   Chariya in the 1980s. Image courtesy of Prince Sisowath
         Chariya.

p. 112   Thach Soly © Kevin Peyok.

p. 119   Sinan digitising his collection at the CVMA © Martin Jay.

p. 127   Sophoan band. Image courtesy of Thach Soly.

p. 138   Master Kong Nay © Tom Whittaker/Alamy Stock.

p. 153   Kong Nay © Dee Peyok.

p. 155   Ros Sereysothea. Image courtesy of CVMA.

p. 168   Sinn Sisamouth and Ros Sereysothea. Image courtesy
         of CVMA.

p. 169   Ros Sereysothea record sleeve. Image courtesy of Greg
         Cahill.

p. 172   Saboeun looking through the CVMA archive © Dee Peyok.

p. 174   Saboeun's wall of photos © Dee Peyok.

p. 195   Sinn Sisamouth and his beloved VW Bug. Image courtesy
         of CVMA.

p. 199   Vintage Sisamouth songbook © Dee Peyok.

p. 205   Sophorn, Oro, Dee, Gnut © Martin Jay.

p. 209   Cover and page from 1950s RNK Radio programmes ©
         Reahoo Publishing.

p. 215   Sinn Sisamouth record sleeve. Image courtesy of CVMA.

p. 226   Dee, Gnut, Oro, Martin and Sophorn © Martin Jay.

p. 232   Sinn Sisamouth's childhood home © Martin Jay.

p. 234   Drakkar 1974 album cover. Image courtesy of Touch
         Chhattha.

p. 239   Touch Chhattha in the late 1960s. Image courtesy of Touch
         Chhattha.

p. 264 Baksey Cham Krong. Image courtesy of Mol Kamach.
p. 274 Tana, Kagnol and Sothivann at the City Winery Show ©
        Dee Peyok.
p. 301 Lon Nol soldier running, guitar in one hand, gun in the
        other © by Roland Neveu/RNBK.INFO.
p. 310 Nate Hun, CVMA co-founder, with his collection. Image
        courtesy of Nate Hun.
p. 318 Dee Peyok in Bokor Palace's abandoned newly rendered
        ballroom in 2012 © Kevin Peyok.

SONG CREDITS

Lines from 'Pleine Lune' by Baksey Cham Krong, released by
    Chanchhaya, 1964 © reissue by Akuphone, 2016.
Lines from 'Under the Sound of Rain', composed and performed
    by Sinn Sisamouth. Reproduced by kind permission of the
    Cambodian Ministry of Culture and Fine Arts.
Lines from 'We Sing Together', composed by Sinn Sisamouth,
    performed by Ros Sereysothea and Sinn Sisamouth.
    Reproduced by kind permission of the Cambodian Ministry of
    Culture and Fine Arts.
Lines from 'Dying Under a Woman's Sword', unknown composer,
    performed by Yol Aularong and Va Savoy.
Lines from 'The King Sold the Land to the Viet Cong', composed by
    Samneang Rithy, performed by Sinn Sisamouth.
Lines from 'Don't Think I've Forgotten', composed and performed
    by Sinn Sisamouth.

Index

A-Rex (later Lotus D'Or), 18
Addrisi Brothers, 21–2
agriculture, 30–1
AIDS *see* HIV/AIDS
Akuphone, 33, 274–6, 282, 296
Amara, 49, 242
Amatak Festival, 138–40
Ancestor's Day *see* Pchum Ben
Anderson, Marian, 101–2
Angkor Wat, 4, 5
Animals, 14, 222, 245–6
animism, 4–5, 8
Anka, Paul, 16, 211, 270, 280
Anlong Veng Peace Center, 312
Anthony, Richard, 16
Antoine, 25, 241
apsara, *66*, 69, 110–11, 209
Apsara, 19, 68, 74–8, 75, 80, 286; *see also* Sisowath Panara Sirivudh
Apsara (film), 63, 64, 102
Archies, 221
arek, 5, 6
Armed Forces Vietnam Network, 14, 177–8
Army of the Republic of Vietnam (ARVN), 147
art and architecture, 4, 87–8
Arthur Lyman Group, 77
Asakawa, Maki, 275
Association, 22, 129

Axel, 297
Aznavour, Charles, 12, 128

Baksey Cham Krong: background of members, 74–5; and *Don't Think I've Forgotten* reunion tour, 272; early days, 127; French reissue of singles, 33, 296; influences on, 16; legacy, 299–300; name's origins, 268–9; overview, 264, 266–70, 278–88, 292–3; *see also* Mol Kagnol
SONGS: 'Adios, Mama and Papa', 281; 'BCK', 286–7; 'Pleine Lune' ('Full Moon'), 281–3, 296, 298; 'The Rose of Battambang', 283
Bangkok, 109
Banner, Linda, 304, 306
Baramey, 316
Bare, Bobby, 14
Baribo River, 135
Baribour, 122–3, 134
Barigozzi, Giancarlo, 101
Barroso, Ary, 211
Bassac theatre, 5
Battambang, 156–7, 162, 164, 165, 173
Bayon, 19, 293–4; *see also* Hong Samley

Beatles: cover versions, 135, 221, 293; and Khmer Rouge, 257; Paris concerts, 102; popularity and influence, 88, 125, 237, 240
Bee Gees, 242, 294
Berrocal, Jay, 275
Berry, Chuck, 270, 284
birthdays, 206
Bo Hein, 2
Bodhi Villa, 95–6
Bodiansky, Vladimir, 87
Bokor Palace Hotel, *xv*, xvi–xvii, 317, *318*
Booker T. and the MGs, 21, 129
Boone, Pat, 16, 270
Bopha Devi, Princess *see* Norodom Bopha Devi, Princess
Borey Pen, 139
Boswell, Steven, 106
Bou Meng, 302
Bounrith, 264
Bouw, Josh, 92–3
Brassens, Georges, 12
brothels, 105–6
Brown, James, 21, 241
Buddhism: death rituals, 110–11, 157, 192–3; on divorce and remarriage, 213; fight against French, 11; funerals, 157; and hornbills, 317–18; and Khmer culture, 4–5; languages, 207; the middle path, 306–7; pagoda boys, 206–7; Pchum Ben, 94, 120, 192–3; *sampeah krou* ceremonies, 43; temples, 4, 5, 156, 192–3; Vietnamese treatment of monks, 124
buffaloes, 131
Burma, 1, 2
Burnett, Dick, 62

Caldwell, Malcolm, 183
calendars, 206
Cambodia: Angkorian period, 3–4, 8–9; attitude to Vietnamese, 125; caste system, 284–5; civil war (1970–75), 26–9, 107–8, 116–17, 128–9, 131–2, 147–8, 180–5, 246, 294–5; under French, 1, 5, 9–11, 43–6, 121; indigenous hill tribes, 48; under Khmer Rouge, 29–34, 51–3, 64, 79, 84–7, 116–18, 121, 132–4, 148–50, 185–91, 222–5, 254–60, 288–9, 311; under Lon Nol, 22–9, 50–1, 108–9, 178–85, 219–22; map, *ix*; in nineteenth century, 6–7; path to reconciliation, 301–14; role of family, 130; survivor's guilt and refugees, 295; in twenty-first century, 67–8, 304; under Sihanouk, 1, 11–23, 46–50, 96–7, 101–4, 105–7, 125–8, 178, 208–19, 292–4; US bombing, 216; US invasion, 25–7; and Vietnam War, 216; Vietnamese invasion and occupation, 52–3, 58, 78–9, 87, 118, 134, 149–50, 252, 261–2
Cambodian Cassette Archives (compilation), 33
Cambodian Living Arts organization, 139, 308–10
Cambodian music: archives, 5, 33, 70, 82, 119, *119*, 158, 170–1; classical, 5–15; compilations, xvii–xviii, 8, 32–3, 81; mid-twentieth century song structures, 63; now vs 1960s and 1970s, 262–3; percentage of musicians killed during genocide, 309; sales statistics, 253–4; use of influences, 237–8

Cambodian National Rescue Party
(CNRP), 67–8
Cambodian People's Party (CPP),
68, 79
Cambodian Rocks (compilation), xvii–
xviii, 32–3, 81
Cambodian Space Project *see* CSP
Cambodian Vintage Music Archive
(CVMA), 70, 82, 119, *119*,
158, 170–1
Carpenters, 179
Cascades, 212–13
cassettes, 17
caste, 284–5
Catholicism, 57–61, 64–5
Caylee So, 212
CBC Band, 2
Celestial Harmonies, 5
ceremonies *see* Buddhism
Chanchhaya, 221
Chantays, 287
Chao, Lily, 275
chapei dang veng, 62, 141,
142–5, 152–3
Chariya, Prince, *see* Sisowath
Chariya, Prince
Charles, Ray, 72, 140
Chay Lay, Colonel, 164
Chea Savoeun, 128
Checker, Chubby, 16–17, 125
Cherk, Mr, 255–6
Chhom Nimol, 99–100, 272, 273,
315; *see also* Dengue Fever
Chhuon Malay, 20
Chicago, 294
Chiemi Eri, 275
Chim Chhuon, Brigadier
General, 184
China: Cambodian attitude to,
10, 285; and Cambodian music
industry, 315; Chinese-Khmers,

217, 261; Chinese musicians
in Cambodia, 50; influence on
Cambodia, 8, 12, 13, 97; and
Khmer Rouge, 27, 117, 216–17;
and Sihanouk, 216, 217, 219
Chinith River, *31*
Chlangden, 32, 81
chok krapeus, 20
Chorn-Pond, Arn, 308–10
Chou, Davy, 195
Chum, Mme, 106
Chum Kem, 17, 73, 211, 284
Chum Mey, 302
CIA, 96, 216
class issues: caste, 284–5; and rock
bands, 74
clubs *see* nightclubs
CNRP *see* Cambodian National
Rescue Party
cockroaches, 172
Cohn, Nik, 160, 241
Community Favoured by the People
see Sangkum Reastr Niyum
Comrade Duch (Kaing Guek
Eav), 305
Congress Day, 125–6, 165, 292
copyright, 80–2, 191, 197–9, 201,
213, 315
CPP *see* Cambodian People's Party
Creedence Clearwater Revival, 179
CSP (Cambodian Space Project),
99, 314
CVMA *see* Cambodian Vintage
Music Archive
cyclo riders, 18

Dale, Dick, 287
dams, *31*
Dâmrei Mountains, xv–xvii, 317–19
dance and dances: apsara, *66*, 69,
110–11, 209; *chok krapeus*, 20;

Index

the jerk, 100; *khene*, 236; modern
forms, 311; *rom kbach*, 20; *rom lam
leav*, 20; *romvong*, 20, 131; Royal
Ballet, 9, 44, 208–9, 210; *saravan*,
20; the twist, 16–17, 20
Dara Puspita, 2
DC-Cam *see* The Documentation
Center of Cambodia
Dean, John Gunther, 182–4
Deang Dell, 131
Delpeuch, Edouard Degay, 235, 262,
277, 296–7
Denacio Saem, 45–6, 102, 126
Dengue Fever, 99–100, 271–2, 273,
314–15
La Dépêche du Cambodge, 2
Diệm, President, 1
divorce, 213
Doch Chkae, 316
The Documentation Center of
Cambodia (DC-Cam), 271, 301,
311–13
*Don't Think I've Forgotten:
Cambodia's Lost Rock and Roll*
(film): aim, 86; content, 177, 225,
270–1; executive producer, 313–
14; Mol Kamach on, 299; Paris
screening, 296, 297–9; reunion
tour organized by, 264–74;
soundtrack, 33, 70, 167
Dontrey Phirum, 15
Doors nightclub, 160
Drakkar, *234*; under Lon Nol,
28–9; their music and shows,
24–5; overview, 234–43, 249–52;
revival, 262; *see also* Touch
Chhattha; Touch Tana
SONGS AND ALBUMS: 'Boer Bang
Min Mayta?' ('Have You
No Mercy?'), 137; *Drakkar
74*, 33, *234*, 249–52, 253–4,

262; 'Sarawan Chhan Penh
Boromei' ('Dancing Saravan
under the Full Moon'), 62, 251
Dust for Digital, 33
Dy Saveth, 100, 195
Dylan, Bob, 62–3

Écran Voisin, 297
education: Cambodian children
sent to France for, 12, 16, 60;
Cambodian secular school
system, 267–8; under French, 10;
palace, 44; Phnom Penh schools,
74; UBA, 57–8, 62, 64–5, 138–40;
women's, 205
Eldred, Paul, 38
Ell Bunna, 89
Epplay, Vincent, 275
*Ethnic Minority Music of Northeast
Cambodia* (compilation album), 8
Everly Brothers, 84, 89–90

FANK *see* Forces Armées Nationales
Khmères
Fennech, David, 275
festivals, 94, 138–40, 192–3
Fex, Jan, 93, 95, 98
Fex, Sokheng, 93
Filipino Constabulary Band, 45
Filipino music, 6–8, 45
film industry, 29, 31–2, 63
Fishery ministry band, 260
folktales, 144
food, 10, 153, 277–8
Forces Armées Nationales Khmères
(FANK), 147
Forest, Alain, 9
43 B1, 131
France: as Cambodia's colonizer, 1,
5, 9–11, 121; Cambodian children
sent to be educated in, 12, 16, 60;

Cambodian refugees in, 276–7, 285; French music's influence on Cambodian, 12, 16, 25, 75–6; *see also* Paris
FUNCINPEC, 54, 79
funerals, 157
Furie, Sidney, 16

GANEFO Games (1966), 107
gem mining, 252–4
Gerry and the Pacemakers, 73
Géry, Fabrice, 274–6, 296, 298
Golden Slumbers (film), 195
Golden Tequila Mile, 104–5
Goodman, Ben, 50
Goodman, Benny, 50, 102
Gourevitch, Philip, 148
Grand Funk Railroad, 87
Granddad, xix
Groove Club series, 33
guitars, 270, 293
gungteng, 8

Haley, Bill, 125
Hallyday, Johnny, 16
Hancock, Herbie, 56–7
Hass Salan, 55, 248, 249
Hathaway, Donny, 179
Hazlewood, Lee, 193
Heart of Darkness bar, 104
Hendrix, Jimi, 14
Heng Heng, 221, 285
Heritage of Survivors programme, 151
Hin Kraven, 74–8, 75
Hinduism, 3, 318–19
HIV/AIDS, 48
Holtzmann, Zac, 315; *see also* Dengue Fever
Hong Kong, 17, 214
Hong Sambath, 293–4, 295

Hong Samley, *264*, 272, 284–5, 289–96; *see also* Baksey Cham Krong; Bayon
Hong Samlot, 293–4, 295
Horn, 71
hornbills, 317–19
hostess bars, 104
Hour Lonh, 74–8, *75*; *see also* Apsara
Hsu, Michael 'Big Mike', 104, 271
Hun, Nate, 33, 70, *310*
Hun Sen, 68, 79, 203, 304, 305
Huoy Meas, *49*; death, 133; husbands, 114, 133; under Khmer Rouge, 133, 190–1; and Magetat, 19; overview, 132–3; and Ros Sereysothea, 133, 165; and Sinn Sisamouth, 214
Huoy Siphan, 166, 180

ICP *see* Indochinese Communist Party
Ieng Sary, 28, 148
Ieu Pannaker, 39
Im Song Seum, 164, 165, 190
In the Life of Music (film), 212
Indochinese Communist Party (ICP), 27
Indonesian music, 2
Infantry Brigade 13, 108

Jack Adaptor, 92
Jackson, Will, 196
Jay, Martin, *226*; and Akuphone, 274, 275; and author's Paris trip, 274, 276–7; and *Don't Think I've Forgotten* Paris screening, 296; and Keo Thorng Gnut interview, 202, 204, 226–7, 231; and Mol Kamach interview, 277–8, 284, 285, 289–90, 291, 296
Jay, Peter, 283

Jayavarman II, King of Cambodia, 3
the jerk, 100
Joe, Mr, 60
Joe and the Jumping Jacks, 93–9
La Joie de Vivre (film), 102–3
Jomreang Eth Preang Thok (*The Song
    Extemporaneous*; film), 170

Kaing Guek Eav *see* Comrade Duch
Kak Channthy (aka Srey Thy), 99
Kampong Chhnang city, 121–2
Kampong Chhnang province, 120–3
Kampong Song province, 100–1
Kampong Thom province, *31*, 113–
    14, 116–17
Kampong Trach, 141–2,147
Kampot, 95–6, 100–1
Kampuchea Krom, 124–5, 149
Kampuchean People's Revolutionary
    Party *see* People's Republic of
    Kampuchea
Kampuchean United Front for
    National Salvation (KUFNS), 150
Kandal province, 100–1
Kansaing Sar (White Scarves), 216
karaoke, 80–1, 104, 315–16
Kbal Thnal, 55–6, 208, 209–10,
    237, 244–5
Keo Sinan, 112, 113–20, *119*
Keo Sokha, 210, 251
Keo Thorng Gnut, 201–28, *205*, *226*,
    229–30, 231–2
Kersalé, Patrick, 311
Kes Sarol, 133
Khao-I-Dang camp, 53–4
Khatharya Um, 295
khene, 8, 236
Khieu Ponnary, 74
Khieu Samphan, 28, 148, 253,
    301–3, 305
Khmer Issarak, 11, 27, 147

Khmer Krom people, 124–5
Khmer Republic, 22–30, 50–1,
    108–9, 178–85, 219–22
Khmer Rocks, xvii
Khmer Rouge: attitude to music,
    116, 117, 134, 148–9, 257, 308–9;
    and Cambodian civil war, 26–8,
    108, 116–17, 147–8, 182–5;
    and the disabled, 149, 150;
    founders' background, 27–8;
    and indigenous hill tribes, 48;
    leaders' fate, 253, 301–5; life
    under, 29–34, 51–3, 64, 79, 84–7,
    116–18, 121, 132–4, 148–50, 185–
    91, 222–5, 254–60, 288–9, 311;
    nowadays, 228–31, 304; origins,
    23–4; propaganda against, 178–9;
    public attitude to nowadays,
    304–5; and reconciliation, 301–14;
    and Sihanouk, 54, 148, 183,
    216–17, 219; and slave labour, 121;
    tribunal cases, 301–6
Khmer Serei, 23, 216
Kiernan, Ben, 26
King's Guard Orchestra, 24
Kissinger, Henry, 25–6
KlapYaHandz, 316
Ko Shin Moon, 275, 297
Kong Nay, *138*, 140–53, *153*, 311
Kong Sam Oeun, 214
Kong Tith, 143–4
kongvong, 5
Koppe, Victor, 305
Kornfield, Jack, 306–7
Kosal, 244–5
Kosnaka, 15, 51
Kossamak, Queen *see* Norodom
    Kossamak, Queen
krolan, 153
kse diev, 9
KUFNS *see* Kampuchean United

Front for National Salvation

Lac Sea, 17
language and languages, xiii–xiv, 10, 38–9, 207
Laos, 1, 8
Lara *see* Yol Aularong
Larks, 100
Latiff, Roziah, 2
Lay Mealea, 91–9, *91*, 131, 155, 194
Lay Mealai, 93
Lee Him Uon, 243
Liébot, Maurice, 46, 60, 126
Liev Tuk, 21–2, 128–9
Lim Sophorn, *205*; background and character, 40, 41, 110, 228–9; film job, 69–70; and Keo Thorng Gnut interview, 202, 210, 226–7, 231; and Kong Nay interview, 141–2, 153, 154; and Mam Boutnaray interview, 58–9, 61, 63; and Minh Sothivann interview, 82–3; and Sinn Chanchhaya, 201; and Sisowath Chariya, 110; and Svay Sor interview, 40–2, 57; and Thach Soly interview, 120, 122–3, 130, 131
Lion Productions, 33
literature, 10
Little Richard, 72
Lomorpich Rithy, 316–17
Lomhea Yothea, 164
Lon Nol, General: character, 218; later life, 183; overthrown, 29–30; and propaganda, 50; regime, 22–9, 50–1, 108–9, 178–85, 219–22; rise to power, 23, 107–8, 218–19
Lon Non, 184
London, 102
Long Boret, 183, 184

Long Soda, 128
Lopez, Trini, 16, 102
Lotus D'Or (formerly A-Rex), 18, 128, 165
Lu Ban Hap, 87
Luk Thung country music, 2
Lumumba, Patrice, 275
Ly Tai Cheng, 49, *49*, 242

Ma Lopy, 115
McGilligan, Clancy, 194
Magasin d'État (Magetat) club, *103*; acts at, 19, 49, 165; atmosphere, 19, 102–3; closure, 107–8; establishment, 19; house band, 293–4; music programme manager, 106–7
mahori, 5–6, 8, 9
Malis, Mme, 94
Mam Bophani, 46, 57–8, 60–1, 63, 64
Mam Boutnaray (aka Mono Cakey), 58–63, 64, 65, 115, 124, 240
Mam, Laura, 316–17
Mam Molivan, 236, 240–3, 245
Mam, Mme (Mam Molivan's mother), 236
Mam, Mrs (Mam Boutnaray's wife), 58–9, 60, 61
Manila music, 7, 45
Mao Sareth: and code of conduct for women, 20; and Drakkar, 251; hits, 248–9; live sets, 18; singing style, 14; and Sinn Sisamouth, 210, 214, 248
marching band music, 9, 45–6, 89, 101, 107
Marie (Géry's girlfriend), 296, 298
Marley, Bob, 275
marriage, 236; arranged, 207–8
Maxine's, 104
Mech Dara, 65, 67

Mekong nightclub, 284
Mekong Studio, 169
La Melodie, 114–15
Mer Bun, 58, 210
Mermaid Bar *see* Sovanmancha
Metal Postcard, 33, 262
Mic, Master, 308–9
Minh Prahul, 74–8, 75, 82, 83–4, 89;
    see also Apsara
Minh Sothivann, 66, 82–90, 260,
    266, 272, 273, *274*
Ministry of Culture and Fine Arts,
    197–8; band, 89
Ministry of Industry band, 134
Ministry of Information recording
    studio, 76–7
Ministry of Interior band, 89
minivans, public, 154
Miss Sarawan, 91–9, *91*
Moeun Chhean Nariddh, 225
Mol Kagnol, *264, 274*; and Baksey
    Cham Krong, 264, 267–70, 279,
    281–8; and *Don't Think I've
    Forgotten*, 266–7, 270–3; and
    Drakkar, 250–1; his guitar, 283–4;
    see also Baksey Cham Krong
Mol Kamach, *264*; and Baksey Cham
    Krong, 264, 267–70, 277–88; and
    Don't Think I've Forgotten, 296,
    298, 299; later life, 288–91, 297–8;
    see also Baksey Cham Krong
Mol Minh, 267, 278–81
Mol Saem, 270, 278–9, 289
Mol Samel, 278, 280, 281–3, 289; *see
    also* Baksey Cham Krong
Mol Samine, 278, 280, 281, 288, 289;
    see also Baksey Cham Krong
Mol Samkot, 279, 289
Mol Samot, 278, 280, 289; *see also*
    Baksey Cham Krong
Mondulkiri, 8

Monica (Ros Sereysothea's great
    niece), 191, 192–3
Monique, Queen *see* Norodom
    Monique, Queen
Mono Cakey *see* Mam Boutnaray
Montand, Yves, 12
Morrison, Van, 248
Mortar Round, 104–5
Mushapata, 275
music notation, 45
Music of Cambodia archives, 5
music shops, xvii, 17–18
musical instruments: Cambodian
    classical and folk, *6*, 8, 9, 62–3;
    chapei dang veng, 62, 141, 142–5,
    152–3; guitars, 270, 293; *khene*,
    8, 236; rebuilding extinct
    instruments, 311; *roneat thung*,
    161, 163
Myanmar *see* Burma

Nagara Vatta (*Notre Cité*)
    newspaper, 10–11
Naradipo, Prince *see* Norodom
    Naradipo, Prince
Nath Samean, 163–4, 165, 187–9
national anthems, 45
National Congress *see* Congress Day
Neveu, Roland, 185
New Cambodian Artists, 311
new people (Khmer Rouge term), 86
New York, 264–6, 271–4
Nget Rady, 311
nightclubs: closure, 29, 107–8; under
    Lon Nol, 28–9, 50, 246; under
    Sihanouk, 18–19, 50, 102–4,
    112–15, 165; *see also* Kbal Thnal;
    Lotus D'Or; Magasin d'État
Nil Nonn, 302–3
Nil Thera, xix
Nixon, Richard, 26

Nong Neang *see* Sisowath Panara Sirivudh, Prince

Nop Nem, 114

Nop Noeun, 114

Norodom I, King of Cambodia, 6–7

Norodom Bopha Devi, Princess, *66*, 69, 110–11

Norodom Kossamak, Queen: and Cambodia's health, 209–10; and dance, 12, 69, 208, 209; favourite singers, 12, 132; and Khmer Rouge, 222; and palace education, 44; role, 209; and Sinn Sisamouth, 200, 208, 209–10

Norodom Monique, Queen, 67

Norodom Naradipo, Prince, 45

Norodom Narottama, King of Cambodia, 289

Norodom Ranariddh, Prince, 42, 45

Norodom Sihamoni, King of Cambodia, 67

Norodom Sihanouk, Prince, *13*; abdication, 1; and the arts, 12–16, 46; in exile, 109; fall from power, 22–3, 108, 216–19; favourite singers, 132, 167; films by, 63, 64, 102; and Hong Samley, 292, 293, 294; Khmer Republic's attitude to, 50–1; and Khmer Rouge, 54, 148, 183, 216–17, 219; later life, 54–5; and Magetat, 19, 103, 294; and Mol family, 278; policies and regime, 1, 11–23, 46–50, 96–7, 101–4, 105–7, 125–8, 178, 208–19, 292–4; propaganda against, 178–9, 180; and Sinn Sisamouth, 212, 219–20; and Sisowath Thomico, 67; and Svay Sor, 46–7; and Vietnam War, 96–7, 216

North Vietnam: Cambodian massacre of migrant Vietnamese, 27; relations with Cambodia, 50

North Vietnamese Army (PAVN): and Cambodian civil war, 23, 26, 50; invasion of Cambodia, 32, 52–3; and Sihanouk, 216; and Vietnam War, 96

Notre Cité (newspaper) *see* *Nagara Vatta*

Le Nouveau Tricon, 105–6

Novak, Professor David, 33

novels, 10

Nuon Chea, 28, *28*, 253, 301–3, 305

Oer Sam Ol, 244, 245–6, 249–52, 260; *see also* Drakkar

Ok Silyauth, 100, 170

old people (Khmer Rouge term), 117–18

Olympia club, 50, 294

One Thousand Memories (film), 116

Operation Eagle Pull (1975), 182–3

Operation Freedom Deal (1970–73), 26

Operation Menu (1969–70), 25–6

opium dens, 106

Oro *see* Oum Rattanak Oudam

Osborne, Milton, 217

Ouk Sam Ath, *234*; appearance, 25; background, 164, 244; and Drakkar, 245–6, 249–52; later life, 260, 266; *see also* Drakkar

Oum Dara, 275–6

Oum Rattanak Oudam (Oro), *205*, *226*; at Amatak Festival, 139; background, 70; character, 171–2, 228; on copyright, 80–1; and CVMA, 70, 170–1; and Keo Sinan, 113; and Keo Thorng Gnut interview, 202, 204, 210, 226, 231, 232, 233; Khmer Rouge encounter, 230; and Ros Saboeun

interview, 158–9, 170–2, 191; and
Sinn Chanchhaya interview, 196;
and Sisowath Panara Sirivudh
interview, 70–1
Owen, Taylor, 26

pagoda boys, 206–7
Pailin city, 29, 252–6
palace music, 8–9, 24, 40–50, 209–10
Pankhurst, Chris, 196
Parallel World, xvii, 32, 81
Paris, 102, 274, 276–7, 295,
296, 297–8
Paris Peace Agreements (1991), 79
Paris Set, 27–8, 148
Parsons, David, 5
PAVN *see* North Vietnamese Army
Pchum Ben (Ancestor's Day), 94,
120, 192–3
Pech Saloeun, 187
Pen Ram, *1*, 49–50, 190, 270–1,
294, 295
Pen Ran: childhood, 165; death, 190;
and *Don't Think I've Forgotten*
reunion tour, 273; and Drakkar,
251; 'Farewell Song', 62–3;
and Huoy Meas, 133; and Lay
Mealea, 95; popularity, 22; and
Ros Sereysothea, 165; singing
style, 20–1; and Sinn Sisamouth,
210, 214; songwriters for, 77; at
Van Chann studio, 247
Penhsamnang Kan, 301–2
People's Republic of Kampuchea
(PRK), 53, 79, 261–2, 304
Peou Sipho: brother, 55; favourite
singers, 132; influence, 74, 115;
overview, 73–4; pupils, 102, 281;
and RNK, 73, 208; and Royal
Palace, 200
Peou Vanchon, 55

Perruchot, François, 45
Peter Jay and the Jaywalkers, 283
Peyok, Dee, *205, 226, 318*;
childhood, 36–7; and cigarettes,
229; in Dâmrei Mountains,
xvi–xviii, 317–19; journey to
Cambodia, 36; Khmer Rouge
encounter, 228–31; life in Phnom
Penh, xviii–xx, 36–40; musical
career, 92, 267; pregnancy, 265;
return to UK, 264–5; speaks at
Don't Think I've Forgotten Paris
screening, 296, 298–9; on tour
with Miss Sarawan, 92–9
Peyok, Kevin: appearance, 37, 123,
157; Battambang trip, 156–7;
on Borey Pen, 139; at Buddhist
festival, 192–3; character, 177;
childhood favourite music, 135;
in Dâmrei Mountains, xvi–xviii,
317–19; guitar purchase, 175–7;
home town, 121; journey to
Cambodia, 36; and Kong Nay
interview, 141–2, 153, 154; life in
Phnom Penh, xviii–xx, 36–40;
musical career, 92; New York
trip, 265; Paris trip, 274, 277, 285,
289, 296; return to UK, 264–5;
and Ros Saboeun interview, 191;
as teacher, xviii, 36, 156–7; and
Thach Soly interview, 120, 121,
122, 130, 131; on tour with Miss
Sarawan, 92–9
Philippines, *1*, 6–8, 45
Phnom Penh: BKK1 district, 71;
BKK2 and BKK3 districts,
82–3; Bophana Center, 39–40;
Catholic churches in, 64; during
civil war, 181–2; under Khmer
Rouge, 30, 52–3, 182–7, 288–9,
303; life in and atmosphere,

xviii–xx, 18, 36–40; live music
scene and nightlife, 18–19, 24–5,
28–9, 50, 55–6, 102–8, 112–15,
160, 165, 208, 237, 244–5, 246,
293–4; under Lon Nol, 24, 52;
nicknames, 3; Olympic Market,
242; schools, 74; White Building
(Municipal Apartments),
87–8, 103
Phú Quốc island, 149
Piaf, Édith, 12, 280
Pickett, Wilson, 21
pinpeat/piphat, 8, 9, 44
piracy *see* copyright
Pirozzi, John, 70, 86, 194, 239, 265,
271; *see also Don't Think I've
Forgotten: Cambodia's Lost Rock
and Roll*
pizza joints, 104
Platters, 73
Pol Pot, *28*; background, 23, 27–8,
74; and Caldwell, 183; grave, 312;
and Sihanouk, 148
polygamy, 236
Pond, Peter, 308
Potter, Andy, 93
Potter, Rattana, 93
Pou Vannery, 25, 28–9
Poulson, Julien, 99
Prach Chhoun, 152
*Preah Leak Sinavong Neang Pream
Kesor* (film), 165
Presley, Elvis, 237, 270
pressing plants, 17
PRK *see* People's Republic of
Kampuchea party
Procol Harum, xvi–xviii, 221
Pry Nehru, 173–5, 190–1, 192

radio: under Lon Nol, 24; under
Sihanouk, 13–14; US stations

broadcasting to Cambodia, 177–8
Radiodiffusion National Khmère
(RNK): band, 15, 73, 208, 210;
and Bayon, 293; creation, 13–14;
and Huoy Meas, 133; mission
and achievements, 51; mixing
facilities, 126–7; programmes,
209; and Ros Sereysothea, 165;
staff levels, 262; studio, 169;
Touch Chhattha at, 243, 262;
Touch Tana at, 243–4, 252
Ramayana (aka *Reamker*; Sanskrit
epic), 4
Ranariddh, Prince *see* Norodom
Ranariddh, Prince
Ratanakiri, 8
record labels: Akuphone, 33,
274–6, 282, 296; Baramey, 316;
overview of Cambodian, 17, 115;
Wat-Phnom, 77, 212, 248
recording studios: Ministry of
Information, 76–7; RNK,
169; Van Chann, 77, 169, 220,
246–7, 285
records *see* vinyl
religion: animism, 4–5, 8;
Catholicism, 57–61, 64–5;
Hinduism, 3, 318–19; place in
Khmer culture, 4–5; *see also*
Buddhism
Richard, Cliff, 16, 283
Rin Chhoum Virak, 32
Rithy Panh, 39
ritual *see* Buddhism
RNK *see* Radiodiffusion National
Khmère
Robert (American writer), xix–xx
Rolling Stones: cover versions, 246,
293; popularity and influence, 25,
125, 237, 240, 241
rom kbach, 20

rom lam leav, 20
romvong, 20, 131
roneat thung, 161, 163
Ronnie Scott's, 102
Ros Saboeun, 157–94, *172*, 215–16
Ros Saboeuth, 157–8, 161, 162–3
Ros Sabun, 161, 163–4, 191
Ros Sareth, 161
Ros Saroeun, 161
Ros Sereysothea, *155*, *168*, *169*,
    174; appearance, 22; childhood,
    161–4; death, 187–8; and *Don't
    Think I've Forgotten* reunion
    tour, 273; and Huoy Meas, 133,
    165; influences on, 248; and Lay
    Mealea, 94, 98–9, 155; marriages
    and relationships, 165–6, 179–81;
    overview, 157–94; popularity and
    influence, 146, 160; and Sinn
    Sisamouth, 22, 164, 165, 166–9,
    170, 214–15; songwriters for, 77; at
    Van Chann studio, 247
    SONGS: 'Chnam Oun Dop-Pram
        Muy' ('I'm Sixteen'), 160;
        'I'm Ticklish! I'm Ticklish!',
        116; 'Karma', 116; 'Memory
        of Kampong Som', 101;
        'Snaeh Yerng' ('Love Us'),
        167; 'Thavary My Love', 167;
        'Tomorrow I Will Leave You',
        116; 'We Sing Together', 167
Ros Sokunthea, 161, 162–3, 180
Ros Sophean, 161, 180
Rossi, Tino, 16, 280
Roussillon, 297
Roxas y Manio, Josefa 'Pepita', 7
Royal Ballet, 9, 44, 208–9, 210
Royal Fanfare Band, 45
Royal University of Fine Arts
    (RUFA; formerly Université des
    Beaux-Arts), 138–40

Roziah Latiff and the Jayhawkers, 2

S21 detention centre, 302, 305
Sacred Dancers of Angkor, 110–11
St Marks hotel, 265
Saksi Sbong, 214
Sam & Dave, 245
sampeah krou ceremonies, 434
sampots, 223
Sangkum Reastr Niyum
    (Community Favoured by the
    People), 11–16, 22–3
Santana, 222, 249, 294
Santiago, Luciano P. R., 7
Saphan, LinDa, 271, 292
saravan, 20
Savoy, 178–9
Schanberg, Sydney, 184
Schwartz, Andre, 93, 95
Scorpio, 156, 157
sculpture, 4
Seng Dara, 161
sex industry, 104–6, 282
sex workers *see* sex industry
Shadow Over Angkor (film), 63
Shadows, 16, 270, 283, 286, 287
Sharky's, 104–5, 105–6, 271
Siem Reap, 32
Sieng Dy, *103*; character, 109; and
    code of conduct for women,
    19–20; death, 109–10; in films, 64,
    102; hits, 102; later life, 108–10;
    at Magetat, 102–3, 294; marriage,
    102, 109; and Sinn Sisamouth,
    208, 210
Sieng Vanthy, *1*, 20, 270–1, 294
Sihamoni, King of Cambodia *see*
    Norodom Sihamoni
Sihanouk, Prince *see* Norodom
    Sihanouk, Prince
Sihanoukville, 96–7

Sim Samuth, 198
Simoeun, Mme, 56
Sinatra, Frank, 135
Sinn Chanchhaya, 196–202, 225, 233
Sinn Leang, 205–6
Sinn Sethakol, 272–3
Sinn Sisamouth, *168*, *195*, *199*, *215*;
    as businessman, 17; childhood,
    205–7; childhood home, 232–3,
    232; death, 224–5; early career,
    50, 208–12; in films, 64; films
    by, 169; grandson, 272–3; and
    Khmer Rouge, 24, 29; marriage
    and family, 207–8, 213, 220, 226;
    and the Mol brothers, 285–6; and
    Oum Dara, 275–6; overview, 195–
    233; popularity and influence,
    15–16, 146, 160, 196, 280; and Ros
    Sereysothea, 22, 164, 165, 166–9,
    170, 214–15; songwriters for, 73;
    soundtracks by, 214; stage fright,
    210, 215
    SONGS: 'A Go-Go', 220; 'Away
        from Beloved Lover',
        xvi–xviii, 221; 'Champa
        Battambang' ('The Flower
        of Battambang'), 211–12, 285;
        'Don't Be Mean', 221; 'I Love
        Petite Women', 221; 'I'm Still
        Waiting for You', 245; 'I'm
        Ticklish! I'm Ticklish!', 116;
        'Kampot From the Bottom
        of my Heart', 100–1; 'Kandal
        Goddess', 100–1; 'Karma',
        116; 'The King Sold the
        Land to the Viet Cong',
        219–20; 'Malavy's Tears',
        116; 'Sat Stiang Heur Stuoy'
        ('Stingray'), 62; 'Snaeh Yerng'
        ('Love Us'), 167; 'Souvenir
        of Battambang', 193; 'Tasona

Krong Phnom Penh' ('Phnom
    Penh is a Good City'),
    248; 'Thavary My Love',
    167; 'Tomorrow I'll Join
    the Army', 178; 'Under the
    Sound of Rain', 227; 'We Sing
    Together', 167
Sinn Sisamouth Association, 196–9
Sisario, Ben, 241
Sisowath Chariya, Prince, 101–3,
    106–11, *109*
Sisowath Lycée, 74
Sisowath Panara Sirivudh, Prince
    (aka Nong Neang), 68–82, 138,
    141; *see also* Apsara
Sisowath Sirik Matak, Prince, 23,
    108, 183–5, 218–19
Sisowath Sirirath, Prince, 76
Sisowath Thomico, Prince, 67–8
SKD (Société Khmer des
    Distilleries), 15, 107, 108, 165
Sliten6ix, 316
Slur's, 92
smot, 5, 6
So Savoeun, 19–20
Société Khmer des Distilleries
    see SKD
Sok, Mr, 165
Sok Visal, 212
Som Sareth, *234*, 244, 245–6, 249–
    52, 260; *see also* Drakkar
Song Hong, 187
The Song Extemporaneous (film) *see*
    Jomreang Eth Preang Thok
Sonic Sing, 15
Sophoan Dontrey, 126–8, *127*
Sos Mat, 165–6, 200, 210
South Vietnam, 1
Sovanmancha (Mermaid Bar), 114–15
Soviet Union, 150
Spain, 6–7

spiders, 130
Srey Thy *see* Kak Channthy
Srey Ya, 179–81, 187
Sroeng Santi, 2
Stanley Brothers, 63
Stefan (translator), 298, 299
Stung Khieu restaurant, 164
Stung Treng, 202–3, 204–5, 231
Sublime Frequencies, 8, 33
Suramarit, King of Cambodia, 11
Svay Sor (aka White Mango), *35,*
    40–57, *49*, 115, 124
Swain, Jon, 181, 225

Ta Mok, *28*, 147
takhe, 62
Tan Kdompi, 78
Tan Phanareth, 241
Tat Chen, 143, 145–6, 150, 153
taxi girls, 104, 106
Taylor, Vinny, 128
television *see* TVK television
temples, 4, 5, 156, 192–3
Tep Mam, 132
Tep Sodachan (film), 214
Tha Luch, 280, 281
Thach Soly, *112*, 122–37, *127*, 240
Thach, Mme, 123
Thailand: refugee camps for
    Cambodians, 52, 53–45, 308;
    and the Shadows, 16; support for
    Cambodian independence, 11;
    Thai music, 2, 8
Thavary Meas Bong (*Thavary My
    Love*; film), 214
theatre, 5
3rd D.1, 25
Thoeung Son, 32–3
Tomorrow I Will Leave You (film), 116
Tong Sany, 74–8, *75*; *see also* Apsara
Tonlé Sap River, 18, 259

Touch Chhattha, *49, 234, 239;*
    childhood, 240; and Drakkar, 237,
    238–41, 249–52; later life, 261–3,
    266; at RNK, 243, 262; teacher,
    128, 137; *see also* Drakkar
Touch Tana, *234, 274;* appearance,
    235; childhood, 236–8; and *Don't
    Think I've Forgotten* reunion tour,
    266, 272, 273; and Drakkar, 25,
    234, 240–3, 249–52, 253–4; gem
    mining, 252–4; under Khmer
    Rouge, 254–60; later life, 260–1,
    262–3; non-Drakkar musical
    career, 243–9; overview, 240–61;
    at RNK, 243–4, 252; and Yol
    Aularong, 241–3, 244–5, 247–8;
    see also Drakkar
Trashmen, 287
tro, 9, 62–3
Trudeau, Justin, 299
Tuol Po Chrey, 303, 305
TVK television, 49, *49*, 51, 77–8;
    band, 239
the twist, 16–17, 20

UK: and Khmer Rouge, 304; UK
    music's influence on Cambodian,
    14, 16
Université des Beaux-Arts (UBA;
    later Royal University of Fine
    Arts), 57–8, 62, 64–5, 138–40
urbanization, 12–13
USA: bombing of Cambodia, 216;
    Cambodian relations with, 96;
    evacuation of Phnom Penh,
    182–4; invasion of Cambodia,
    25–7; and Khmer Rouge, 304;
    and Sihanouk, 216; US music's
    influence on Cambodian, 7, 14,
    16–17, 177–8

Va Savoy, 248
Van Chann, 166; studio, 77, 169, 220, 246–7, 285
Vann Molyvann, 87–8, 139
VannDa, 311, 316
Vartan, Sylvie, 16, 102
Vartey Ganiva, 316
Ventures, 16, 270, 284
Vibrations, 133
Vichara Dany, 187
Viet Cong, 23, 26, 50, 96, 216, 218
Vietnam: invasion and occupation of Cambodia, 52–3, 58, 78–9, 87, 118, 134, 149–50, 252, 261–2; Khmer Rouge incursions, 149–50, 189; in nineteenth century, 6; treatment of Khmer Krom people, 124–5; Vietnamese music, 2, 8; *see also* North Vietnam; South Vietnam
Vietnam War (1955–75): and Cambodia, 25–7; and Sihanouk, 216; and Sihanoukville, 96–7; troop entertainments, 245–6
vinyl: Cambodian, 16; digitizing, 171; first 33⅓ rpm record, 280
Voice of America, 14, 177–8, 240
Vorn Vet, *28*
Voy Ho, 115, 133, 162, 220, 222, 247

Walkabout pub brothel, 105
war tribunals, 301–6
Wat Damrey Sor, 156, 192–3
Wat-Phnom, 77, 212, 248
water festivals, 9
Waxwings, 92
Wheeler, Paul, 32
White Mango *see* Svay Sor
White Scarves *see* Kansaing Sar
Williams, Andy, 179
Williams, Hank, 96

Winery, 271–4, *274*
Wise Hippies, 78
women: and divorce, 213; education, 205; status of Cambodian, 19–21, 236, 278, 282
Woodstock (film), 271
Wrigley, Joe, 91–9, *91*

Yab Moung Records, 316
Yanko, Kristina, 92–3, 96, 97–8
Yel Om Sophanarak (Mr Yel), 114, 165
yé-yé groups: definition and etymology, 16
Yil Chathou, 89
Yin Dykan, 89
Yol Aularong (Lara), *1*; background, 241; death, 260; and *Don't Think I've Forgotten* reunion tour, 273; film of, 270–1; at Kbal Thnal, 244–5; and Lon Nol regime, 28–9, 178–9; songwriting, 249; style, 25; and Touch Tana, 241–3, 244–5, 247–8; SONGS: 'Café Kmao' ('Black Coffee'), 243; 'Dying under a Woman's Sword', 178–9; 'Navanny' ('Number One'), 247–8
Yothea Phirum (Youth Band), 14–15, 102
Youk Chhang, 271, 311–14
The Young Ones (film), 16, 283

Zhou Enlai, 13, 42